Atlas of the Ancient Nea

This atlas provides students and scholars with a broad range of information on the development of the Ancient Near East from prehistoric times through the beginning of written records in the Near East (c. 3000 BC) to the late Roman Empire and the rise of Islam. The geographical coverage of the Atlas extends from the Aegean coast of Anatolia in the west through Iran and Afghanistan to the east, and from the Black and Caspian Seas in the north to Arabia and the Persian Gulf and Indian Ocean in the south.

The Atlas of the Ancient Near East includes a wide-ranging overview of the civilizations and kingdoms discussed, written in a lively and engaging style, which considers not only political and military issues but also introduces the reader to social and cultural topics such as trade, religion, how people were educated and entertained, and much more. With a comprehensive series of detailed maps, supported by the authors' commentary and illustrations of major sites and key artifacts, this title is an invaluable resource for students who wish to understand the fascinating cultures of the Ancient Near East.

Trevor Bryce is an Honorary Professor at the University of Queensland and Fellow of the Australian Academy of the Humanities. He has held positions as Reader in Classics and Ancient History, University of Queensland, Professor of Classics and Ancient History, University of New England (Australia), and Deputy Vice-Chancellor, Lincoln University, New Zealand.

Jessie Birkett-Rees is Lecturer in the Centre for Ancient Cultures at Monash University, Melbourne. She is an archaeologist of the ancient Near East and a specialist in cultural landscape analyses. Her fieldwork and research have focused on the emergence and development of complex societies, and the changing relationships between humans and their environment in Turkey, South Caucasia, Africa and Australia.

Atlas of the Ancient Near East

From Prehistoric Times to the Roman Imperial Period

by

Trevor Bryce

with an introductory section on

The Prehistoric Near East

by

Jessie Birkett-Rees

Routledge
Taylor & Francis Group

NEW YORK AND LONDON

First published 2016
by Routledge
2 Park Square, Milton Park, Abingdon, Oxon OX14 4RN

Simultaneously published in the USA and Canada
by Routledge
711 Third Avenue, New York, NY 10017

Routledge is an imprint of the Taylor & Francis Group, an informa business

British Library Cataloguing in Publication Data
A catalogue record for this book is available from the British Library

Library of Congress Cataloging in Publication Data
A catalog record for this book has been requested

ISBN: 978-0-415-50800-1 (hbk)
ISBN: 978-0-415-50801-8 (pbk)
ISBN: 978-1-315-73481-1 (ebk)

Typeset in Minion Pro and Myriad Pro
by Swales & Willis Ltd, Exeter, Devon, UK

Contents

Figures

Acknowledgements

I would like to thank once more the scholars who acted as consultants for *The Routledge Handbook of the Peoples and Places of Ancient Western Asia*, and wrote some of the entries in it; namely Heather Baker (Mesopotamia), Dan Potts (Iran), Jonathan Tubb (Syria and Palestine), Jennifer Webb (Cyprus) and Paul Zimansky (Urartu). The benefits of their advice and expertise extend to the present volume, with additional information provided by Dr Webb on Cyprus. I am also very grateful to my co-author Jessie Birkett-Rees both for her own substantial contribution to this book and for her advice and assistance to me on a number of technical matters to do with the maps and images. It has been a pleasure to work with Jessie. My thanks are due too to the School of Historical and Philosophical Inquiry, University of Queensland, and especially to Lucy O'Brien, for their invaluable infrastructural support in the preparation of this book.

Trevor Bryce

My thanks go to Trevor Bryce for the benefit of his advice and expertise throughout the preparation of this volume. It has been a great experience to work with Trevor, who is an inspiration to many of us working in the Near East. I am also grateful for the support of Monash University and thank the Centre for Ancient Cultures and the School of Philosophical, Historical and International Studies at Monash University for providing the vibrant environment of teaching and research in which this work was prepared. I thank La Trobe University Archaeology Department for their support during the initial stages of this project. Last but not least, I am grateful to Professor Tony Sagona for his invaluable guidance over many years.

Jessie Birkett-Rees

We both warmly thank our editor, Matthew Gibbons, and assistant editor, Lola Harre, for their advice and guidance through the various stages of this project. Our warm thanks also to Colin Morgan and his associates at Swales & Willis for their excellent work in the design and layout of the book. And finally, we would like to acknowledge, with our great appreciation, the enormous contribution to the project by Richard Talbert and his colleagues at the Ancient World Mapping Center.

Abbreviations

AANE – Potts, D.T. (ed.) (2012), *A Companion to the Archaeology of the Ancient Near East* (2 vols), Chichester: Wiley-Blackwell.

BNP – *Brill's Encyclopedia of the Ancient World. New Pauly (Antiquity)*, Leiden and Boston: Brill (2002–).

CANE – Sasson, J.M. (ed.) (1995), *Civilizations of the Ancient Near East* (4 vols), New York: Charles Scribner's Sons.

CS I-III – Hallo, W.W. and Younger, K.L. (eds) (1997, 2000, 2002), *The Context of Scripture* (3 vols), Leiden, New York and Cologne: Brill.

GEAW – Harrison, T. (ed.) (2009), *The Great Empires of the Ancient World*, London: Thames & Hudson.

HCBD – Achtemeier, P.J. (ed.) (1996), *The HarperCollins Bible Dictionary*, New York: HarperCollins.

HE – Finkelberg, M. (ed.) (2011), *The Homer Encylopedia*, Chichester: Wiley-Blackwell (3 vols).

NEAEHL – Stern, E. (ed.) (1993), *The New Encyclopedia of Archaeological Excavations in the Holy Land*, New York, London, Toronto, Sydney, Tokyo and Singapore: Simon & Schuster (4 vols).

OCD – Hornblower, S. and Spawforth, A. (eds) (1996), *The Oxford Classical Dictionary*, Oxford: Oxford University Press (3rd edn).

OEAGR – Gargarin, M. and Fantham, E. (eds) (2010), *The Oxford Encyclopedia of Ancient Greece and Rome*, Oxford: Oxford University Press (7 vols).

OEANE – Meyers, E.M. (ed.) (1997), *The Oxford Encyclopedia of Archaeology in the Near East*, Oxford: Oxford University Press (5 vols).

OHAA – Steadman, S. and McMahon, G. (eds) (2011), *The Oxford Handbook of Ancient Anatolia*, Oxford and New York: Oxford University Press.

OHBAA – Cline, E.H. (ed.) (2010), *The Oxford Handbook of the Bronze Age Aegean*, Oxford and New York: Oxford University Press.

OHIH – Daryaee, T. (ed.) (2012), *The Oxford Handbook of Iranian History*, Oxford and New York: Oxford University Press.

PECS – Stillwell, R. (ed.) (1976), *The Princeton Encyclopedia of Classical Sites*, Princeton: Princeton University Press.

PPAWA – Bryce, T.R. (2009/2012), *The Routledge Handbook of the Peoples and Places of Ancient Western Asia: From the Early Bronze Age to the Fall of the Persian Empire*, Abingdon and New York: Routledge.

SB – Rainey, A.F. and Notley, R.S. (2006), *The Sacred Bridge: Carta's Atlas of the Biblical World*, Jerusalem: Carta.

Chronological note

Ma: mega-annum = million years

BP: years 'Before Present', in which the present is defined as 1950.

C + no. = a particular century. Thus C5 BC = 5th century BC.

M + no. = a particular millennium. Thus M2 AD = 2nd millennium AD.

Introduction

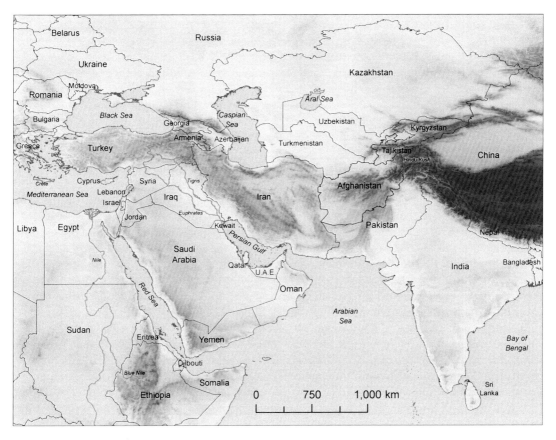

The Near East in its modern context

In 1985, Croom Helm published an *Atlas of Classical History* edited by Richard Talbert, intended primarily for high school and undergraduate students. Its aim was to provide 'a reasonably comprehensive, up-to-date and scholarly coverage of Classical history down to the time of Constantine'. The book's success is reflected in its numerous reprints by the publisher Routledge, from 1985 to 2008. Encouraged by this, Matthew Gibbons, Routledge's current editor for Classics, Archaeology and Museum Studies, asked me to write a complementary volume on the ancient Near East, catering primarily for the student market, but with appeal for a broader reading public as well. The present volume is the outcome.

One of my initial problems in embarking on this enterprise was to decide on what lands, regions and periods should actually be covered by the term 'Near East'. As it is widely used by scholars, the term is generally applied to the ancient civilizations that arose, flourished and fell throughout a large part of Western Asia, extending from the Aegean coast of Turkey through modern Syria, Lebanon, Palestine, Israel and Jordan, then eastwards across Iraq to the eastern fringes of Mesopotamia. (Much of this area is today referred to as the Middle East.) But some scholars broaden the term to cover lands even further east, including Iran (where several great empires rose and fell), Afghanistan and other Central Asian regions. This poses an important question. If there is no agreed limit on how far the term's coverage can be extended, is there any reason for not including under its umbrella Cyprus and Egypt as well? Indeed some scholars have done so. Both certainly had close and regular contacts, cultural, political and commercial, and sometimes military, with the Near Eastern world, even if, strictly speaking, they are not generally considered a part of it. This Atlas in fact covers all the abovementioned lands and regions, including Cyprus and Egypt. But I should hasten to say that its treatment of the latter in particular is a very limited one. There is clearly scope for a more detailed and more specialized treatment of Egypt – perhaps as a third volume in this series.

Then there is the question of the Atlas' chronological limits. After consultation with the editor, I have included sections on Greece's and Rome's involvement in the Near Eastern world, beginning with the Bronze Age Mycenaean presence on the fringes of this world and continuing through the periods of later Greek settlement in it, and in the Atlas' final sections, Roman domination of much of it through the Roman imperial era. I am aware that this means some overlap with Talbert's Atlas, which provides a relatively detailed account, in a number of its sections, of the Greeks and Romans in the East. But there are several reasons for re-covering some of Talbert's ground. In the first place, my treatment of the relevant topics is quite different in approach and content to that of Talbert and his co-authors. Further, a number of the eastern sites which were supposedly Greek and Roman foundations were settled well before any Greek or Roman presence there. Thus while Talbert's Atlas provides an account of the city of Miletus, near Turkey's Aegean coast, in its Classical phase, my own treatment of it places it in a broader historical context; the city had already achieved prominence during the Bronze Age and is referred to in a number of Hittite texts of the period; it was an indigenous foundation, but was also extensively settled by Minoan and Mycenean colonists in M2 BC.

Another important reason for assigning space to the Greeks and Romans in the East has to do with the Atlas' most important feature – its maps. The fact that Talbert's Atlas was published in black and white significantly limited the possibilities for displaying clearly on its maps (by using, for example, contrasting colours) a number of geopolitical features, like the territorial extent of particular kingdoms or states or provinces, especially ones adjacent to each other, and the physical features of the regions where they were located. Access to improved technology, courtesy of Richard Talbert and his colleagues at the Ancient World Mapping Center, and the publisher's decision to print the maps in colour have provided greater opportunities for enhancing both the maps' visual appeal as well as their value as sources of information.

Let me return to the question of the Atlas' actual timeframe. I should stress that it is primarily an historical Atlas, in the sense that its information is based to a large extent on written sources, and that it deals mainly with political and military events throughout Near Eastern history, and the peoples and individuals who were participants in these events. Thus an obvious starting-point for it is late M4 AD, when writing first becomes evident in southern Mesopotamia and Egypt. Nonetheless when the initial proposal for the Atlas was sent out for peer review, it came back with the advice that a brief treatment of the prehistoric Near East would provide a useful introduction to the later historical phases. I took that advice on board, and am delighted that Dr Jessie Birkett-Rees agreed to provide maps and archaeology-based texts for the section on prehistory with which the Atlas begins. I should add that the later sections also contain accounts of a number of the material remains of the regions and periods dealt with and the societies and cultures associated with them – though an atlas dedicated to the archaeology of the Near East would obviously treat such matters much more comprehensively.

The Atlas concludes with a survey of Roman rule in the Near East up to the Islamic conquests in C7 AD. This end-point means that *in addition to* the millennia covered by the introductory pre-historic material, the Atlas' historical timescale covers a period of about four millennia, beginning with the emergence of writing in the late M4 BC. Inevitably, Dr Birkett-Rees and I have had to be highly selective in the material we have chosen for representation on the maps and discussion in their accompanying texts. We have also included brief accounts of specific sites, sometimes with accompanying site-plans. The number of these is relatively small, and they are simply a personal selection from a large range of possibilities.

It will be clear from the Contents pages that though the Atlas extends to the late Roman period, its chief emphasis is on a time-span that extends from the prehistoric period to the fall of the Persian empire in 330 BC. Thus, its appeal as a potential textbook may be primarily to students of the ancient Near East whose courses cover the Bronze Ages (and their prehistoric antecedents), the Iron Age, including the Neo-Assyrian empire, and the Babylonian and Persian periods. The greater part of the book is devoted to the civilizations, kingdoms, countries, cities and inhabitants of these periods (including the Greek settlements established in the Near East within this time-frame). I have dealt with many of them at greater length in *The Routledge Handbook of the Peoples and Places of Western Asia: From the Early Bronze Age to the Fall of the Persian Empire* (2009, paperback 2012; cited as *PPAWA*). But I am conscious that *PPAWA*'s bulk – at almost 1,000 pages – makes it more suitable for use as a reference work to be plucked off a library shelf and consulted as the need arises, than as a concise, portable student companion that fits comfortably into a carry-bag or rucksack along with a tablet, smartphone, and other accessories of student life. Much of *PPAWA*'s material, however, is directly relevant to high school and university student programmes on the Near East, and with this in mind, I have adapted and condensed a number of relevant entries in it for the texts that accompany the maps in this Atlas (for example, the entries on the Diyala and Habur regions and sites, and the kingdoms of M1 BC Cyprus).

The Atlas is more compact and cheaper than *PPAWA* (though with many more maps, and in colour), and students may well find it practicable and within their resources to have their own copies of it. If they have access to *PPAWA* as well, that will provide them with more detailed infor-mation on the archaeology and history of the sites, regions, kingdoms and peoples of the ancient Near East – up to 330 BC – together with frequent citations of the relevant ancient written sources. Let me also add that the Atlas closely complements the excellent survey of ancient Near Eastern

Part I

The prehistoric Near East

1

The geography and geology of the ancient Near East

The ancient Near East is at the junction of three continents: Africa, Asia and Europe. It includes territory from Turkey to eastern Iran and is encircled by the Mediterranean, Black Sea, Caspian Sea, Persian Gulf and Red Sea.

The patterns of the human past are better understood when seen as interacting with physical features, climatic elements and dynamic environmental conditions through time, and the cultural diversity of the ancient Near East has been supported by equally great geographic diversity. This region has sustained a broad spectrum of human lifestyles, partly as a result of the variety of topographic and climatic zones found in close proximity to one another; from lowland plains to upland plateaus, mountains, coasts, marshes and deserts, the landscapes of the Near East are varied and dynamic.

This introduction to the prehistory of the Near East will provide an overview of the geological formation of the region and its principal geographic features, including the Taurus and Zagros Mountains and the Tigris and Euphrates Rivers (see map on p. 10). The physical landscape, climate and ecology of the Near East contribute to its human geography, influencing early human settlement and underlying the changing relationships between people and environment which resulted from the development of agriculture. The factors influencing the domestication of plants and animals, which occurred some 11,000 years ago in the Near East, will be addressed, and discussion of several key sites presented to illustrate the range and complexity of human cultures in the millennia before the rise of the first literate civilizations.

The Near Eastern landscape was formed two hundred million years ago by the collision of two supercontinents, Gondwanaland and Laurasia, and their fragmentation into several smaller continental plates. These plates continue to move relative to one another, causing rift and convergence, uplift and subsidence at the plate boundaries.

Through these processes the great Mesopotamian plain was formed and the Zagros Mountains rose between the Arabian and Iranian continental plates (see map on p. 11). Likewise, as the Arabian plate moved north towards the Anatolian plate and away from the African plate, the Taurus Mountains, the Dead Sea and Jordanian rift valley were created. It is at these plate boundaries that structural weaknesses are greatest, resulting in earthquakes and the extrusion of metamorphic and volcanic rock types, including obsidian (volcanic glass) which was traded from its mountain sources throughout the Near East in prehistory. The majority of surface rocks in the Near East are sedimentary rocks, the marine sediments accumulated from the closing of the ancient Tethys Sea around 50 million years ago. Above these mudstones, sandstones and limestones, the river valleys are filled with more recent alluvial silt eroded from the mountains.

Long-term geological processes have combined with more recent effects of wind, water and ice to shape the landscapes of the Near East. At the height of the last Ice Age (or *Last Glacial*

The physical geography of the Near East

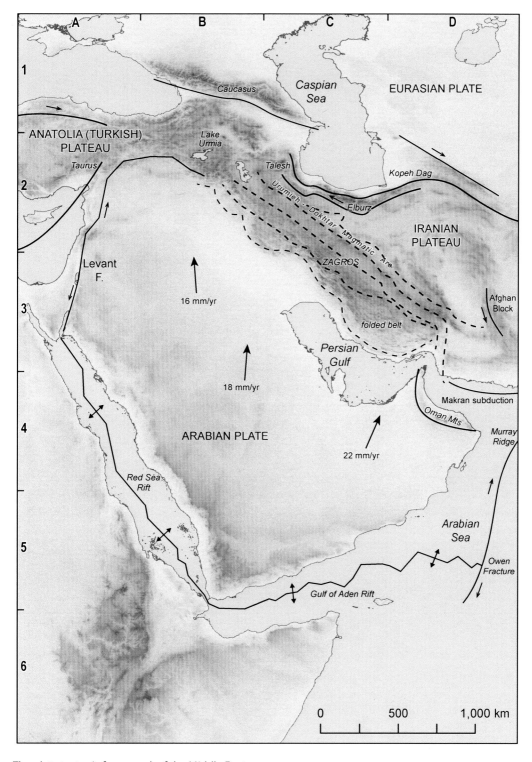

The plate tectonic framework of the Middle East

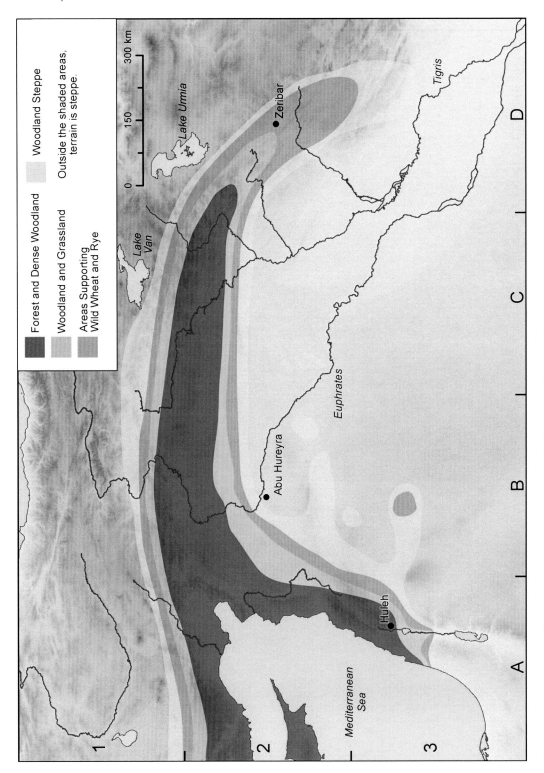

The approximate extent of forest and open woodland during the Holocene climatic optimum

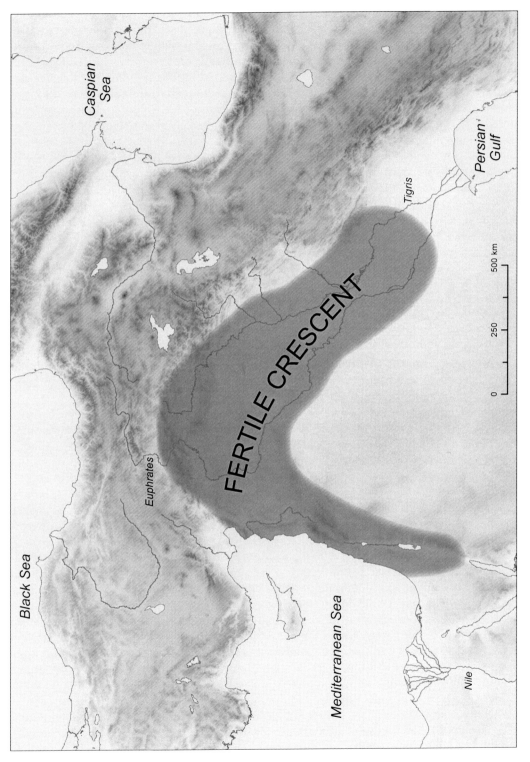

The Fertile Crescent

Maximum 26,500–19,000 BP) ice sheets up to 3 km thick blanketed northern Europe and North America and the world climate was markedly more arid than today. Around 19,000 years ago the world began the slow and irregular process of warming, reaching temperatures similar to the present day around 13,000 BP before another cold snap, known as the *Younger Dryas* (12,800–11,600 BP). Warmer conditions re-established around 11,600, marking the beginning of the *Holocene* period. A second cold episode known as the *8.2 kiloyear event* occurred around 8200 years ago and lasted only a few centuries before the generally stable trends of the Holocene climatic optimum returned. This interglacial period saw forests spread across the Zagros and Taurus Mountains and a moister climate in the Near East (see map on p. 12).

Humans were one of the species to benefit from the changes in vegetation and the increasing stability, warmth and moisture in the Holocene climate.

The Taurus and Zagros Mountains form the backbone of the Near East. The Taurus Mountains run east–west across south-eastern Turkey and meet the Zagros Mountains in western Iran, which run north-west–south-east to the Persian Gulf. These mountain ranges are flanked by great plateaus; to the north of the Taurus is the plateau of central and eastern Anatolia and to the east of the Zagros is the Iranian plateau. The mountain ranges provided shelter for early human settlers in the region, who favoured cave sites along river valleys as seasonal dwellings. The snowmelt from the mountain ranges also feeds the great rivers of the Near East; both the Tigris and Euphrates originate in the mountains of eastern Turkey before flowing southwards across Syria and Iraq, meeting in the marshy margins of the Persian Gulf (Shatt al-Arab).

On the other side of these mountain chains lies the 'Fertile Crescent', the well-watered foothills and lowland plains which were home to some of the world's first farmers (see map on p. 13). Archaeologist James Henry Breasted popularized the term 'Fertile Crescent' to denote an arc stretching from the southern Levant (Jordan, Lebanon, Israel and Palestine) north and eastward across Syria and Iran into northern Iraq.

In this geographic zone, the foothills of the Taurus and Zagros Mountains capture the moisture carried by the westerly winds travelling over the Mediterranean and bring rainfall, sustaining a productive ecosystem in an otherwise arid area. The region is rich in natural resources including wild wheat and barley, and supported populations of wild animals including sheep, goats, cattle and pigs. These are the ancestors of the plants and animals that would be domesticated during the Neolithic.

The southern arm of the Fertile Crescent also forms a corridor between Africa and Eurasia in which populations of plants and animals have intermingled over many thousands of years, resulting in rich biodiversity. In the southern regions of the Crescent we find evidence of the earliest human habitation in the Near East, including pre-modern and early modern humans. In this same region, also known as the Levantine corridor, Late Pleistocene hunter-gatherers and Epipalaeolithic semi-sedentary communities took advantage of the oases in the Jordanian rift valley and the Syrian desert. To the north, where the crescent curves to the east, the Taurus foothills provided important connections with the resource-rich Anatolian highlands and central plateau. To the east of the Fertile Crescent is Mesopotamia, between the Tigris and Euphrates Rivers, long referred to as a 'Cradle of Civilization'. The levels of rainfall in northern Mesopotamia made some farming possible without irrigation (dry-farming), but in southern Mesopotamia early farmers had to make further modifications to their environment, including building irrigation canals to water fields and levees to protect against seasonal flooding.

Beyond the Fertile Crescent, the central Anatolian plateau and the Iranian plateau are important geographic regions. The Iranian plateau extends for some 2,000 km east of the Zagros Mountains and includes several mountainous regions (Elburz, Köpet Dağ, Jebel Barez) and two great deserts: the Dasht-e Kavir and the Dasht-e Lut. The Anatolian plain lies north of the Taurus Mountains, a semi-arid highland plateau at the heart of modern Turkey. Several drainage basins, including the large Konya basin, provide fertile areas within the region and were focal points of Neolithic settlement.

The geography of the ancient Near East, at local and regional scales, has been a major contributor to the long human history of the region. Human societies and the environments they inhabit have influenced and transformed each other over both short- and long-term interactions. A remarkable example of this interaction between people and environment is in the early development of agriculture in the Near East.

Roaf (1990: 18–25); Liverani (2014: 17–33); Peregrine and Ember (2002: xvii–xxi).

2

Foragers and farmers

Early agricultural communities

The domestication of plants and animals in the ancient Near East produced new farming economies which could support larger populations, resulting in the growth of settlements, the development of new technologies and increasing social complexity. Several key terms, regions and theories contribute to our ongoing interpretation of the processes and motivations behind the development and spread of agriculture in the Near East.

Terminology

Continual and prolonged interaction between plants, animals and humans can cause the physical characteristics or the genotypes of plants and animals to change as these species become dependent on humans for reproductive success. This is the process of *domestication*, which can occur naturally through ongoing interaction between people and wild species, or can be actively promoted by human communities through preferential selection of plants or animals based on desirable attributes. For instance, wild cereal grains with brittle rachis (the connection between grain and ear) naturally release the cereal grains once ripe, allowing wide dispersal of seeds; human selection of wild cereals favoured varieties which did not easily drop the ripened grain and which had larger or more numerous seeds for harvesting. The seeds which are stored and sown by people then bear these preferred characteristics and, over time, the species is modified such that it is physically and genetically distinct from wild populations. *Cultivation* and *herding* are two practices which represent the active promotion of domestication, whereby fields are prepared and seeds sown or groups of animals (herds) are brought together, kept together and actively managed. Both these practices, which do not always occur together, entail new relationships between humans and their environment, new behaviours within human communities and new technologies required to carry out agricultural practices. *Agriculture*, the practices of farming domesticated plants and animals, in turn produces a modified ecosystem through the selective cultivation of plants and rearing of animals for primary food production. The domestication of animals also produces important secondary products, including milk, wool and manure for soil improvement.

Domestication of species is not restricted to agricultural or sedentary communities, with considerable evidence for the early domestication of dogs by hunter-gatherer societies. Genetic studies of canine DNA indicate that domestic dogs evolved from a group of wolves that came into contact with European hunter-gatherers over 18,000 years ago. Likewise, hunter-gatherers are known to have resource management practices verging on domestication of plants, including selective harvesting and partial replanting of yams by northern and western Australian Aboriginal groups. Similar selective practices may have led to the earliest domestication of cereals in the Fertile Crescent some 11,000 years ago.

Regions

The development of agriculture has diverse manifestations worldwide.

Research in recent decades has shown that agriculture developed independently in several geographically dispersed regions of the world at different periods during the Holocene, with core areas being the Fertile Crescent in the Near East (c. 9000 BC), the Yangzi and Yellow River basins in East Asia (c. 7000 BC), highland New Guinea (c. 7000–4000 BC), sub-Saharan Africa, Andean South America and central Mexico (3000–2000 BC) and north-eastern America (2000–1000 BC) (see map on p. 18). Different plant varieties formed the foundation of agricultural systems in different geographic regions – wheat and barley in the Near East, millet and rice in east Asia, maize in central America. The differing geographic context of centres of agricultural development, the varying timeframes and the different foundation species suggest that the development of agriculture is best considered as multi-causal. There was no singular 'invention' of agriculture, rather a series of adjustments and adaptations by humans made according to their differing social, demographic and environmental contexts.

In the Near East, people began to cultivate wild plant species at the end of the Epipalaeolithic and beginning of the Neolithic. At this time, the Near East possessed the largest number of potential and future domesticates in the world, including the eight Neolithic 'founder crops': emmer and einkorn wheat, barley, lentils, pea and chickpea, bitter vetch and flax. Sheep, goats, cattle and pigs are four primary domesticated animal species also native to parts of the Near East. The varied geography of the Near East appears to have influenced the composition and spread of agricultural practices in the early Holocene; the early instances of domestication and farming in this region are best conceived of as a mosaic, since people appear to start cultivating locally available species at different times in different parts of the Near East.

Reasons

Once agriculture had been developed or adopted, early societies for the most part show an ongoing preference for food production over hunting and gathering; this is certainly the case in the ancient Near East. Theories as to how and why, not just what, when and where, agricultural practices originated and dispersed during the Neolithic have been debated by archaeologists and other scientists for over a century. These hypotheses have shifted over the years to arrive at the current frameworks, under which researchers balance the results of increasingly precise scientific analyses with awareness of the complexity of foragers' and farmers' decision-making processes. Archaeological evidence for early agricultural practices includes the preserved remains of plants and animals, the form and function of different artefacts, and identification of storage spaces, animal pens, irrigation canals and other structural features employed in agricultural life. More recently, advanced scientific techniques have been applied to the origins of agriculture, including the isotopic analysis of bone chemistry for information on diet and studies of ancient DNA (aDNA) from bones and seeds to trace the processes of genetic change linked to domestication. Analyses of ice cores, tree rings and sediment cores provide proxies by which to reconstruct palaeoenvironmental conditions. Linguistic patterns have also contributed to our understanding of the mosaic of agricultural development and to debate on the tempo and mode of the spread of agricultural practices.

Key variables contributing to the development of agriculture are environmental conditions, demographic pressures and social choices. The trajectory of theories on the development of agriculture has been influenced over the years by new analytical techniques employed in the discipline

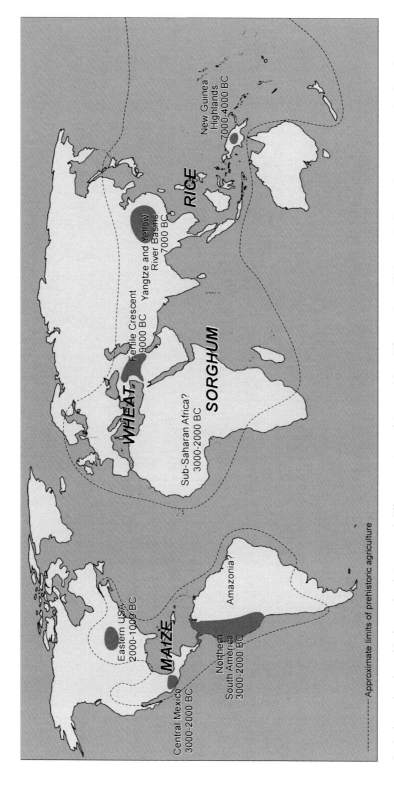

Agriculture developed independently in several different regions of the world at different times. This map indicates the core areas, the foundation crops and the various dates of agricultural origins

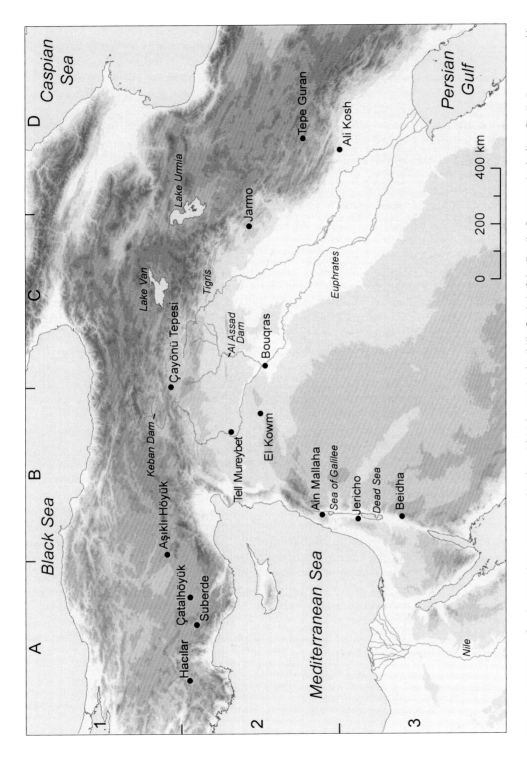

The principal sites of early agriculture excavated in the mid 20th cent. in the 'hilly flanks' of the Fertile Crescent, including Çayönü, excavated by Robert Braidwood

of archaeology and new discoveries in the Near Eastern record. Yet by and large the ways in which archaeologists evaluate the variables that motivated the development and spread of agriculture keep step with wider theoretical developments within archaeology. Some of the most influential theories include V.G. Childe's 'oasis theory' (1928), Robert Braidwood's 'hilly flanks hypothesis' (1960) (see map on p. 19), the development of multi-causal models focusing on demographic pressures and systems theory, proposed by Lewis Binford (1968) and Kent Flannery (1969, 1973), and theories emphasizing the role of social and ideological strategies offered by Ian Hodder (1982, 1990) and Barbara Bender (1978).

These theories move from Childe's broad culture-historical synthesis, to theses drawing on developments in archaeological science from the late 1950s onward. Interrogations of palaoeconomies and applications of systems theory in the 1970s were countered by increasing concern with social context and symbolic processes, influencing the approaches of the 1980s onward. The shifting ideas about how and why foragers became farmers highlight the complex motivations for the development of agriculture in the Near East and the multiple factors influencing the spread of this way of life: geography and ecology, climatic changes, demographic pressures and social frameworks.

We know that agricultural practices developed under relatively stable environmental conditions in the early Holocene which permitted ongoing experiments with plant domestication. These experiments evidently took place alongside significant changes in human behaviour, whereby a series of decisions were made to influence and control food supply. Early theories on the development of agriculture, such as those of Childe and Braidwood, typically considered farming a natural preference to foraging. However, research since the 1960s has articulated the efforts required to successfully initiate agriculture, indicating that farming requires *more* effort than foraging. In the initial stages of farming, this economy also has less reliable results than foraging. The decision to begin farming, or to integrate agricultural practices into a mixed economy, is therefore not driven simply by convenience. Rather, it is part of a broader shift in the relationship between humans and their environment and indicates considerable investment in a local area.

As agricultural lifestyles spread from their initial points of origin, the human and natural environments of the Near East were transformed. This occurred at the local scale of cultivation and, over the long-term, promoted population growth and economic specialization throughout the region. The adoption of agricultural ways of life permitted the development of non-food specialists, including craftspeople and bureaucrats, scientists and authors. Not only did agriculture entail new relationships between people and environment, it fostered new roles and structures within society. The food surplus which early farmers were able to generate facilitated, and in some cases demanded, innovations such as writing, administration and scientific scholarship. In terminology still familiar today, V.G. Childe labelled the development of agriculture in the Fertile Crescent the 'Neolithic Revolution', in association with the establishment of urban lifestyles and population increase. Although the processes of agricultural development were protracted and dispersed around the Near East, revolutionary status is justified in view of the profound and enduring consequences of agricultural practices.

Barker (2006); Scarre (2013: chapter 5); Liverani (2014: 34–58); Sherratt (1981: 261–306); Roaf (1990: 18–41); Zohary and Hopf (2000).

3

The prehistory of the Near East

Key sites

Late Pleistocene and Early Holocene

Throughout the Pleistocene the Levant formed a major corridor between Africa and Eurasia for human and animal populations.

The earliest human settlements in the Near East were caves or open air camps, such as Mughara Es Skhul cave on Mount Carmel in Israel and Jebel Qafzeh rockshelter on Mount Kedumim in Galilee. The skeletal remains of more than twenty early modern humans have been found at these two sites, dated to 90–110,000 years ago. These individuals exhibit modern features, including a pronounced chin and long, slender postcranial remains, which differ from Neanderthal populations who lived in the region some 40,000 years later. Kebara cave in the Carmel Range has yielded Neanderthal remains (61–48,000 BP), as has Shanidar cave in the Zagros Mountains, Iraq (65–35,000 BP).

The limited evidence from these earliest periods of modern human and Neanderthal habitation of the Near East produces a somewhat confusing chronology which implies that these different species may have coexisted in parts of the Levantine corridor. An alternate explanation is that the finds of early modern humans and Neanderthals reflect biogeographic variations in the dispersal of these different populations, in which the early modern human population known from Es Skhul and Qafzeh may have become locally extinct when Neanderthals occupied the region during a period of harsh climatic conditions between 70–60,000 years ago. Movement along the Levantine corridor is not unidirectional, of course, and the varied geography of the region permitted oscillations in populations. Modern humans and Neanderthals also used the landscape differently, reflected in studies of their stone tool technology and faunal assemblages at Kebara and Tabun in the Carmel Range, and employed different patterns of mobility and seasonal exploitation strategies. Modern humans seem to have moved between several camps according to seasonal change, whereas Neanderthals lived and hunted year-round within fairly small areas.

Modern humans became established in the Near East by the Late Pleistocene, around 55–35,000 years ago. In addition to rock shelters and caves, several important sites reveal human settlement in 'open air' locations and highlight increasing sedentism and growing communities in the Levant. The site of Ohalo II, dated to 20,000 BC, is a long-lived settlement of oval huts on the shore of Lake Lisan in northern Israel. The huts at Ohalo II were built of wood and grasses and were destroyed by fire, leaving an invaluable record of the more than 100 plant species used by this Epipalaeolithic community, as well as the bones of gazelle, hare, birds and fallow deer which they hunted. Neve David in Israel and Uyun al-Hammam in Jordan are also early sites which indicate the establishment of long-lived base camp sites at the boundary of different ecological zones, a strategy which providing the inhabitants with access to a broader range of resources. Very early

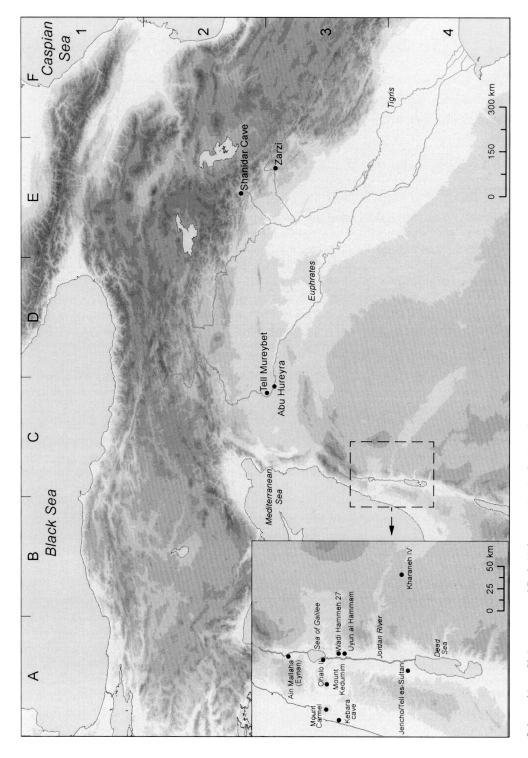

Selected Late Pleistocene and Early Holocene sites in the Near East

stone structures occupied between 18,000 and 14,000 BC have also been excavated at Kharaneh IV, in Jordan; ongoing excavations at this site stand to reveal more.

In the terminal Pleistocene and very beginning of the Holocene, a period also called the Late Epipalaeolithic in the ancient Near East, several significant, early sites were established in present-day Palestine, Jordan, Israel, Lebanon and Syria (see map on p. 22). In the well-watered areas of this Levantine corridor, where a range of wild plants and animals thrived, people established year-round settlements. These sites belong to the Natufian culture, a name given by British archaeologist Dorothy Garrod after her work at Shuqba cave in Wadi an-Natuf. Garrod also provided the names for the preceding communities in the region: the Kebaran in the west, following her excavations of Kebara cave in Mount Carmel in 1931, and the Zarzian in the east, named after the cave of Zarzi in Iraq, excavated in 1928.

The Natufian communities represent an important phase in human prehistory, the antecedent to agrarian village life in the ancient Near East which saw people begin to establish settlements and cultivate plants. There are numerous significant Natufian sites in the ancient Near East, including Abu Hureyra and Jericho (below), Tell Mureybet, Ain Mallaha and Wadi Hammeh 27. New lifestyles and subsistence strategies saw the development of innovative assemblages of artefacts for the procurement and processing of plant resources, particularly basalt grinding stones, pestles and mortars and sickles made of bone and flint. The lustre on the flint blades shows that these tools were used to cut grasses or cereals, which grew wild in the region. The mortuary rituals of Natufian people, which saw burials placed beneath and between the floors of some houses, also indicate a florescence of symbolic behaviour.

The Holocene era saw a rise in global temperatures, in which rainfall increased and plant and animal species flourished. Human populations took advantage of the opportunities these natural conditions afforded and in turn shaped their environments in novel ways. The foundations of settled village life and the developments of agriculture are of fundamental importance in these prehistoric periods, during which we can trace increasing social complexity in the ancient Near East.

Edwards (2007); Garrod (1932); Lieberman and Shea (1994); Scarre (2013: chapter 4).

Abu Hureyra, 11,500–7000 BC

Tell Abu Hureyra in Syria is significant as a site of two early occupations, the first an Epipalaeolithic Natufian settlement at c. 11,500–10,000 and the second a Neolithic settlement c. 9000. These distinctive settlements are separated by a period of abandonment of around a thousand years. Abu Hureyra settlement was located on a plateau on the southern bank of the Euphrates River and was excavated in 1972–3 before being flooded by the construction of Lake Assad.

Abu Hureyra is remarkable for the evidence it provides for economic shifts in diet and food production between the Late Palaeolithic and Early Neolithic. The nearby site of Tell Mureybet, which was occupied from around 10,200–8000 provides additional information on the transition from Natufian to the Pre-Pottery Neolithic period. The first settlers at Abu Hureyra lived in clustered 'pit-houses', small circular dwellings with a slightly sunken floor excavated into the sandstone. The walls of these houses were likely built of degradable materials, such as wood and mud, with central wooden posts supporting rooves of reeds. The community at Abu Hureyra, estimated to be up to 200 people in the Epipalaeolithic, were permanently settled hunter-gatherers who lived off the abundant resources near their home. The site is on the migration route of wild gazelle, which was the main animal hunted here, with other large animals such as wild sheep and cattle also hunted.

Selected Neolithic sites in the Near East

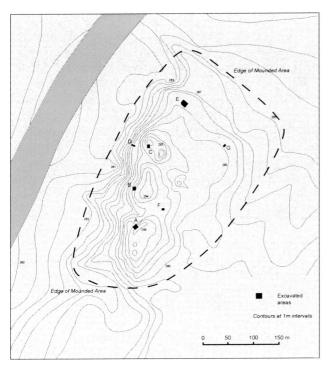

Site plan of Abu Hureyra

More than one hundred types of wild plants and fruits were gathered by the people living at Abu Hureyra and at Tell Mureybet, including wild cereals of einkorn wheat, emmer wheat and two varieties of rye. Radiocarbon dating of the rye seeds returned a very early date of 11,050 BC. These rye seeds also show evidence of selective planting, resulting in characteristics of cultivation and providing slender evidence for very early domestication of cereal grains. Abu Hureyra is situated in a marginal environment and was settled just before the Younger Dryas cooling phase. The cooler and drier climate which came around 11,000 BC could have motivated people to begin cultivating a hardy cereal like rye, which can tolerate harsh conditions. No other cereal except rye seems to have been domesticated during the Epipalaeolithic and there was then a break of several thousand years before the next evidence for cereal domestication. This find is significant, though contentious; these rye seeds have been argued to represent the earliest domestication of cereal crops in the ancient Near East.

Following a break in occupation at Abu Hureyra, people re-settled the site around 9000 BC, establishing a Neolithic village which became one of the largest in the Near East at the time. These people built rectilinear houses of mud brick, gradually creating a large anthropogenic mound (*tell*) as old houses collapsed and new ones were constructed on top of the remains. There is substantial evidence of domesticated wheat, barley and pulses in this second occupation level, which continued through the Pre-Pottery Neolithic A and B (PPNA, PPNB) and into the Ceramic Neolithic, before the site was abandoned at around 7000 BC. The terms PPNA and PPNB, used in the ancient Near East to classify the periods after the Natufian settlements and before the development of pottery in the Neolithic, were defined by archaeologist Kathleen Kenyon during her excavations of Jericho in 1952–8. By the end of the Pre-Pottery Neolithic, villages such as Abu Hureyra, Ain Ghazal and Jericho had populations of over a thousand and occupied areas greater than 10ha. Several of these sites were abandoned in the later Neolithic.

Peregrine and Ember (2002: 12); Scarre (2013: 212–13); Roaf (1990: 18–57).

Jericho (Tell es-Sultan) 10,000–1100 BC

Jericho's history of occupation extends from the Epipalaeolithic period to the Iron Age – from c. 12,000 to 600 BC. The site of Jericho in the Jordan Valley was first inhabited in seasonal occupations of Natufian hunters and gatherers, before becoming an important settlement in the Pre-Pottery Neolithic A and B periods. The site is located near a freshwater spring and a permanent settlement was established here from the PPNA. Investigations, conducted from 1930 to 1936 by John Garstang and from 1952 to 1958 by Kathleen Kenyon, brought to light large areas of the city's Epipalaeolithic and Neolithic phases. A series of round huts about 5 m in diameter with a sunken floor, a stepped doorway and walls of sun-dried mud brick were built by the Neolithic villagers. As the mud brick of house walls collapsed and was rebuilt upon, a mound of twenty-five successive building levels gradually accumulated at Jericho, providing a well-stratified sequence of late Epipalaeolithic and Neolithic material culture. Although the houses were built of mud and straw the early town also featured a substantial stone wall, enclosing the village except for the spring to the east. This enclosure wall stands almost 4 m high and built against it was a stone tower with an internal staircase, an unprecedented structure in the PPNA. Obsidian tools are found in this PPNA settlement, sourced from Çiftilik in central Anatolia. Obisidan from the mountains of central Turkey present at Jericho indicates the distances which valuable materials could be transported even in this early period. There is also evidence for plant cultivation, but animal husbandry begins later in PPNB.

One of the main excavators of Jericho, Kathleen Kenyon, noted that the construction of houses changes from the use of rounded 'hog-backed' bricks to build round huts in the PPNA to rectilinear structures in the PPNB, in a settlement established around 6800 BC. Burials from this period indicate complex rituals, in which skeletal material was inhumed in the walls, or beneath the floors of houses. In one house a series of ten human skulls were found, with facial features reconstructed using plaster and shells set in place of eyes. Two wicker and plaster figurines were also discovered, similar in style to the thirty-five such figurines found at the settlement at Ain Ghazal, contemporary with Jericho. These plastered skulls and figurines found interred within house walls and beneath floors are features of several Neolithic sites in the ancient Near East, including Jericho, Ain Ghazal, Nevalı Çori and Çayönü. Ancestor worship has been inferred as a motivation for the careful reconstruction and treatment of these skulls and remains.

Jericho is one of the world's oldest settlements, but there were long periods in its existence when it appears to have been uninhabited; for example, there is no evidence of settlement in the Chalcolithic period (M5–4). Again, in the later years of the Early Bronze Age, the city was abandoned around 2300 BC. It was partially reoccupied from c. 2100 to 1950, in the transitional period between the Early and

Figure 3.1 A plastered skull from Neolithic Jericho © Ashmolean Museum, University of Oxford.

Middle Bronze Ages, before a Middle Bronze Age city was built, and substantially fortified. After a further violent destruction (perhaps due to earthquake or enemy attack) at the end of the Middle Bronze Age, the site was again abandoned, and then reoccupied, by 1400, in the Late Bronze Age.

Gates (2011: 17–19); Kenyon (1957); Peregrine and Ember (2002: 16); Roaf (1990: 32); Scarre (2013: chapter 6).

Çayönü, 7400–6880 BC

Çayönü was an aceramic Neolithic site in south-eastern Turkey, located at the foot of the Ceramic Mountains on routes connecting the Levantine corridor, the Fertile Crescent and the resource-rich mountains of Anatolia. Its strategic location helps explain the site's longevity and its repeated changes of architectural style.

Providing continuity with sites like Jericho, as well as evidence of settlement into the Ceramic Neolithic, Çayönü demonstrates the great variety of architectural styles and materials found across this period (see site plan on p. 28). It is also significant as a centre of early metal-working.

Between 1964 and 1991, the archaeologists Robert Braidwood and Halet Çambel, Mehmet Özdoğan and Wulf Schirmen unearthed a large expanse of the village, covering three hectares. Its six sub-phases of architecture each appears to have been deliberately buried before the next was constructed. Çayönü's first stage of settled life began with sunken round houses of wattle-and-daub, comparable to those found at other aceramic Neolithic sites including Jericho, Abu Hureyra and Hallan Çemi. The second sub-phase shows a similar reconfiguration of house style, in which the sunken, rounded design is replaced by rectilinear stone foundations resembling a grill plan, onto which wooden flooring covered with lime and clay was laid. This was the living area to which an enclosed courtyard and a small storage area were attached, with mud and straw continuing in use for the walls. These '*Grill Plan*' houses are similar in plan, size and orientation, indicating a well-defined architectural style and shared concept of spatial organization. This Neolithic house-plan is also known from Basta in southern Jordan, Beidha near Petra, at Qal'at Jarmo in north-eastern Iraq, and from Nevalı Çori in south-eastern Turkey, which is contemporary with Çayönü and whose housing designs change in step with Çayönü.

In the subsequent *Channelled Building sub-phase* house foundations were filled in, leaving only drainage channels to protect the structures from groundwater. The houses were dispersed around the site and the villagers built a significant 'Plaza', an open space presumed to be communal in nature. This Plaza is used over several building phases at Çayönü, from sub-phase 3 through sub-phases 4 and 5 (*Cobble-paved Building sub-phase* and *Cell Building sub-phase*, respectively). The Cell Building sub-phase saw the Plaza encircled by the site's largest houses. They are built on cell-plan stone foundations with sturdy mud-brick walls replacing the earlier wattle-and-daub construction technique. The house-plans vary in size and the finds within the houses also differ, suggesting social differentiation between households at Çayönü. The village decreased in size in sub-phase 6, the *Large-room sub-phase*, and the Plaza was used as a rubbish dump.

Çayönü's Neolithic settlements feature significant communal buildings, some of which were maintained and rebuilt throughout the site's history. These include a large round-house, the 'Flagstone Building' with a floor of polished limestone slabs, and the 'Terrazzo Building' whose floor was made of polished stones and specially heat-treated, pink limestone. The most famous of these communal buildings is the 'Skull Building', which contained over seventy skulls and skeletal fragments within and beneath its walls, estimated to be from around 450 individuals. This building, with its intramural burials, recalls the decorated skulls found at Jericho and also known from

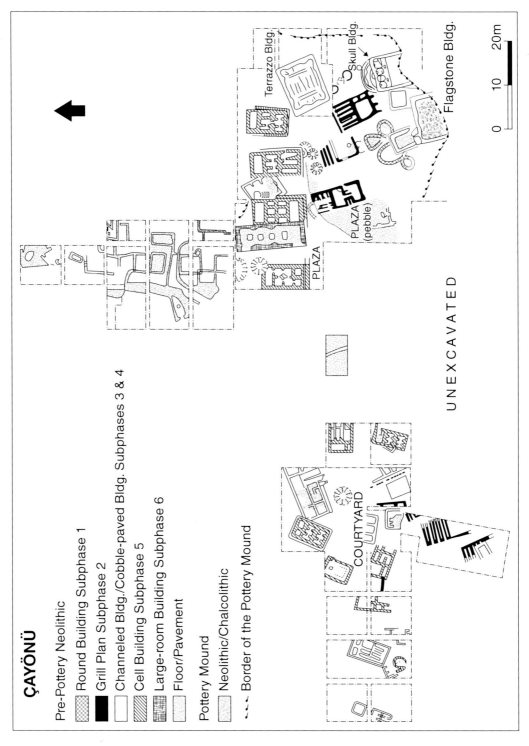

The Neolithic and Chalcolithic levels of Çayönü, showing the location of the Plaza, the Flagstone Building, the Terrazzo Building and the Skull Building

Ain Ghazal in north-west Jordan. As at these sites, the building may have been a place of secondary burial (a charnel house) and possibly connected with ancestor veneration.

Çayönü's villagers experimented with metallurgy early in the site's history, during sub-phases 2, 3 and 4. The working of copper and the copper-bearing mineral malachite provide one of our earliest cases of metallurgy in the Near East. Sourced from the Ergani Maden copper deposits, in the Taurus Mountains some 20 km from Çayönü, the ore was hammered into shape or annealed, a process by which the ore is heated without being smelted. Working of native copper does not seem to have continued long at Çayönü, nor did it spread; it is not until the later M7 at Çatalhöyük that metallurgy is again practised. Pottery arrives at Çayönü c. 6000, without any apparent developmental phase.

In addition to the changing architectural styles of the early Neolithic villagers, the construction of several communal buildings, and the technological experiments with pottery and copper, Çayönü is significant for showing a changing food economy and lifestyle. During sub-phases 1–5, the villagers hunted wild animals and gathered wild plants whilst supplementing their diet by cultivating pulses, lentils, vetch and einkorn wheat. Grapes, figs, rye and domesticated emmer and einkorn wheat are known from the earliest occupations. During the later occupations (sub-phase 5), this strategy shifted to include large quantities of domesticated sheep and goat, with wild animals such as aurochs and red deer hunted less frequently as a result. Domesticated dogs are also evident at Çayönü. For these reasons Çayönü was important in Braidwood's work on early agriculture in the foothills of the Taurus Mountains; Çayönü provides important evidence for a significant shift from hunter-gatherer to agricultural lifestyles between 12,000 and 8000 years ago in the 'hilly flanks' of the Fertile Crescent.

Gates (2011: 19–22); Rosenberg and Erim-Özdoğan (2011); Roaf (1990: 33–5).

Göbekli Tepe

The 'ceremonial centre' of Göbekli Tepe is changing the way that archaeologists think about the role of ideology in the early Neolithic world. The site is dramatic, situated on a hilltop in south-eastern Turkey, and comprises at least twenty circular features, the earliest of which were carved around 9700–9300 BC. The circular features are formed by stone walls, some of which are concentric and the largest of which is 12 m in diameter (Enclosure C) in the interior and 30 m in diameter at its outermost concentric wall. Within these walls stand monumental limestone stelae (pillars) carved with the images of wild and dangerous animals: lions, scorpions, foxes, snakes and vultures. These T-shaped stelae, embedded in the ground and carved in relief, stand at right angles to the walls. The circular rooms were intentionally buried when they came to the end of their use, in a practice similar to the deliberate burial of successive domestic levels at Çayönü, leading to the excellent preservation of the structures and relief sculptures. The only site to have revealed similarly monumental carved pillars is Nevalı Çori, a PPNB settlement where a 'cult complex' dated to around 8000 BC was excavated in 1993. Here, monumental pillars were embedded into the dry-stone walls of a rectangular structure which had been cut into a hillside in the north-west of the village. Nevalı Çori is just 70 km from Göbekli Tepe, once on the shore of the Euphrates but now beneath the Atatürk Dam.

Göbekli Tepe has been hailed as the worlds 'first temple' and pre-dates the development of pottery, of metalworking and of other megalithic sites. It also appears to pre-date settled village life in this part of the world. The early levels of Göbekli Tepe (Level III, dated to the PPNA) have not revealed any trace of houses, hearths or refuse pits to indicate settlement at this site. However, it is clear that this monumental site would have required considerable time, skill and teamwork to construct. There is evidence of tool use, including stone hammers and blades, and animal bones at the site also show the cut marks of butchery. It seems that Göbekli Tepe was a place of feasting, with wild gazelles making up over 60 per cent of the assemblage, along with wild sheep, cattle and pigs. The

Figure 3.2 Excavations at Göbekli Tepe in eastern Anatolia, showing the circular enclosures lined with carved, T-shaped pillars. Teomancimit via Wikimedia.

people building and visiting Göbekli Tepe were hunting wild animals and harvesting wild crops, and do not appear to have been sedentary. The excavation director, Klaus Scmidt, believed that Göbekli Tepe served as a central place for many hunter-gatherer communities living in the region.

What Göbekli Tepe appears to indicate is that monumental architecture and highly developed symbolic repertoires were present without people having sedentary lifestyles. Göbekli Tepe demonstrates that village life and the practice of agriculture were not required in order for people to have the time, marshal the resources and employ the organizational skills to build temples and sustain complex social systems. Later in the site's history there was settlement at Göbekli Tepe, but this came in the PPNB in the form of small oval huts, rectilinear house foundations and small circular structures (Level II). Excavations continue at Göbekli Tepe, with the likelihood that this site and its surrounding region in south-eastern Turkey will reveal further important evidence for the lifestyle and traditions of the early Neolithic people.

Dietrich and Schmidt (2011); Gates (2011: 22–5); Peregrine and Ember (2002: 15); Scarre (2013: 20–1).

Çatalhöyük

Occupied from c. 7300 until at least 6200, Çatalhöyük was one of the first Neolithic villages discovered in the Near East. The site was investigated in the 1960s by James Mellaart, British Institute of Archaeology at Ankara, and since 1933 by Ian Hodder of Stanford University, who headed a large, multidisciplinary investigation. Celebrated for its size, symbolic material culture, and

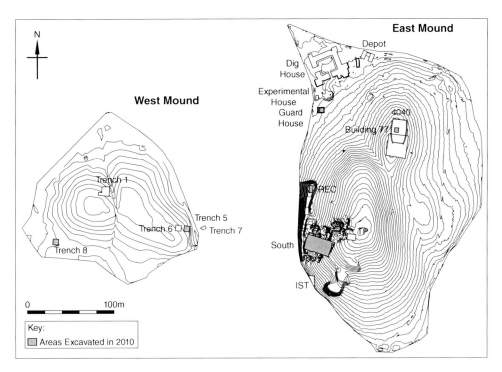

Site plan of Çatalhöyük showing the east and west mounds

complex, early urban structures, Çatalhöyük lies in the Konya basin on the Central Anatolian Plateau, where the moist climate which developed in the Holocene led to the formation of alluvial fans and wetlands. In this favourable environment, a substantial Neolithic village of terraced mud-brick houses arose on what is now the east mound of Çatalhöyük. A settlement from the subsequent Early Chalcolithic period developed on the west mound.

The east-mound village contains many mud-brick houses, clustered in a 'honeycomb' arrangement whereby the walls of one house adjoined its neighbours. Though each house is small, with c. 30 m² of floor-space, the village encompasses 13 ha, a substantial area for the time. Relatively uniform in design, the houses comprise a main room and adjacent storeroom, with small windows high in the walls and an opening in the roof for ventilation. The inhabitants could access their homes via ladders from openings in the flat rooftops. Inside, a clay hearth or oven was usually positioned below the roof-opening. The walls were often painted white with clay and the floors red, red plaster-paint being used to create wall-designs. Low platforms and raised benches were built into the walls, with burials often placed beneath the plastered platforms.

The mud-plaster walls of several buildings were decorated with reliefs of human and animal figures, female breasts and animal heads. Over forty such 'shrines' were discovered within the different building levels. Animal sculptures included the horned heads of cattle (*bucrania*), representations of a stag and a ram, and several pairs of intricately decorated leopards. Painted with stylized, geometric markings, the leopards were often replastered and renewed. Some animal heads integrated the real skull or horns of the animal as a core, which was then plastered over. Likewise, the representations of breasts sometimes used the jaw of a boar, or the skull of a fox, weasel or vulture as a core for the plastered form. Bulls, leopards and vultures appear frequently in Çatalhöyük's shrines, in plastered and painted forms.

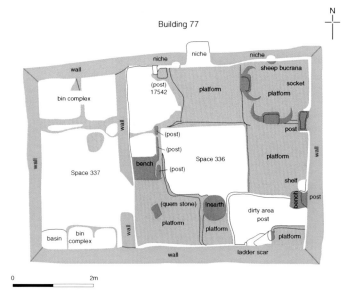

Figure 3.3 Plan of Building 77 at Çatalhöyük, showing the main room and adjacent storeroom, the circular hearth and platforms adjoining the walls. Bucrania are mounted in the wall in the north-east corner. Drawn by David Mackie.

Painted scenes and geometric designs also distinguish the shrines and include intriguing images of life in this Neolithic town. In one scene, stylized vultures appear to circle headless human forms; other scenes depict figures in leopard loincloths, large bulls and wild animals such as boar, wolves, lions, bears, deer and onagers. One mural shows a cluster of rectilinear, geometric shapes and has been interpreted as a representation of the village itself – hence the first known map or town-plan. An abstract shape above the geometric design has been taken to depict an erupting volcano, possibly the nearby mountain Hasan Dağ. But we should be cautious in reading specific events or beliefs into such abstract imagery from 7500 years ago. Alternative interpretations include the suggestion that the 'volcano' represents a leopard hide stretched to dry and the 'village plan' a geometric design, as both leopards and geometric designs commonly occur in the symbolic repertoire of Çatalhöyük.

The shrines' elaborate decoration has led to speculation about the roles of ritual activities in this Neolithic society. In the upper levels of the site, archaeologists found distinctive clay figurines depicting voluptuous female forms, typically linked to fertility rituals and beliefs. The best known figurine, the so-called 'Seated Mother Goddess', represents a female, apparently giving birth while flanked by two felines (leopards or panthers).

The people at Çatalhöyük had domesticated animals but also hunted wild sheep, deer, boar and onagers. Einkorn and emmer wheat were domesticated, and diet was supplemented by other plants native to the area. The villagers made pottery vessels and wooden bowls, cups and boxes, and stone was an important utilitarian and luxury material. The lithic assemblages from Çatalhöyük provide insight into Neolithic exchange networks, through which the central Anatolian villagers could source flint from Syria, turquoise from Sinai, and obsidian from Göllü Dağ and Nenezi Dağ, 125 km to the north-east in Cappadocia. Fine, pressure-flaked spearheads and arrowheads, polished beads and mirrors were made from this obsidian. Most copper objects at Çatalhöyük were of hammered native copper, like earlier examples from Çayönü, but a lump of copper slag implies that copper-smelting was also part of the repertoire of Çatalhöyük's craftspeople.

Similar contemporary (but smaller) sites in Çatalhöyük's region include Hacılar, Suberde and Can Hasan II. Çatalhöyük itself was abandoned near the end of M7, but by about 6000, villages of various appearance and economy were well established throughout the Near East.

Gates (2011: 25–8); Hodder (2006); Roaf (1990: 44–5); Scarre (2013: chapter 6).

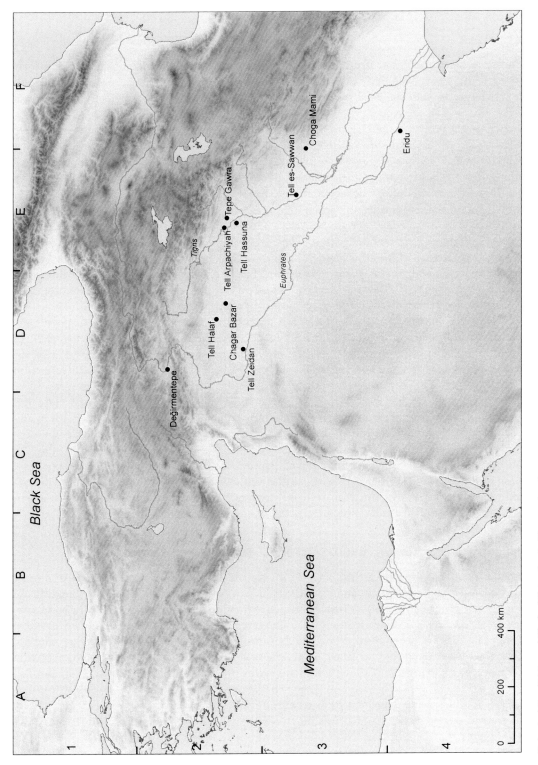

Selected Neolithic and Chalcolithic sites in Mesopotamia

Neolithic Mesopotamia: Hassunan and Samarran cultures (6500–5500)

Tell Hassuna

The previous sites have highlighted the western Fertile Crescent and Anatolian plateau. By the early 6M, people had also moved into the foothills of northern Mesopotamia, a region which could support agriculture without the need for irrigation ('dry' agriculture). These people are known from Tell Hassuna in Iraq, the type-site of the Neolithic Hassuna culture. Tell Hassuna is located beside two wadis on the border of the Tigris valley and was excavated by British archaeologist Seton Lloyd and Fuad Safar of the Iraqi Directorate General of Antiquities in 1943–4. The site extends across 2 ha and contains multiple cultural levels in which the development of the Hassuna culture and its relationship with subsequent regional cultures can be traced. The initial settlement at Tell Hassuna (Level 1) is represented only by hearths and pits, after which people began to construct rectilinear houses of two to three rooms using packed mud (variously termed *adobe*, *pisé* or *tauf*). The early houses included storage spaces beneath the floors, lined with plaster or bitumen. In later levels 2–6, the Hassuna people built larger adobe homes and arranged them around open, central courtyards. These villagers were agriculturalists and left behind stone axes, sickles and grinding stones, which they used to harvest and process grains and pulses including einkorn, emmer and bread wheat, spelt and barley, lentils and peas. Baking ovens and refuse pits also provide insight into their economy, showing that they kept domestic cattle, sheep, goats, pigs and dogs.

The Hassuna cultural traditions of central and northern Mesopotamia intersect with the Samarran traditions of central and southern regions. The Samarran culture marks the extension of agricultural societies southwards from central Mesopotamia, where people established large villages and developed irrigation systems at sites such as Tell es Sawwan and Choga Mami. Irrigation allowed the villagers to increase their crop yields and settle the Mesopotamian plains.

The stratigraphic sequence at Tell Hassuna documents the development of the Hassuna-type ceramic tradition, the introduction of Samarran pottery into the Hassuna assemblage and the Samarran replacement by the successive Halafian traditions. The pottery produced by the Hassuna people was initially coarse, chaff-tempered ware, which was decorated by burnishing to create a 'shiny' exterior. From Level 1c onward, painted decoration is found on Hassuna pottery, shifting to more complex assemblages of painted and incised ceramics in Levels 3–5. Elaborate black-painted pottery in the Samarran-style is introduced in Level 3 (Figure 3.4) and overlaps in later stages with burnished and painted Halafian ceramics in Levels 7–10.

Halaf and Ubaid cultures (c. 6000–5400 and c. 5900–4200)

The majority of Halafian sites are small (1–3 ha), such as Tell Hassuna and Tell Halaf, and seem to have been self-sufficient village communities. Halafian cultural elements include increasing use of copper and bronze, imported obsidian, distinctive handmade pottery, richly decorated by specialist potters, as well as geometric stamp-seals and circular mud-brick buildings known as *tholoi*. Halafian ceramics are easily distinguished by their form and decorative style, typically geometric or animal motifs in red or red and black paint. The peoples of the Halafian culture lived primarily in northern Mesopotamia but their characteristic pottery has been found far afield; the sites of Tell Arpachiyah (Tepe Reshwa) in Iraq and Chagar Bazar in Syria are thought to have functioned as specialized pottery manufacturing and distribution centres.

There was considerable regional variation in local ceramic styles in M6, and so the Halaf ceramic wares are significant as one of the few styles to be found across sites with diverse traditions, from south-east Anatolia to southern Mesopotamia.

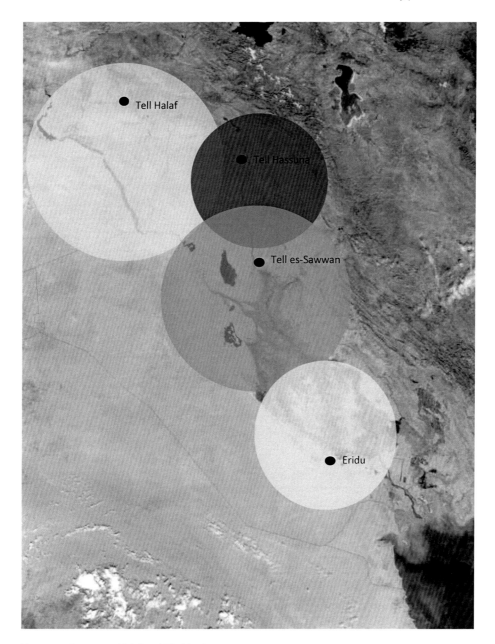

Hassunan, Samarran, Halaf and Ubaid spheres.

Figure 3.4 The general distribution of Hassunan and Samarran sites, in relation to the successive Halaf and Ubaid traditions. Composition by author, satellite photo by Jacques Descloitres, MODIS Rapid Response Team, NASA/GSFC.

Figure 3.5 Black-painted pottery in the Samarran-style, decorated with geometric birds and fish © PRISMA ARCHIVO/Alamy. Peregrine and Ember (2002: 44, 46, 50); Scarre (2013: 433–8).

The Halafian culture overlaps with the start of the Ubaid tradition (evident in Level 11 of Tell Hassuna), a late Neolithic group of villagers who settled in southern Mesopotamia. The transition to Ubaid sees the amount of obsidian at Tell Hassuna fall, indicating reduced contact with the northern sources. The Ubaid culture had a very long duration in the southern Mesopotamian alluvial plains, initially developing alongside Samarran traditions as early as the M7, and being replaced by the Uruk culture in the late M5. Ubaid traditions spread to northern Mesopotamia from around 5300, following the Tigris and Euphrates Rivers and gradually replacing the Halafian traditions. The Ubaid period sees the development of large urban settlements comprised of multi-roomed, rectilinear mud-brick houses. Some of these settlemens spread over 10ha with smaller villages developing nearby, in a pattern of urban development at the heart of Mesopotamian civilization. Large-scale irrigation systems were also built by the Ubaid peoples to manage the land and expand agricultural practices. The culture is named for Tell Ubaid, excavated by Sir Leonard Woolley in the 1920s, and includes important sites such as Eridu, founded in 5400 and arguably the oldest city in the world, Choga Mami and Tepe Gawra in Iraq, Tell Zeidan in Syria and Değirmentepe in Anatolia.

Southern Ubaid: Eridu

Both the southern and northern Ubaid communities appear to have been made up of a series of small, localized, ideologically connected chiefdoms. In the north, these people coexisted with the Halaf in apparent harmony. There are few exotic or prestige items evident in these communities, in which it appears that control of land, water and staple resources were markers of power. The settlement of Eridu was located next to a branch of the Euphrates and its inhabitants practised agriculture, kept domesticated animals including sheep, goats and cattle, hunted wild game from the nearby wetlands and steppe, and fished in the river. Eridu is a large 'city' mound surrounded by six smaller 'village' mounds, providing one of the best stratigraphic sequences for the Ubaid tradition. Fourteen levels of Ubaid period settlement have been excavated here (levels 19 to 6), beginning with small huts constructed of reed matting plastered with mud, and later buildings constructed of sun-dried mud brick. From levels 16–19 the village included a clearly identifiable temple precinct, beginning as a single-roomed structure and developing in later levels into an

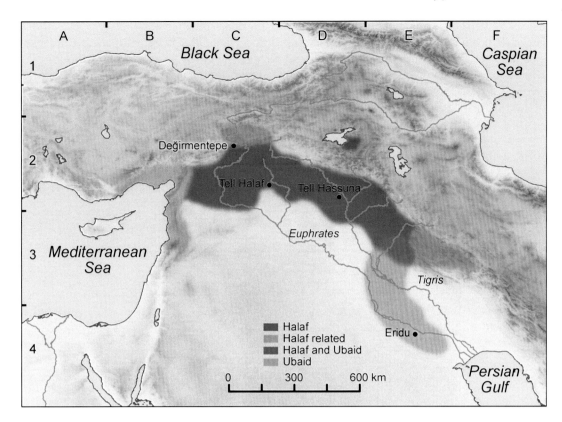

The general distribution of sites from the Halaf and Early Ubaid periods

imposing Mesopotamian temple with buttressed walls and recessed niches. In the later Ubaid period a large cemetery of over 1,000 burials was established near Eridu. Two hundred graves were excavated, many containing two interments, along with painted ceramic vessels, obsidian and shell beads. Eridu continued to be inhabited into the Uruk period, with a later Uruk temple complex overlaying the Ubaid period settlement.

Regional networks in the Ubaid period were evidently extensive, with Ubaid pottery found at several sites along the west coast of the Persian Gulf. Analysis of Ubaid pottery at these sites indicates that the pottery was produced in southern Mesopotamia and transported to the Persian Gulf sites, several hundred kilometres away. The Ubaid culture also spread northward through Mesopotamia, gradually replacing the Halaf traditions.

Peregrine and Ember (2002: 383–5); Scarre (2013: 436–7).

Northern Ubaid: Tepe Gawra

The northern Ubaid culture is well represented at Tepe Gawra, a site in the piedemont of the Zagros Mountains, which revealed eight levels of Ubaid occupation before a transition to the related Uruk tradition. The site is about 2 ha in size and its inhabitants lived in rectilinear houses of 2–3 rooms, some having a central hallway. Narrow alleyways separate some of these dwellings whilst many of the houses share walls with their neighbours. The site appears to have been more densely settled as the Ubaid period progressed, with the open areas between houses in lower levels gradually taken up by newer houses in later levels. Incorporated into the village was a drainage system of brick- and pottery-lined channels and basins throughout the settlement. Kilns for pottery production are found in groups at Tepe Gawra, indicating that some areas of the settlement were set aside as pottery workshops. Other areas defined for specific purposes include a complex of three temple structures established in the late Ubaid period, c. 5200.

The Ubaid period provides the first evidence for regional centres with satellite villages, development of temples within larger settlements, established irrigation economies and new forms of social complexity and identity. In Mesopotamia, these characteristics lead directly into the first urbanized states of the Uruk period (M5).

Peregrine and Ember (2002: 377–9, 389–90); Stein and Rothman (1994); Scarre (2013: 437).

Part II

Background to the historical era

4

The homelands of the major
Near Eastern kingdoms

Anatolia is a name first used in C10 AD for the land mass lying to the east across the Aegean Sea. It comes from the Greek word *anatole*, 'rising', which refers to the region where from a Greek perspective the 'rising (of the sun)' takes place. The name is still often used for modern Turkey (or at least the western two-thirds of it, and sometimes more specifically for Turkey's central highlands). *Anadolu* is the Turkish form of the name. The western half of Turkey, roughly the area extending between the Aegean coast and the Euphrates, is sometimes called Asia Minor, a name first used in Classical Greek sources. One of the most distinctive features of Anatolia's topography is the highland plateau which rises 1000 m above sea level. On the north it is bounded by the Pontic Mountains, on the south by the Taurus Mountains, and in the east it merges into the Armenian Mountains. These mountain ranges sharply differentiate the plateau from the rest of the Anatolian region. In the west, the plateau slopes down more gently to the Aegean coast. Anatolia is often referred to as a landbridge between the Near Eastern and western worlds, for across it passed many important routes of communications which conveyed population groups, trade, cultures, ideas and armies from east to west, and from west to east. It was the homeland of many ancient civilizations, notaby the Late Bronze Age Hittite kingdom of Hatti, and the Iron Age kingdoms of Phrygia, Lydia, and, in the east, the kingdom of Urartu.

Mesopotamia, another ancient Greek name, means 'the land between the rivers'. It broadly defines the region bounded by the Euphrates and Tigris and their tributaries. Much of this region today lies within Iraq, but in the north Syria and Turkey also extend into it. Broadly speaking, it consists of two main parts: (1) northern or Upper Mesopotamia (north of modern Baghdad, where the two rivers most closely approach each other), homeland of the Old, Middle and Neo-Assyrian empires (M2 and M1), and the Mitannian (Mittanian) empire (M2); (2) southern Mesopotamia, often called Babylonia, the homeland of the Sumerian city-states (M3) and the Babylonian empires of Hammurabi (early M2), the Kassites (later M2), and the Neo-Babylonian kings of whom Nebuchadnezzar II was the most famous (mid M1). Following the conquest of the Neo-Babylonian empire by the Persian king Cyrus the Great in 539, Mesopotamia was incorporated into a succession of empires, beginning with the Persian (Achaemenid) empire, and subsequently, in the wake of Alexander the Great's conquests, the Seleucid empire. In the latter's declining years, Mesopotamia came progressively under the control of the Iran-based Parthian empire. But as Rome extended its imperial sway through the western half of the Near Eastern world, particularly from 64 BC when Syria was made a Roman province, sovereignty over Mesopotamia became a major source of conflict between Rome and Parthia. The contests with Rome was one of the legacies inherited from the Parthians by their Sasanian successors, whose empire was founded by Ardashir I in AD 224.

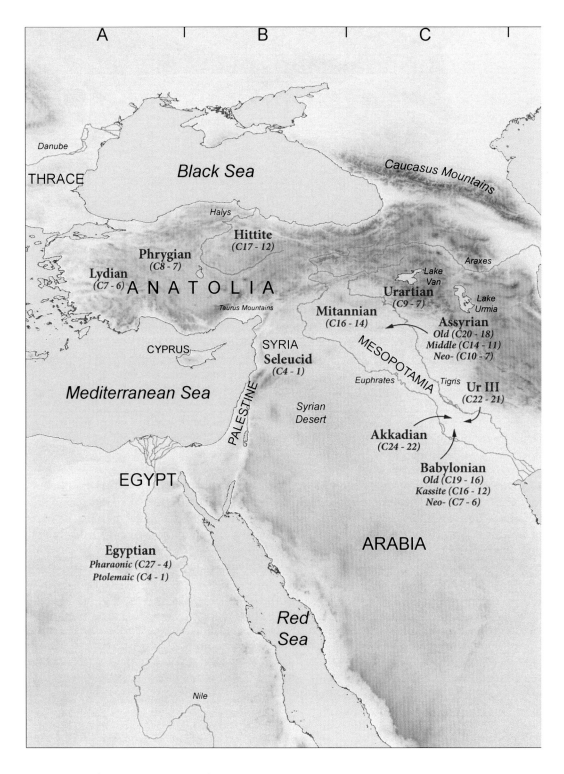

Core regions of the Near Eastern kingdoms

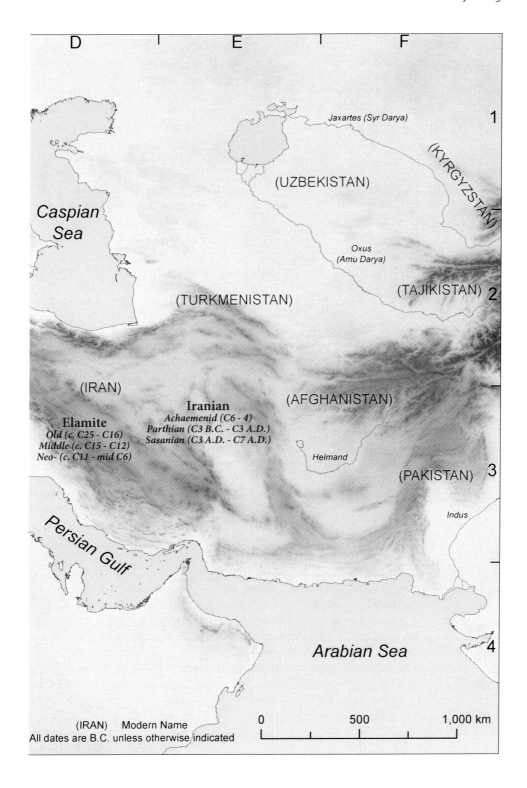

D　　　　E　　　　F

1

Jaxartes (Syr Darya)

(KYRGYZSTAN)

(UZBEKISTAN)

Caspian Sea

Oxus (Amu Darya)

(TAJIKISTAN)　2

(TURKMENISTAN)

(IRAN)

Iranian

(AFGHANISTAN)

Elamite
Old (c. C25 - C16)
Middle (c. C15 - C12)
Neo- (c. C11 - mid C6)

Achaemenid (C6 - 4)
Parthian (C3 B.C. - C3 A.D.)
Sasanian (C3 A.D. - C7 A.D.)

Helmand

(PAKISTAN)　3

Indus

Persian Gulf

Arabian Sea　4

(IRAN)　Modern Name
All dates are B.C. unless otherwise indicated

0　　　500　　　1,000 km

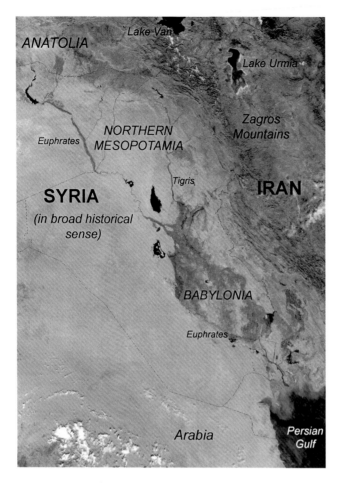

ANATOLIA

Lake Van

Lake Urmia

NORTHERN
MESOPOTAMIA

Euphrates

Zagros
Mountains

Tigris

IRAN

SYRIA

(in broad historical sense)

BABYLONIA

Euphrates

Arabia

Persian
Gulf

Mesopotamia and surrounding territories (NASA satellite image)

The name **Syria**, which first appears in Greek in the *Histories* of Herodotus (C5), is a variant of 'Assyria'. The variants are earlier attested in a C8 Luwian-Phoenician bilingual inscription found at Çineköy in south-eastern Turkey, in the form 'Sura/i' and 'Assura/i'. When speaking of Syria in its ancient context, scholars commonly use the name in a broad geographical sense, to cover a conglomerate of lands that stretch southwards from south-eastern Anatolia to Arabia, through the Amuq plain of Turkey, and the modern country of Syria west of the Euphrates. The term is sometimes extended to include the territories of Israel, Palestine, Lebanon and Jordan as well. Of course, such a definition excludes the large triangular area of modern Syria that extends east of the Euphrates through the Habur river region to the banks of the Tigris. (We shall include this area in the region broadly referred to as northern or Upper Mesopotamia.) Whatever their compass, the lands comprising 'ancient Syria' retained throughout the ages a relatively high degree of ethnic and cultural homogeneity, despite their populations being intermixed with constant influxes of immigrants into their communities and cities – new settlers sometimes forcibly transplanted from other parts of the Near Eastern world.

Topographically, Syria consists of widely contrasting regions. Its westernmost component, a narrow fertile strip along the Mediterranean coast with typically Mediterranean climate and vegetation, is separated by mountainous terrain, like the Jebel Ansariyah and the Lebanon and Anti-Lebanon ranges, from semi-arid and arid plateaux. Despite its vast tracts of inhospitable territory, control of Syria was much sought after by the great powers of the day, since through it passed many of the routes of communication which linked the lands of the east – Mesopotamia, Iran and central Asia – with the ports and land-routes that provided access, for both commercial and military purposes, to the Mediterranean world. Indeed, much of Syria's history has to do with the imposition of foreign sovereignty over it, by the superpowers of the various epochs who were fully aware of its strategic importance – Egypt, Mitanni and Hatti in the Late Bronze Age, Assyria, Babylon, Persia and the Seleucid kingdom in M1 BC, and Rome from mid C1 BC onwards. The task of imposing administrative uniformity on the region was generally not an easy

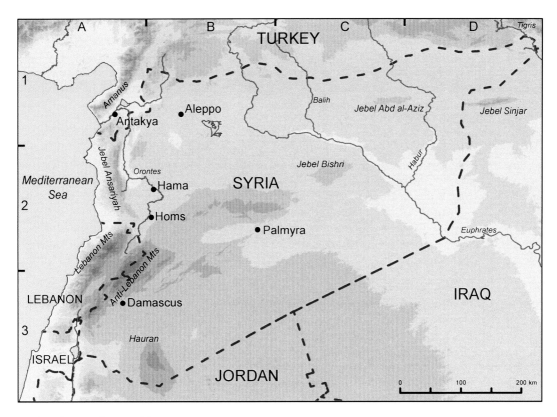

Modern Syria and its neighbours

one, for throughout its history Syria was a patchwork of many independent cities, principalities and sub-regions.

In AD 135, the Roman emperor Hadrian reconstituted the Roman province of Judaea as a new province under the name Syria Palaestina. A further administrative reorganization in the region took place under the emperor Septimius Severus (193–211), who split the old Roman province of Syria into two: Syria Phoenice along the Phoenician coast, and the much larger Syria Coele ('Hollow' Syria), which extended through the northern Orontes river valley, and eastwards from the river to the Euphrates. First attested in the Hellenistic period, the term Coele Syria was originally used to designate the region of the ('hollow') Biqaʻ valley in Lebanon, extending between the Lebanon and Anti-Lebanon ranges. Its northern limit was marked by the Eleutheros river (modern Nahr el-Kebir), which forms the northern boundary of modern Lebanon, and was for long the boundary between Seleucid- and Ptolemaic-controlled territory in Syria. But the term was flexible in its definition. W.G. Dever notes that under the Ptolemies and Seleucids, all of Phoenicia, and even Palestine, could be designated Coele Syria (*OEANE* 2: 41). In later periods, the term was sometimes used to designate the whole of Syria from the Orontes valley eastwards to the Euphrates.

The name **Levant**, first used in Medieval times, is derived from the Italian word 'levante' which means 'rising' (from the Latin verb *levare*, 'to raise'). Like Greek *anatole*, it signifies the rising of the sun in the east. In its most comprehensive sense, the term has been applied to all the lands lying east of Europe – from the western coast of Turkey to the Euphrates, southwards through Syria, Lebanon,

Jordan and Palestine to the borders of Egypt, with the inclusion of Cyprus and other islands of the eastern Mediterranean. It is now mostly associated with Jordan and the eastern Mediterranean coastal lands and hinterlands of Syria, Lebanon, Israel and Palestine. But in the context of Roman rule in the Near East, it is given broader application, being applied to the Roman-controlled territories lying between the Taurus Mountains in the north and the Red Sea in the south, and between the Mediterranean coast and the Euphrates.

(After D.F. Graf, *OEAGR* 4: 247–8).

Palestine has also had a wide range of meanings throughout its history, its locations and its limits shifting, expanding, or contracting from one period to another. The name is commonly believed to have originated from the people called the Peleset, one of the groups of so-called Sea Peoples, who in C12 BC settled in the southern coastal plain of the Levant (in the restricted sense of this term), where they re-emerged in biblical tradition as the Philistines. Their land was called Philistia. Greek sources preserved their name as *Palaistine Syria* (Palestinian Syria), which gave rise to *Palaestina* as a stand-alone place-name covering the region of the Levant between Phoenicia and Egypt. *Palaestina* was the abbreviated name that came to be used of the Roman province which the emperor Hadrian designated as *Provincia Syria Palaestina* in AD 135 (in place of the earlier *Provincia Iudaea*).

Jordan is the name of the Arab state which became the independent Hashemite Kingdom of Jordan in 1946 after it was first created as a British protectorate called Transjordania in 1921. From the area east of the Jordan rift valley, it extends southwards to the head of the Gulf of ʿAqaba. The modern term 'Transjordan' is generally applied, by archaeologists and others, to all the territories lying within the present kingdom of Jordan. However, it reflects a perception, dating back at least to Old Testament sources, that the area east of the Jordan river was a separate geographical entity 'beyond the river' – i.e. across the Jordan river from Palestine. Our biblical sources provide much of our information about the principal countries which occupied the region both east and south of the river, particularly during late M2 and M1 BC – most notably, Gilead, Ammon, Moab and Edom. Topographically, Jordan is a highly diverse region. The more elevated westward-oriented parts of the plateau on which much of it is located enjoys a Mediterranean-style climate well suited to agricultural activity, whereas the plateau's lower parts slope down eastwards towards the Arabian desert with the attendant arid conditions thus entailed.

The modern country ***Iran*** extends over the high Iranian plateau (more than 1,500 m above sea level) from the Caspian Sea in the north to the Persian Gulf in the south. It shares land borders with Iraq and Turkey on the west and north-west, Armenia, Azerbaijan, and Turkmenistan on the north, and Afghanistan and Pakistan on the east. The name 'Iran' is derived from *ariyanam*, which comes from *ariya*, an Old Persian word meaning 'noble, lordly'. In Old Persian, *ariyanam* (*khshathram*) means '(land) of the Aryans'. Initially, the term *ariya* was applied to several Indo-European groups, who are believed to have entered the Iranian plateau around the middle of M2 BC (or later), perhaps from a homeland east of the Caspian Sea. *Ariya* also provided the basis for the Middle Persian name *Eran*, from which the Sasanian kings adopted the political concept *Eranshahr* ('Empire of the Aryans'). And from this concept comes the name *Iranshahr*, shortened to *Iran*, which was adopted (in place of 'Persia') as the modern country's official name in 1935. Three great Iran-based empires arose and flourished in the Near Eastern world throughout the course of its history, each of them extending its power and influence well beyond the frontiers of its homeland. We now commonly refer to them by the names of their founders (or their alleged ancestors): (1) the Achaemenid empire (559–330 BC), founded by Cyrus II (the Great), allegedly a descendant of the house of Achaemenes; (2) the Parthian (Arsacid) empire (c. 247 BC–AD 224), founded by Arsaces I; (3) the Sasanian empire (AD 224–651), founded by Ardashir I, and named after Sasan, a legendary ancestor of the Sasanian royal line.

5
Writing systems

When human beings began to draw, impress or inscribe symbols on pieces of clay and other suitable surfaces, for the purposes of recording information, the age of writing began in the Near East, pretty much around the same time as it did in Egypt – in the last centuries of M4 BC. The invention of writing marks the beginning of the historical era in the Near Eastern and Egyptian worlds. (Scholars are uncertain whether the development of one was in any way linked to the development of the other, though they observe that the systems are quite different to each other.) The earliest examples of writing in the Near East come from the southern Mesopotamian city Uruk, where roughly square and rectangular clay tablets have been found, dating to c. 3300 BC, with some 700 different signs represented on them. Clay writing surfaces of other shapes were also used at this time, including cones, cylinders and spheres. As writing developed, the clay sufaces, especially tablets, were impressed with what we now call the cuneiform script. The term meaning 'wedge-shaped' is adopted from the Latin word for a wedge – 'cuneus'. It indicates that the signs of the script so called were made by pressing into soft clay the triangular ends of reeds cut from the banks of the Mesopotamian and other rivers. This script was preceded by a relatively simple pictographic script, in which the signs mostly represented easily identifiable objects; thus an ox is represented by the picture of an ox-head, a human by a human head, barley

PICTOGRAPHIC SIGN c. 3100 BC						
INTERPRETATION	?stream	ear of barley	Ox-head	bowl	head + bowl	?shrouded boby
CUNEIFORM SIGN c. 2400 BC						
CUNEIFORM SIGN c. 700 BC (turned through 90˚)						
MEANING	water, seed, son	barley	ox	food, bread	to eat	man

Figure 5.1 The development of the cuneiform script. Adapted from Roaf (1996: 70).

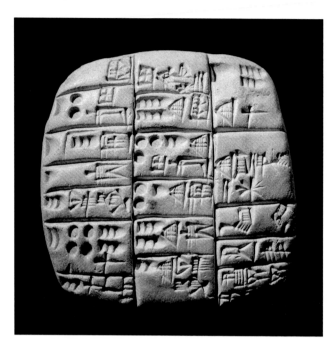

Figure 5.2 Sumerian tablet recording goats and sheep, c. 2350 BC. © The Art Archive/Alamy.

by an ear of grain. Two pictograms together could represent a slightly more abstract or complex idea, or an action; thus a combination of a human head and a bowl could be used to represent the action of eating.

The earliest cuneiform tablets were used for recording business transactions, or a farmer's produce or assets, in the form (for example) of a specified number of livestock and a specified quantity of grain. We can still detect the pictographic origins of a number of cuneiform signs in the group of wedge-shaped impressions making up a particular cuneiform representation of a word; thus the original pictographic representation of an ox is easily detectable in the cuneiform sign-group for this word. But the cuneiform script grew ever more complex as it was called upon to record the activities and transactions and assets of increasingly complex societies. And the more sophisticated a society, the greater the need for putting into written form abstract concepts and other kinds of information which were very difficult, if not impossible, to represent by simple pictograms. Inevitably, writing-systems became increasingly detached from their pictographic origins.

The cuneiform script represents a predominantly syllabic system of writing, made up of a series of syllable signs and what are called ideograms and logograms. In general, syllable signs represent a combination of vowels + consonants, or vowels on their own – e.g. *a, na, nan*. Words in the syllabic script are made up of at least one syllable. Ideograms are signs indicating a concept, logograms a single word. These signs are generally represented in transliteration by upper case letters (e.g. LUGAL – king) or are used as determinatives to identify the nature of a word to which they are attached; thus the name of a deity is preceded by the sign for a deity, and that of a city by the sign for a city.

The cuneiform script, first evolving in southern Mesopotamia, was adopted as the writing system of the Sumerian city-states. It then passed to a succession of other Near Eastern states, from the Akkadian and Ur III empires in late M3 through the Middle and Late Bronze Age kingdoms of Mesopotamia and Syria, the Middle and Late Bronze Age Anatolian-based kingdom of Hatti and well down into M1 BC, when it served to record the exploits of Persian Achaemenid kings. For much of its history, the script was impressed on clay tablets, but it was inscribed on other writing surfaces as well, painted on wood and carved on stone. Throughout its existence, cuneiform was most frequently employed for fairly mundane purposes – the recording of inventories, business transactions, routine administrative activities and the like – but its use extended well beyond this, to records of a king's achievements, of military conquests and political coups, to exchanges of correspondence between the great rulers of their days, to treaties concluded between royal peers or kings and their vassal rulers, to hymns, prayers and mythological texts, and to literary classics like the Gilgamesh epic. The various tablet archives unearthed from palaces, administrative buildings, temple repositories and private houses provide us with the basis of most of our information for the history of the Near East throughout the Bronze Ages and for much of it during the succeeding Iron Age and later periods.

The ability to read simple, basic cuneiform texts may have been fairly common in many Near Eastern societies. But reading and writing skills of a more complex order, encompassing both technical and scholarly literacy, were probably largely con-

Figure 5.3 The 'alphabet' of Ugarit. Photo of replica from the collection of Trevor Bryce.

fined to a select scribal class within the Near Eastern palace and temple bureaucracies, whose members must have taken years to master the complete cuneiform system with its hundreds of sign groups. The first substantial example of an alphabetic script, or at least one to which the name 'alphabet' is commonly applied, was found in the tablet archives of Ugarit; the oldest of the tablets are of C14–13 date (the alphabet's invention may date back several centuries before this), but the tablets belong mostly to Ugarit's last years in early C12 BC. An obvious advantage that alphabetic scripts have over syllabic ones is that they are made up of much simpler and much smaller sign-lists. There are only thirty-three symbols in the most extensive of them (the Georgian alphabet). With regard to the Ugaritic script, each sign in it appears to represent a consonant only – which presumably would mean that the combination of consonants making up a word were considered sufficient to identify the word without the need for vowels. On the other hand, it might be argued that the Ugaritic script should really be categorized as a short syllabary, in which each sign represents a consonant and (implied) vowel combination (cf. Powell, 2007: 35, on the Phoenician 'alphabet').

However we categorize it, this type of script was used to write the Ugaritic language (just one of the languages represented on the tablets from Ugarit). The scholar P.T. Daniels devised for it the name 'abjad', from the first two letters of the Arabic alphabet. The signs making up the very first, pre-Ugaritic, 'alphabetic script' were probably linear ones, drawn or painted onto writing surfaces. In this category we can perhaps include the (as yet unreadable) linear signs, dating to c. 1800 BC, carved on rock-faces in Egypt. But in the Ugaritic version of the script, wedge-shaped signs were used. This was clearly in imitation of the long-established cuneiform system. But the 'alphabetic signs' are not related, except in appearance, to the traditional cuneiform ones; rather, they are an adaptation of earlier linear signs, as evidenced by the few remaining examples we have of earlier scripts of this kind. The reason for the use of cuneiform for the Ugaritic writing system was that the script was incised on clay tablets, perhaps reflecting, the scholar D. Pardee suggests, a shortage of papyrus on which a linear script could more easily have been used.

By the early Iron Age, the alphabetic script was being used by Phoenicians, or their Canaanite predecessors, and from there passed to the Aramaeans and Hebrews, henceforth becoming widespread throughout the Near East. The Arabs also adopted the alphabetic script, tailoring it to suit the particular phonemes of their own language. And from the Phoenicians the alphabet spread westwards into the Greek world. We cannot be sure when the Greeks began using the Semitic-originating script – though a C8 date is widely accepted. The Greeks' particular innovation was that they incorporated into their alphabet explicit vocalic as well as consonantal sounds, to help accommodate their wide range of vowels

Figure 5.4 Luwian hieroglyphic inscription © Mike P. Shepherd/
Alamy.

and diphthongs. This could be done by using a number of Phoenician alphabetic signs that represented sounds not used in Greek. Thus the first letter of the Greek alphabet was called alpha, a vowel and an adaptation of the Semitic sign aleph which represented a sound that had no Greek equivalent.

We should also mention here a distinctive form of writing in M2 and M1 BC, in Anatolia and Syria, which bore no relationship to any other Near Eastern script. This was the hieroglyphic script used by one of the Indo-European-speaking groups who arrived in Anatolia probably during M3. Occupying large parts of central, southern and western Anatolia in M2, they were a people we call the Luwians. The archives of the Hittite capital Hattusa indicate that cuneiform was used for recording the Luwian language on clay tablets. But more conspicuous examples of the language are provided by a hieroglyphic script, once misleadingly referred to as 'Hittite Hieroglyphic'. Towards the end of the Late Bronze Age, Hittite kings used this Luwian-language script for recording their exploits on public monuments such as built stone walls and cliff-faces. Like its cuneiform counterpart, the hieroglyphic script is a syllabic one, also containing many ideograms and determinatives. After the collapse of the Hittite empire, Hittite cuneiform died out, but the hieroglyphically-written Luwian language survived, becoming the official language of many of the Iron Age kingdoms of southeastern Anatolia and northern Syria referred to now as the Neo-Hittite kingdoms.

Seals

Seals were another important means of recording information in the Near Eastern world. They could be used to identify the owner of a piece of property, to ensure that access to certain containers (jars, boxes, bags, etc.) or storerooms was limited to authorized persons, and to validate a range of documents which bore the sealing, or seal-imprint, of a person or persons for whom the document was drawn up. Thus peace treaties were validated by the seal-imprints of their signatories. The use of seals for identification purposes dates back to the Late Neolithic period (7600–6000) in Syria. No more than a few centimetres in length, breadth or diameter, seals were incised with a design or inscription which was unique to individual owners and thus served as their owners' particular form of identification. The majority of seals were made of stone, but various other metals were also used, as well as baked clay, faience, wood, bone, ivory and shell. The earliest seals had flat or slightly convex surfaces whose incised design or inscription was stamped on soft clay, to indicate ownership. This form of seal, the stamp seal, remained the most common one in Anatolia, Egypt and the Levant. But in Mesopotamia, a different form of seal, in the shape of a cylinder, became the preferred type from the Early Dynastic Sumerian period (c. 2900–2334 BC) onwards, as also in Iran and Syria-Palestine. Cylinder seals were generally c. 2.5 cm long and 1.5 cm in diameter, and often conveniently pierced lengthwise, to enable their owners or delegates to thread them and wear them around their necks. They were rolled over the surface of pieces of clay and thus produced imprints that could be repeated a number of times, depending on the size of the space available, in a continuous band.

Figure 5.5 Stamp seal of the Hittite king Mursili II. Photo of replica from the collection of Trevor Bryce.

Figure 5.6 Mesopotamian cylinder seal © www.BibleLandPictures.com/Alamy.

The motifs used on seals ranged from abstract patterns, like lozenges, spirals and concentric circles, to mythological scenes and sometimes hybrid monsters, to animals from the natural world, to schematically rendered human figures. Daily activities such as hunting, sailing, grain-collection and storage are also depicted. Many of the representations provide examples of exquisite miniature art, some of the finest from the ancient Near Eastern world. But most important for historical purposes are the seals incised with inscriptions. Some contain prayers and religious dedications, others indicate their owners' titles and professions and the names of the owners' fathers. Among the most valuable of the inscription-bearing seals are those preserved for us in Hittite seal impressions. (Very few actual seals have been found.) Recently, several thousand sealings were discovered in one of the archives of the Hittite royal capital Hattusa, the so-called Nişantepe archive. All the sealings from this archive belong to Hittite kings or members of their families. Typically, the king's name appears in Luwian hieroglyphs in the centre of the seal. His name appears again in a cuneiform inscription inscribed in concentric rings around the outer rim of the seal and often containing valuable information about its owner's genealogy, sometimes extending back several generations.

Articles in *CANE* (4: 2097–209); Robinson (1995); Roaf (1996: 70–3); Daniels (*OEANE* 5: 352–61); Veldhuis (2011).

6

A sample of sites where important inscriptions have been found

Alalah (***Tell Atchana***) The most important periods of Alalah's history are represented archaeologically by levels VII and IV, dating respectively to C17 and C15. Both these levels have produced tablet archives. Almost all the tablets contain Akkadian cuneiform inscriptions. Their contents, covering legal, diplomatic and administrative topics, provide a number of valuable insights into the life, economy and social structure of Alalah in the periods to which they belong. We have almost 200 tablets from level VII, discovered mainly in the palace and the temple, and 300 from the level IV palace archive.

Amarna archive Cache of clay tablets, now 382 in number, discovered in 1887 on the site of el-Amarna (ancient Akhetaten) in Egypt. Three hundred and fifty of the tablets are letters, or copies of letters, exchanged by the pharaoh Amenhotep III (1390–1352) and his successor Amenhotep IV/Akhenaten (1352–1336) with foreign rulers or with the pharaoh's vassal subjects in Syria-Palestine. (A few of the letters also date to Akhenaten's successors Smenkhkare and Tutankhamun.) The remaining thirty-two tablets consist of syllabaries, lexical lists and mythological texts. With the exception of two pieces of correspondence in Hittite, one in Assyrian, and one in Hurrian, the Amarna documents are written in Akkadian.

Bisitun (***Bisutun, Behistun***) Iranian site best known for its rock-cut relief and trilingual cuneiform inscription, carved by order of the Persian king Darius I in 520–519. The three versions of the inscription – Old Persian, Babylonian and Elamite – record Darius' seizure of his throne and his military triumphs at the beginning of his reign. Between 1835 and 1847, a British officer H.C. Rawlinson copied the trilingual and undertook the decipherment of the Old Persian version. His success provided the foundation for all subsequent investigations and translations of the cuneiform languages.

Brak, Tell (**Nagar/Nawar**) Inscriptions of the Akkadian period have been found here, stamped on mud bricks and bearing the name Naram-Sin (c. 2254–2218). A palace-fortress dating to the Mitannian period (C16–14) has produced the earliest known Hurrian text of the Mitannian empire.

Byblos Noteworthy among the city's finds is the so-called Ahiram sarcophagus, dating to late M2 (Ahiram was a king of Byblos), and now in the Beirut Museum. In addition to its artistic motifs, it exhibits the earliest surviving example of a Phoenician alphabetic inscription. The inscription carries a warning against violating the tomb.

Ebla (***Tell Mardikh***) In the remains of Palace G (C24), an archive of c. 2,500 documents was discovered between 1974 and 1976 by an Italian archaeological team led by Prof. Paolo Matthiae. Written in cuneiform in the Eblaite and Sumerian languages, the tablets include a wide range of economic, administrative, legal, lexical, literary, diplomatic and epistolary texts. These provide

Sites of important inscriptions

valuable insights into the administration and daily life of Ebla and its relations with its surrounding region, during a period of approximately 50 years in C24. Lists of names in the texts include many rulers of the city, giving evidence of a succession of Eblaite kings that extends back at least to C27.

Emar (Meskene) Excavations have brought to light approximately 800 Late Bronze Age cuneiform tablets and fragments dating from C14 to C12. A small number are in Hittite and Hurrian, but the great majority are written in Akkadian and Sumerian. Many of them cover a range of economic activities and legal transactions. Others contain lexical, omen and literary texts (including fragments of the Gilgamesh epic), and there are some 200 texts describing festivals and ritual practices. Collectively, the tablets constitute our second most important source of contemporary written information (after the archives of Ugarit) on Late Bronze Age Syria.

Hattusa (Boghazköy, Boghazkale) The city's palace and temple cuneiform archives, containing thousands of tablets and tablet-fragments, provide our main source of written information about the Hittite empire. These are supplemented by a small number of Luwian hieroglyphic inscriptions on stone surfaces and a recently discovered archive of 3,400 royal sealings.

Figure 6.1 The Bisitun monument. Photo by Hara1603 via Wikimedia.

Figure 6.2 Sarcophagus, with inscription, of King Ahiram, Byblos. Photo by DEA/G. DAGLI ORTI/De Agostini/Getty Images.

Kanesh Headquarters of the Middle Bronze Age Assyrian Colony network in central Anatolia. More than 22,000 tablets written in Assyrian cuneiform and providing detailed information about the Assyrian merchants' trading activities in Anatolia have been unearthed from level II of the site (mid C20–early C19), and c. 420 from the succeeding Ib level (late C19–mid C18). The great majority of the tablets are letters exchanged between merchants in the colonies, and business associates and family members in Assyria involved in the trading operations at their home end.

Karabel is located 28 km west of modern Izmir (Turkey), in a pass through the Tmolus mountain. range. It is the site of a Late Bronze Age monument with a relief (originally one of four) and inscription. The relief depicts a male human figure armed with bow, spear and sword. The inscription, carved in Luwian hieroglyphs and translated by J.D. Hawkins, identifies the figure as Tarkasnawa, a late C13 king of the Arzawan land called Mira, a subject state of the Hittite empire.

Mari (***Tell Hariri***) The cuneiform clay tablets excavated at Mari, numbering more than 22,000 and consisting of both state and private archives (the latter belonging to palace personnel), were discovered in various locations, but mainly in and around the great palace. Their contents include letters, administrative documents and a few legal and religious texts. Though the total time-span covered by the archives extends from late M3 until C18, most of the tablets are confined to a quarter of a century at the very end of Mari's existence, from the period of the Assyrian viceroy Yasmah-Addu to the destruction of Mari by Hammurabi at the end of Zimri-Lim's reign (c. 1762).

Nineveh Within the city's so-called North Palace built by the C7 Neo-Assyrian king Ashurbanipal, a library was discovered, consisting of two large chambers stacked with 24,000 cuneiform clay tablets. Its wide range of contents, including copies of literary texts which were gathered from all parts of the empire and whose originals in some cases dated back centuries before the foundation of the Neo-Assyrian kingdom, provide us with one of our most valuable sources of information on Mesopotamian history and culture.

Nippur Excavations have uncovered some 12,000 cuneiform clay tablets. The contents of large numbers of these are economic or lexical in nature, but they also include copies of the great majority of Sumerian literary compositions. The tablets were found mainly in private houses, and range in date from the Old Babylonian through the Kassite and later periods. Nippur was a centre for scribal education in the Old Babylonian period.

Nuzi (***Yorgan Tepe***) Nuzi is best known today for the large quantities of clay tablets which were unearthed from the site's Late Bronze Age phase, roughly between mid C15 and mid C14. Over 5,000 tablets came from both public and private archives, and bear the seal impressions of their authors. Their contents include contracts, legal records, letters, and ration and personnel lists. Written in a distinctive Akkadian dialect, with an admixture of Hurrian names, the tablets have been seen as indicative of declining socio-economic conditions in the region during the period of their composition.

Persepolis The most important tablets unearthed on the site of this the Persian ceremonial royal capital are the 15,000–20,000 Fortification Tablets, so called because they were found in two rooms of the city's fortification-system. Dating to the years 509–494, within the reign of Darius I, they are the earliest administrative documents we have of the Persian Achaemenid empire. They record food distributions made by Treasury officials, from the imperial stores located around the capital, to a large number of recipients (including members of the king's own family, priests and workers in the employ of the royal court), supplies to travellers and donations to the gods.

Qatna German excavations in 2002 unearthed a hoard of sixty-seven tablets and fragments, consisting of letters and judicial and administrative documents, dating to the Amarna period (mid C14). The tablets confirm the existence of a major Hurrian element in Qatna's population at this time.

Shemshara was called Shusharra in the Old Babylonian period. A palace archive dating to this period consists of 250 complete and fragmentary clay tablets – letters, administrative documents and sealings. Most of the letters found in the archive were written to Shusharra's ruler Kuwari by the Old Assyrian king Samsi-Addu (Shamshi-Adad in Akkadian), his son Ishme-Dagan (Assyrian viceroy in Ekallatum), and various Assyrian officials, at a time when the town was becoming caught up in the conflicts between the warring major and petty kingdoms of Mesopotamia. The correspondence can be dated to the mid 1780s.

Sippar Excavations conducted in the city's temple of the god Shamash in the late 19th century uncovered 60,000–70,000 tablet-fragments, mostly dating to the Neo-Babylonian period. A century later in 1986, Iraqi archaeologists discovered in the temple a small Neo-Babylonian library (C6) in which hundreds of tablets were still in their original pigeonholes. Some of the texts they contain are literary in character, and include Standard Babylonian recensions of 'classics' like the Atrahasis myth, and texts of the C18 Old Babylonian king Hammurabi. Other tablets contained hymns and prayers, and mathematical, lexical, divinatory, and astrological texts.

Susa Some 1,550 clay tablets, dating to c. 3100–2900, have been unearthed from an early phase of the city's existence. Written in a pictographic script, and still undecipherable, the inscriptions have traditionally been designated 'Proto-Elamite', on the assumption that they were ancestors of the 'Old Elamite' inscriptions dating to later M3 and early M2. It is now clear, however, that there is no connection between the two. Much later, numerous inscriptions dating to the Persian king Darius I (522–486), including fragments of trilingual inscriptions (in Old Persian, Babylonian and Elamite), provide valuable information on the construction of the city under Darius, the rebellions which Darius put down, and the extent of the empire which he ruled.

Tushpa (Van Kale) Urartian inscriptions written in cuneiform were carved into the natural rock-fortifications of the Urartian fortress settlement, and also on steles and column bases, and royal tombs (identifying their occupants). These written records include a number of 'display inscriptions' which extol the achievements of various Urartian kings. The oldest datable structure of the citadel-complex is a large rectangular platform, on which appear six copies of an inscription of Sarduri I (c. 832–825), written in Akkadian.

Ugarit (***Ras Shamra***) The city's archives constitute one of our most valuable sources of information on international relations in the Late Bronze Age. Most of the documents are written in a local version of the Akkadian language. But some are in Ugaritic, and several other languages are also represented in the archive, e.g. Hittite. A wide range of correspondence with foreign rulers, administrative and legal documents, and ritual, medical and literary texts have been unearthed from six palace archives, from the so-called 'High Priest's House' between the two temples on the acropolis, and from several private houses.

Uruk is considered the birthplace of writing in Mesopotamia, in view of the discovery there of clay tablets containing the first evidence of a pictographic script and numerical notation, dating to late M4.

Xanthus The most important inscription of Xanthus, Lycia's chief city, appears on the so-called Inscribed Pillar which contains a 255-line text – 243 lines in Lycian (in two dialects), and a twelve-line Greek epigram. Dating to the late C5 or early C4 BC, it records, among other things, the military exploits of the city's ruling dynasty. It is the longest surviving inscription in the Lycian language, though – like the Lycian language in general – much of it remains unintelligible. Close by Xanthus is the ***Letoum***, a sanctuary dedicated to the goddess Leto and her children Apollo and Artemis. In 1973, a trilingual inscription, in Lycian, Greek and Aramaic versions, was discovered. Dating to 358 BC, it contains regulations for the establishment of a new cult in the sanctuary.

7

Trade and mineral resources

Regular trading activities between Near Eastern commmunities and regions date well back into prehistoric times. In the Neolithic period, the metal obsidian figured commonly among the items which made up the prehistoric trading repertoire. The Early Bronze Age saw an intense increase in and expansion of commercial enterprises across many regions of the Near East, enterprises frequently asssociated with the spread of cultural contacts from one region to another. Bronze came into common use in this period. Since the tin required for its manufacture could be obtained in relatively few regions, most notably, perhaps, Afghanistan, often far removed from places where it was in demand, large-scale trading operations had to be organized both to access the original sources and to ensure the security of the consignments on the routes along which they had to travel. As international trading ventures developed, so too did the complexity of the societies with which they were associated. This is reflected in the emergence of a number of Early Bronze Age kingdoms in Iran, Mesopotamia, Syria and Anatolia. This period too saw the evolution of writing, used primarily, at least to begin with, as a medium for recording commercial transactions. Cities and kingdoms in resource-poor regions like southern Mesopotamia had a basic need for access to a range of commodities, including timber and various minerals, which they themselves lacked. And what could not be obtained through peaceful commercial enterprises was seized as plunder on military campaigns, like those conducted by the kings of the Akkadian empire into the lands west of the Euphrates. Luxury goods frequently figured in the cargoes brought back from or traded with other lands. They included precious metals, faience, ivory, fine textiles, finely crafted furniture, pottery, perfumes and spices.

Before the invention of coinage in Lydia in C7 BC, a system of barter operated throughout the Near Eastern world. Gold, silver, and bronze ingots were often used as forms of payment, their value depending on the nature of the metal and their weight. Donkeys were commonly used for transporting goods from one region to another, often over considerable distances and rough terrain. The camel was a relatively late introduction as a pack animal, probably coming into regular use for this purpose in Arabia during M1 BC. Water-borne commerce was also a regular feature of trading activity in the Near Eastern world. This began long before there are records of it in our written sources. But the written records provide us with more precise information. They tell us, for example, of late M3 trading expeditions linking the kingdoms of Babylonia with the countries which lay alongside the 'Lower Sea', i.e. the Persian Gulf and the Arabian Sea – in particular, Meluhha, Dagan and Dilmun. Sea trade was also conducted through the waters of the eastern Mediterranean and the Aegean Sea, from ports like Ugarit, Tyre and Sidon on the Syro-Levantine coast, and Troy and Miletus on the western Anatolian coast, to Egypt, Cyprus, Rhodes, Crete, the Aegean islands and mainland Greece. Material evidence for this trade includes the remains of

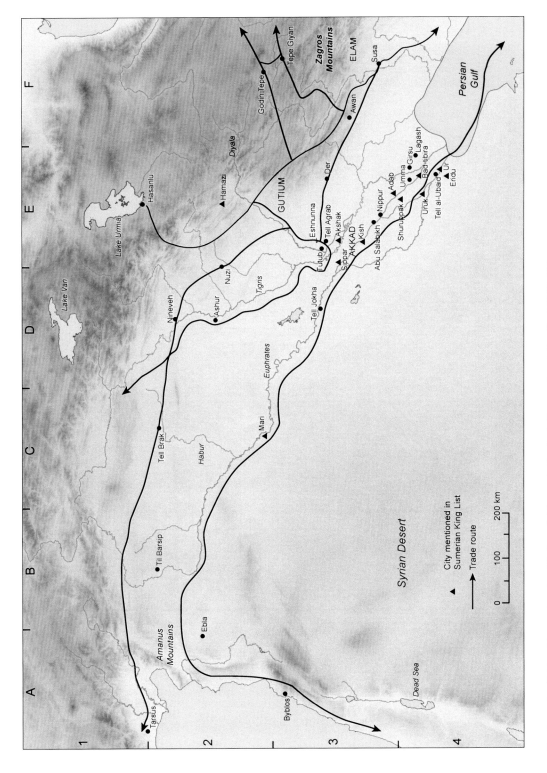

Trade routes linking Mesopotamia with its neighbours in the Early Bronze Age (after Roaf 1996: 83)

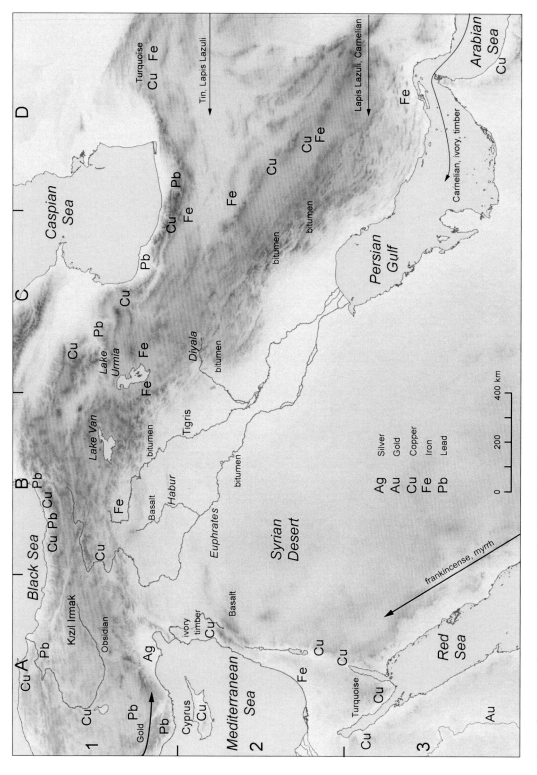

Mineral sources in the ancient Near East (after Roaf 1996: 35)

two Late Bronze Age merchant ships found off the coast of south-western Turkey, the Gelidonya and Uluburun wrecks. The former's cargo consisted principally of copper and tin ingots, but there were luxury goods as well, acquired from all parts of the eastern Mediterranean and Aegean worlds. Luxury items discovered in the Uluburun wreck included faience goblets in the shape of rams' heads, silver bracelets and gold pendants from Canaan, duck-shaped ivory cosmetics boxes, copper cauldrons and bowls, and a trumpet carved from a hippopotamus tooth. Raw materials in the cargo included ebony, ivory and ostrich eggshells.

Astour (*CANE* 3: 1401–20).

Part III

The Early Bronze Age (continuing into the Middle Bronze Age)

8

The Sumerians

The Sumerian civilization arose and flourished in southern Mesopotamia during M3 BC. 'Sumer' and 'Sumerians' are derived from *Shumerum*, the Akkadian word for the region. But in their own language, the Sumerians called their country Kengir, and referred to themselves as the Saggiga, 'the black-headed people'. We do not know whether they were newcomers to Mesopotamia, in early M3, or a continuation of the region's native inhabitants. But in either case, they intermingled with other population groups – primarily those of Semitic origin, who probably arrived in the region around the same time. Out of this ethnic mix, the Sumerian civilization developed. The 'Sumerian' language is unrelated to any other known tongue, but became the dominant language spoken in southern Mesopotamia during the Early Bronze Age.

From written and archaeological sources, we can build up a reasonably comprehensive picture of Sumerian history, in what is known as the Early Dynastic period (c. 2900–2334). Politically, the Sumerian world was divided among fourteen city-states: Sippar, Kish, Akshak, Larak, Nippur, Adab, Shuruppak, Umma, Lagash, Bad-tibira, Uruk, Larsa, Ur and Eridu. Most of these had three main sectors: (a) a walled inner city containing temples, palaces, official administrative quarters, and some domestic dwellings; within the city-centre lay the temple-enclosure, generally surrounded by an oval wall; (b) the *kar*, a business district located on the canal-banks to facilitate trading operations between cities linked by southern Mesopotamia's waterways; (c) a suburban area (*uru-bar-ra*), which included outlying rural districts.

Each city-state was ruled by a king, known as an *ensi* ('lord') or *lugal* ('great man'). Initially, the king's authority was limited by a wealthy temple-priesthood with whom he shared control of the state. But later in the Early Dynastic period, religious and secular authority became increasingly separated. In a number of states, particular kings emerged as powerful absolute rulers, who sometimes extended their authority over other states by military force – like Eannatum, a mid-M3 king of Lagash who conquered Ur, Uruk and Kish.

One of the best known sources of information on Sumerian history is the so-called Sumerian King-List, a document composed in early M2, several centuries after the Early Dynastic period had ended. According to the King-List, the city-states formed some kind of confederation throughout their history, in which one state exercised for a time political hegemony over the others, until the leadership role passed to another state, and then to another. A particular feature of the list is its division of Sumerian history into pre-flood (antediluvian) and post-flood (postdiluvian) eras. The list contains many distortions and exaggerations, not the least of which are the prodigious lengths it ascribes to some of the kings' reigns. And it treats as sequential many kingships which, if they did exist, must have been contemporaneous. But it undoubtedly does preserve some elements of historical truth, and remains for us an important source of information on Sumerian history.

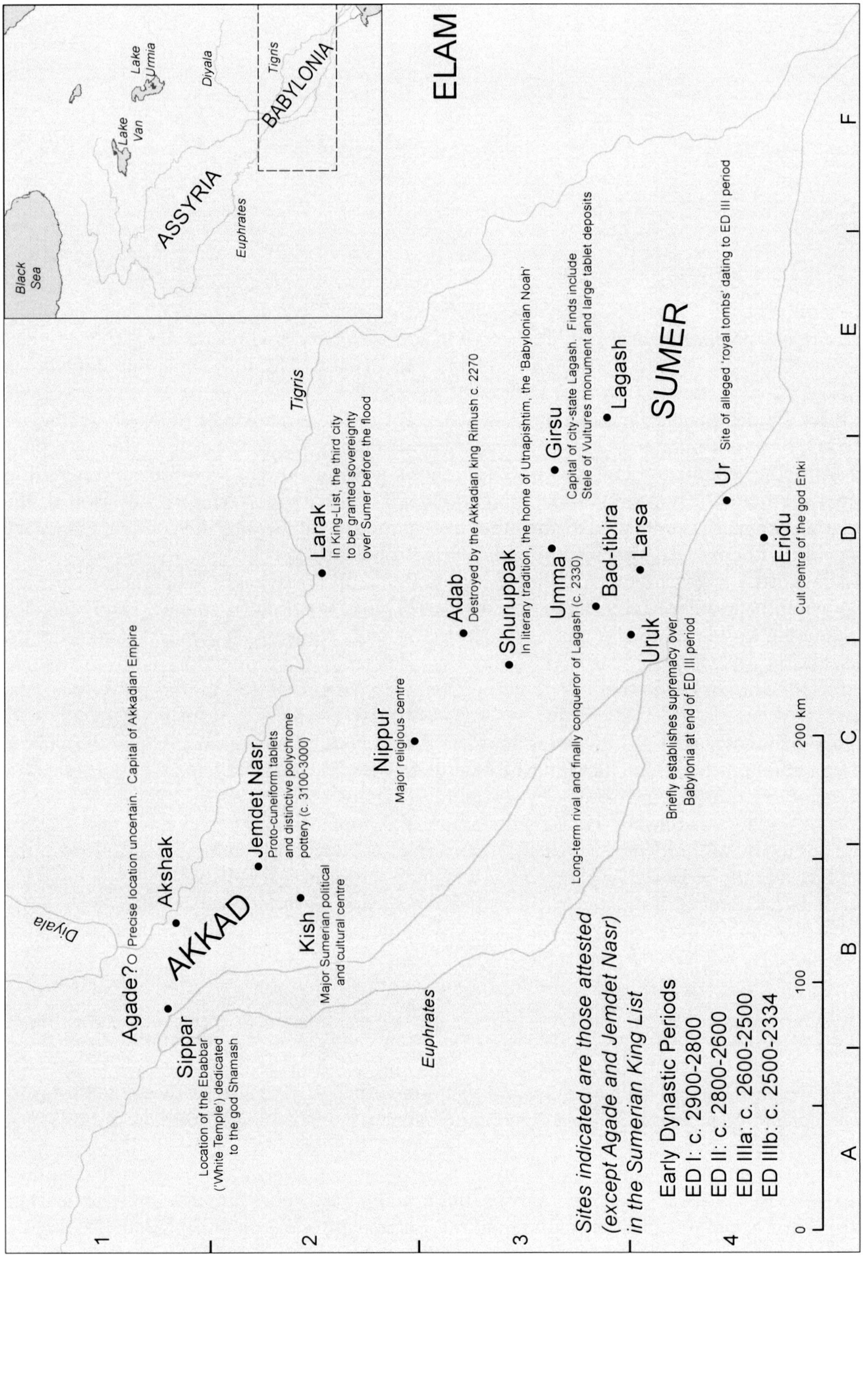

Black Sea
Lake Van
Lake Urmia
Diyala
Tigris
ASSYRIA
BABYLONIA
Euphrates
ELAM
AKKAD
SUMER
Agade? Precise location uncertain. Capital of Akkadian Empire
Sippar
Location of the Ebabbar ('White Temple') dedicated to the god Shamash
Akshak
Kish
Major Sumerian political and cultural centre
Jemdet Nasr
Proto-cuneiform tablets and distinctive polychrome pottery (c. 3100-3000)
Nippur
Major religious centre
Larak
In King-List, the third city to be granted sovereignty over Sumer before the flood
Adab
Destroyed by the Akkadian king Rimush c. 2270
Shuruppak
In literary tradition, the home of Utnapishtim, the 'Babylonian Noah'
Umma
Long-term rival and finally conqueror of Lagash (c. 2330)
Girsu
Capital of city-state Lagash. Finds include Stele of Vultures monument and large tablet deposits
Lagash
Bad-tibira
Larsa
Uruk
Briefly establishes supremacy over Babylonia at end of ED III period
Ur
Site of alleged 'royal tombs' dating to ED III period
Eridu
Cult centre of the god Enki
Sites indicated are those attested (except Agade and Jemdet Nasr) in the Sumerian King List
Early Dynastic Periods
ED I: c. 2900-2800
ED II: c. 2800-2600
ED IIIa: c. 2600-2500
ED IIIb: c. 2500-2334
0
100
200 km
A
B
C
D
E
F
1
2
3
4

Sumer and Akkad

In order to control the harsh natural environment in which they lived, the Sumerians developed a high level of practical and organizational skills. The complex system of irrigation canals which they built to sustain life in the barren tracts of southern Mesopotamia is testimony to this. Amongst the many innovations of Sumerian society, we should give pride of place to what became the Sumerians' most lasting legacy to later civilizations – the technology of writing. Archaeologists have brought to light hundreds of thousands of clay tablets written in Sumerian cuneiform. Their contents include a large array of administrative activities, items for trade and inventories of one kind and another. But they also contain a number of literary texts, most notably poems about a king of Uruk called Gilgamesh. These poems provided the basis for one of the great classics of ancient Near Eastern literature – the Epic of Gilgamesh, composed in early M2 and preserved and redacted in different versions by the Sumerians' successors over a period of almost 2,000 years.

Roux (1980: 85–139); Michalowski (*CANE* 4: 2279–91, *OEANE* 5: 95–101); Crawford (2004).

Nippur

Nippur was Mesopotamia's most important religious centre. It was the site of the Ekur, the temple of one of Mesopotamia's most important gods Enlil. The city's special sacred character, and no doubt its political neutrality, prompted many M3 rulers of both Sumer and Akkad to seek divine endorsement for their regimes there. Resources for many of the city's public building projects, including its temples and fortifications, along with a stream of costly gifts for the temples, were provided by external benefactors. During the first half of M2, Nippur's fortunes declined, but it received a fresh lease of life in C14 under the kings of Babylonia's Kassite dynasty.

Though the worship of Enlil was Nippur's primary focus, the city contained the temples of a number of deities. The most notable of these temples was dedicated to the goddess Inanna. It has a sequence of twenty-two levels, extending from the Middle Uruk through the Late Parthian period. A further sequence of temples, extending from the end of the Ur III dynasty (late M3) through the Neo-Babylonian period (late C7–6), may have been dedicated to the healing goddess Gula, wife of the god Ninurta. Nippur was a centre for scribal education in the Old Babylonian period.

Zettler (*OEANE* 4: 148–52).

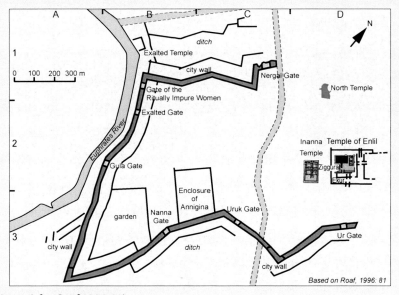

Nippur (after Roaf 1996: 81)

9

Uruk (Warka, biblical Erech)

Uruk's history of occupation extends from the Late Ubaid period (M5) until or shortly before the Arab invasions in C7 AD. The site consisted originally of two settlements, Uruk and Kullab(a); the former was in the area later called Eanna (a Sumerian term meaning 'house of heaven'), the precinct dedicated to the goddess Inan(n)a, the latter lay in the religious complex dedicated to the supreme Mesopotamian god Anu.

In M4 (if not earlier), the settlements were combined into the single city Uruk, which became Mesopotamia's most important political, administrative, cultural, and religious centre. Its significance is reflected in the fact that 'Uruk' is now used as a general designation for the cultural phase which spanned much of M4 in Mesopotamia, between the Ubaid and Jemdet Nasr periods. Uruk is also considered the birthplace of writing in Mesopotamia, because of the discovery there of clay tablets containing the first evidence of a pictographic script and numerical notation; they date to c. 3300. Its importance continued in the Early Dynastic (ED) period of the Sumerian civilization (c. 2900–2334). In fact, the city was now more intensively settled than in any of its earlier phases. It was enclosed by a 9.5 km long mud-brick fortification-wall, which Mesopotamian literary tradition ascribed to Uruk's legendary king Gilgamesh. After a period of apparent decline in ED II, the city seems to have enjoyed another flourishing phase of its existence in ED III (c. 2600–2334), the end of this period being marked by the supremacy which its king Lugal-zage-si established over the whole of southern Mesopotamia. An ambitious building programme was undertaken within Uruk under his rule. But his career ended abruptly when he was defeated in battle c. 2334, by Sargon, founder of the Akkadian empire. Sargon followed up his victory by demolishing Uruk's walls and taking Lugal-zage-si prisoner. Uruk's consequent decline in size and importance was followed by another brief resurgence of power after the destruction of the Akkadian empire by the Gutians, c. 2193. This resurgence was attributed to Uruk's king Utu-hegal (c. 2123–2113) who expelled the Gutians from Sumer, and established his dominance over it – until his rule ended with the rise of the Ur III dynasty founded by Ur-Namma (c. 2112). Uruk continued to prosper under the Ur III kings. Ur-Namma himself commissioned an extensive building programme in the city, which included the construction of a ziggurat.

Figure 9.1 'Warka vase', c. 3000 BC, found in Uruk's temple treasury. Photo by bpk, Berlin/ Art Resource, NY.

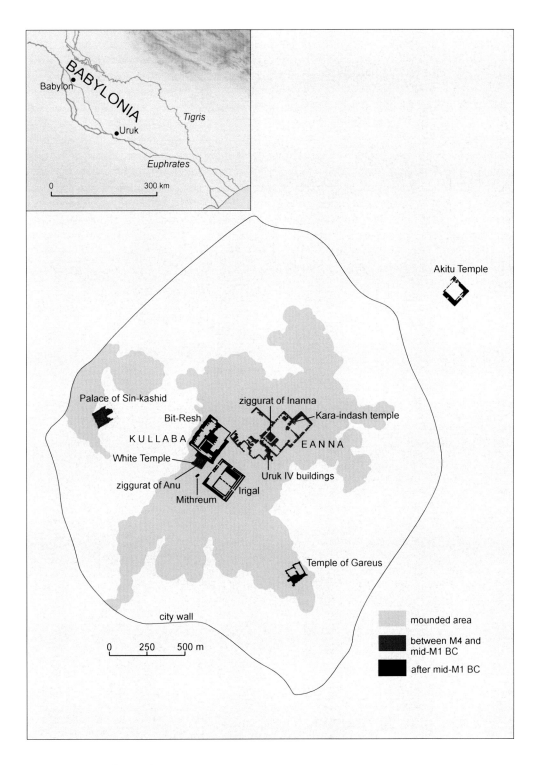

Uruk in context (after Roaf 1996: 60)

With the collapse of the Ur III dynasty at the end of M3, Uruk once more went into decline. After the fall of Ur, it became attached first to the kingdom of Isin, and subsequently to that of Larsa. With Larsa's fall to the Babylonian king Hammurabi in 1763, Uruk was incorporated into the Babylonian empire. When it joined a rebellion against Babylon in the reign of Hammurabi's successor Samsu-iluna (1749–1712), the Babylonian responded with a crushing defeat of the rebel cities, in the process capturing Uruk and demolishing its walls. The city was probably then abandoned, remaining derelict for more than two centuries. However, c. mid C15 the Kassite king Kara-indash undertook another rebuilding programme in Uruk's religious quarter, which initiated a new phase in the city's history. Through the first half of M1, a succession of kings – both Neo-Assyrian and Neo-Babylonian – undertook building and restoration programmes in Uruk, especially within its sacred precincts. But by the later Persian period, the great Eanna temple dedicated to the goddess Ishtar (Sumerian Inan(n)a) had fallen into disuse. In the Hellenistic period, when the region came under Seleucid control, Uruk was the seat of several governors, and two great new temple precincts were built: the Resh, dedicated to Anu, and the Eshgal (sometimes read Irigal), the temple of the goddesses Ishtar and Nanaya. Henceforth, under Parthian and Sasanian rule, the city suffered steady decline until its final abandonment by C7 AD.

Boehmer (*OEANE* 5: 294–8); Rothman (2001); Van De Mieroop (2016: 21–43).

10

Early Dynastic and Old Kingdom Egypt

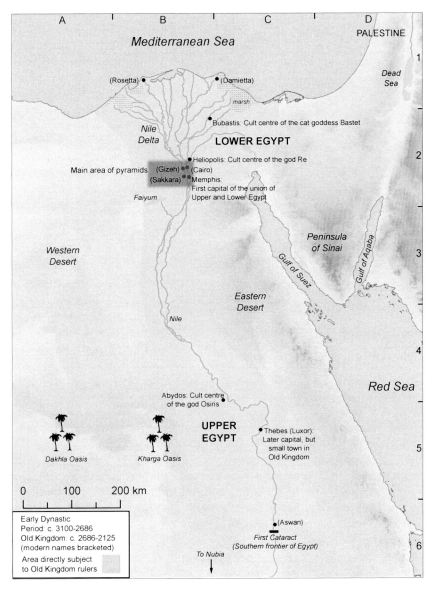

Egypt during the Early Dynastic and Old Kingdom periods

Egypt today (NASA satellite image)

Throughout its recorded history, Egypt had extensive cultural, commercial and political contacts with the Near Eastern world, and was on a number of occasions at war with parts of it. The Greek historian Herodotus referred to the country as 'the gift of the Nile', and indeed the Nile is the lifeblood of this narrow 1,000 km fertile strip of land, which in ancient times extended north from the first cataract near modern Aswan to the Mediterranean Sea. Originally the two main regions of ancient Egypt – Upper Egypt, from the first cataract to the apex of the Delta, and Lower Egypt, comprising the Delta marshlands – formed two separate kingdoms. They were united, according to tradition, by a king of Upper Egypt called Narmer (sometimes identified with a semi-legendary king called Menes). This union marked the beginning of the so-called Early Dynastic period in Egyptian history (c. 3100–2686), which saw many advances in urban civilization including, it was once thought, the development of writing. There is now evidence that writing in Egypt began several centuries earlier. It developed late in the prehistoric Predynastic period (c. 5500–3100), during which a number of links were initiated between Egypt and the Near East, particularly Mesopotamia. Narmer/Menes established his royal seat at Memphis, 24 km south of modern Cairo. The city rapidly became a bustling, cosmopolitan metropolis, capital of a united kingdom whose prosperity increased markedly in the period commonly referred to as the Old Kingdom (c. 2686–2125). This period included the Pyramid Age (c. 2500–2300), so called because of the massive royal tombs built during it. The Old Kingdom saw a significant increase in Egypt's military power and commercial outreach. It established sovereignty over its neighbour Nubia in the south, and constantly extended its commercial links and operations in the lands to its north. The Early Dynastic period and the Old Kingdom span much of M3 BC, the Early Bronze Age in archaeological terms.

Bard (2000); Malek (2000).

11

The Akkadian empire

The Semitic kingdom Akkad arose in the northern part of Babylonia following the end of the Sumerian Early Dynastic period. Its founder Sargon (= Sharrum-kin; c. 2334–2279) established the kingdom by seizing power in a city called Agade. (The unlocated site of this city probably lay near the confluence of the Tigris and Diyala rivers.) Under his rule, Agade became the seat of a royal dynasty which built the first Near Eastern empire. At its greatest extent in the reign of Sargon's grandson Naram-Sin (c. 2254–2218), the Akkadian empire stretched through the whole of Mesopotamia, and reached Kurdistan in the north, Elam in the east, and south-central Anatolia and the Mediterranean Sea in the west (though questions have been raised, e.g. by Van De Mieroop, 2016: 73, about how much direct control the Akkadians actually exercised through all these regions). But after Naram-Sin's death, the empire quickly disintegrated, and ended abruptly in the reign of his son Shar-kali-sharri (c. 2217–2193). Incessant revolts by subject peoples, internal political instability, and a long period of severe drought may all have contributed to the empire's fall. Already in Naram-Sin's reign, there was serious unrest among the subject peoples, including those of its Mesopotamian heartland. This is indicated in a text commonly known as the Great Revolt, which reports a massive uprising against the king. Naram-Sin succeeded in suppressing the rebellion. But it was an ominous warning of things to come. Like many later conquerors and empire-builders, the Akkadian kings lacked both the organizational capacity and the resources to maintain effective control over the vast complex of territories which they had taken by force. But the immediate and specific agent responsible for ending the Akkadian empire was a group of raiders called the Gutians, from the Zagros mountain region.

Despite its relatively short existence and violent end, the kingdom of Akkad left a number of important cultural legacies to the Near Eastern world. The most notable of these was its language, which was to become, for well over a thousand years, the international language of diplomacy throughout the Near East.

Foster, Huehnergard (*OEANE* 1: 44–54); Westenholz (1999); McMahon (*AANE*: 649–67); Van De Mieroop (2016: 68–79).

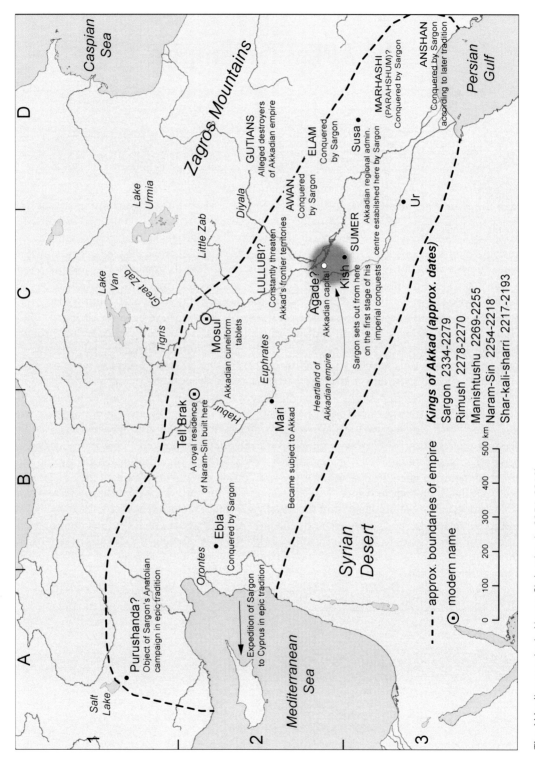

The Akkadian empire in Naram Sin's reign (c. 2254–2218)

Labels on the map:

Caspian Sea

Zagros Mountains

Lake Urmia

Lake Van

Little Zab

Great Zab

Diyala

GUTIANS
Alleged destroyers
of Akkadian empire

AWAN
Conquered
by Sargon

ELAM
Conquered
by Sargon

MARHASHI
(PARAHSHUM)?
Conquered by Sargon

ANSHAN
Conquered by Sargon
according to later tradition

Persian Gulf

Susa
Akkadian regional admin.
centre established here by Sargon

LULLUBI?
Constantly threaten
Akkad's frontier territories

Agade?
Akkadian capital

Kish

SUMER

Ur

Sargon sets out from here
on the first stage of his
imperial conquests

Tigris

Mosul
Akkadian cuneiform
tablets

Euphrates

Habur

Tell Brak
A royal residence
of Naram-Sin built here

Mari
Became subject to Akkad

Heartland of
Akkadian empire

Orontes

Ebla
Conquered by Sargon

Purushanda?
Object of Sargon's Anatolian
campaign in epic tradition

Expedition of Sargon
to Cyprus in epic tradition

Mediterranean Sea

Syrian Desert

Salt Lake

Kings of Akkad (approx. dates)
Sargon 2334–2279
Rimush 2278–2270
Manishtushu 2269–2255
Naram-Sin 2254–2218
Shar-kali-sharri 2217–2193

– – – approx. boundaries of empire

⊙ modern name

500 km

0   100   200   300   400

A   B   C   D

1   2   3

12

Ur and the Ur III empire

The history of Ur (modern Tell el-Muqayyar) in southern Mesopotamia spans some 4,000 years, from mid M5 to mid M1 BC. Ur was already an important site during the prehistoric phases of its existence – from the later Ubaid through the Uruk and Jemdet Nasr periods (i.e. c. 4500–2900 BC). But its main urban development occurred in M3, when it was one of the attested fourteen city-states of Sumer in the Early Dynastic period (c. 2900–2334). A particular feature of Ur's remains in this period is a cemetery containing c. 2000 tombs, ranging in date from Early Dynastic III through and beyond the period of the Akkadian empire (overall, from c. 2600 to 2100). Sixteen of the Early Dynastic tombs have attracted particular interest. They consist of chambers made of brick or stone, and contained numerous burials, most of which are believed to be the bodies of attendants interred with the tombs' principal inhabitants, to serve them in the afterlife. Grave-goods found with the bodies included jewellery made of gold and silver and semi-precious stones, along with finely crafted weapons, musical instruments, furniture and other high quality items, clearly the possessions of an elite social class. All these features have suggested that the tombs were the burial-places of royalty – hence the common designation 'Royal Cemetery' for the necropolis as a whole. But we cannot be sure whether any of their occupants were in fact Sumerian kings or queens or other members of royalty. None of the names inscribed on seals or other objects found in the tombs are known to us from other sources, including the Sumerian King-List.

Ur continued to be an important city during the Akkadian empire, but it achieved its greatest prominence as the capital of the Ur III dynasty and kingdom, which rose after the fall of this empire and lasted just over one hundred years, from c. 2112 to 2004. The dynasty began with a man called Ur-Namma, who founded a new empire which at its peak held sway over southern Mesopotamia and the territories lying to the east of the Tigris, and had extensive diplomatic links with the regions beyond. Vast numbers of bureaucratic documents inscribed on clay tablets provide us with detailed knowledge of the administration of the empire. Written in Sumerian, the empire's official language, the Ur III tablets also provide information about Ur-Namma's ambitious building programme in Ur, particularly in the city's sacred precinct where a great ziggurat was constructed. Following Ur-Namma's death, a major expansion and reorganization of the empire was undertaken by the king's son and successor Shulgi, who greatly extended the empire's peripheral tax-paying subject territories, and established tighter centralized control over its core territory within the regions of Sumer and Akkad.

Shulgi had three successors, Amar-Sin, Shu-Sin and Ibbi-Sin. Under the last of these the empire fell, its death-blow dealt by the Elamites, who attacked, plundered and burnt the royal capital, and carried off the king. But Ur was shortly afterwards rebuilt, by the kings of Isin, who claimed they were the legitimate successors of the Ur III dynasty. Through the early centuries of M2, in the so-called Isin-Larsa period (c. 2000–mid C18), the city remained an important religious

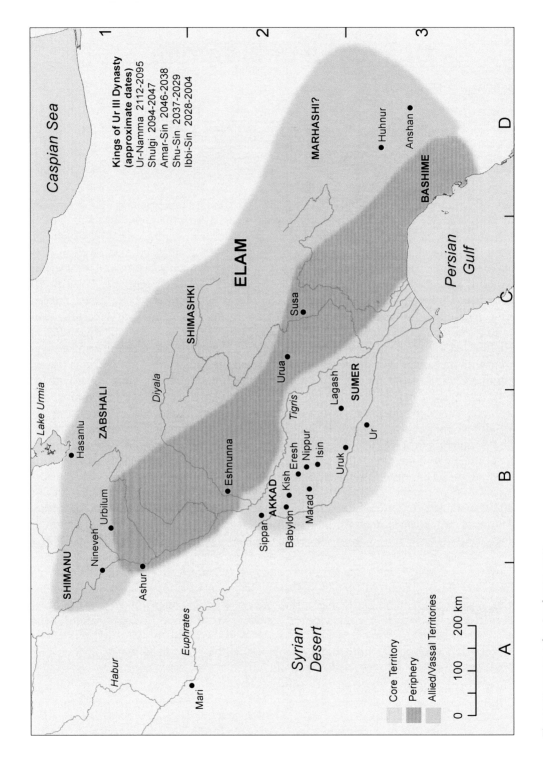

Kings of Ur III Dynasty
(approximate dates)
Ur-Namma 2112–2095
Shulgi 2094–2047
Amar-Sin 2046–2038
Shu-Sin 2037–2029
Ibbi-Sin 2028–2004

The Ur III empire (after Roaf 1996: 102)

Figure 12.1 The 'Standard of Ur', unearthed in the 'Royal Cemetery' of Ur. Photo by Pictures from History/ Bridgeman Images.

and commercial centre. There was some decline in its fortunes in C18, when the Old Babylonian empire was at its height under King Hammurabi. But these fortunes rose again in later periods, particularly in M1 BC, when Ur's revered status as a traditional religious centre prompted a number of kings, like the C6 Babylonian Nebuchadnezzar II, to favour it with major restoration and rebuilding programmes. But Ur's years were now running out. During the Persian period, the city suffered terminal decline, and was abandoned around the end of C4.

In Old Testament tradition, Ur is well known as the birthplace and first home of Abram (later called Abraham), though the fact that Abram's birthplace in this tradition is referred to as 'Ur of the Chaldees' has prompted some scholars to suggest it may be a different city from the one attested in historical and archaeological sources.

Westenholz (1996: 3–30); Pollock (*OEANE* 5: 288–91); *PPAWA* (742–6).

13

The Early and Middle Bronze Age kingdoms of western Iran

The Old Elamite period

Elam became one of the most important and longest-lasting kingdoms of the Near East, with a history extending over 2,000 years, from M3 until mid M1 BC. 'Elam' was the Sumerian name for the country. The Babylonians called it Elamtu, and its own inhabitants 'Haltamti' or 'Hatamti'. By late M3, Elam had established itself as a major international power, with extensive diplomatic, commercial, and military interests in Iran, Mesopotamia, and Syria. It reached the peak of its power during the successive regimes of the so-called Shimashki and *sukkalmah* (Epartid) dynasties (c. 2100–1500), whose sway extended north to the Caspian Sea, south to the Persian Gulf, eastwards to the desert regions of Kavir and Lut, and westwards into Mesopotamia.

Most of our written information about Elamite history comes from Mesopotamian and (much later) Persian sources, from Akkadian texts dating to the second half of M3 down to the records of the Neo-Assyrian and Persian Achaemenid kings in M1 BC. A corpus of c. 1,550 clay tablets, discovered in Susa and dated from c. 3100 to 2900 BC contain a pictographically written language which was once thought to be the ancestor of Elamite, and was thus labelled 'Proto-Elamite'. (Though this language is still undecipherable, we can deduce from the pictograms some of the contents of the tablets.) It is now clear that 'Proto-Elamite' pre-dates the arrival of the Elamites, and is unconnected with their language. The earliest examples of the latter, which was written in a cuneiform script, are inscriptions of later M3–2 in what is called 'Old Elamite'. These inscriptions are not fully understood, and only a few of them have survived. What information we can glean from them is confined largely to the names of kings and their royal capitals.

Henrickson (*OEANE* 2: 228–32); Potts (1999: 43–187); *PPAWA* (219–21); Álvarez-Mon (*AANE*: 747–50).

Awan

Attested in Early Bronze Age Mesopotamian and Elamite texts, Awan was a city and kingdom in south-western Iran. Located either in the region of Susiana or in the highlands lying to its north, it was closely associated with the kingdom of Elam, and is sometimes represented in the texts as part of this kingdom. According to the Sumerian King-List, it ruled over southern Mesopotamia for 356 years. As far as this account has any basis in fact (the length of rule is obviously a gross exaggeration), the events which it records can be attributed to a so-called 'First Dynasty' of Awan. But we have no confirmation from other sources of a period of foreign rule over southern Mesopotamia in this phase (Early Dynastic I) of its history. The most important and best attested of Awan's kings was Puzur-Inshushinak, twelfth and last ruler of the kingdom's second royal line. Attested

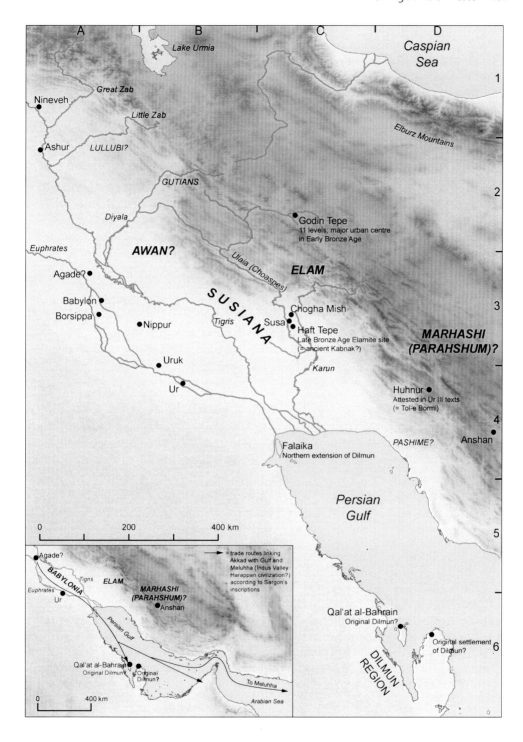

Mesopotamia and western Iran in the 3rd and 2nd millennia BC

Trade routes linking Akkad with the Persian Gulf and Meluhha

in a total of twelve inscriptions, his reign can be dated to early C21. In one of his inscriptions, he claims that his god Inshushinak had given him dominion over the four quarters of the world, an indication that he aspired to becoming the ruler of a large empire. On his way towards achieving this, he had allegedly already conquered eighty-one cities or regions. But Ur-Namma, founder of the Ur III dynasty, abruptly ended his plans when he inflicted a resounding defeat upon him in battle, and incorporated his kingdom into the Ur III empire.

PPAWA (93–5).

Marhashi

Marhashi (= Akkadian Barahshum/Parahshum) was an important Early and Middle Bronze Age kingdom bordering upon Elam which lay to its north-west. The kingdom is attested in Mesopotamian texts of the Akkadian, Ur III and Old Babylonian periods. It was independent of Elam but often allied with it. Frequently attacked by rulers of the Akkadian dynasty, it joined coalitions with Elam and other western Iranian states in attempts to repel the Akkadian invaders or resist subjection to them. For example, it appears in the extensive list of countries which rebelled against the Akkadian king Naram-Sin (c. 2254–2218) at the beginning of his reign. By the end of Naram-Sin's reign, however, its relations with Akkad must have taken a turn for the better, since either Naram-Sin's son Shar-kali-sharri travelled to Parahshum while he was crown prince to marry a local princess, or else Shar-kali-sharri's son was sent there for this purpose.

Through the period of the Ur III empire, Marhashi/Parahshum appears to have retained its independence and to have enjoyed close diplomatic links with at least some of the Ur III rulers. Then after the Ur III dynasty's collapse at the end of M3, conflicts appear to have broken out between it and other states on the Iranian plateau. The last surviving reference to Marhashi/Parahshum, at least as a political entity, occurs in the year-formula of the Babylonian king Hammurabi for his thirtieth year (1762), which records a victory by Hammurabi over the Elamites. By the end of the Old Babylonian period, the kingdom had apparently ceased to exist as a separate political entity, though its name survived down to the very end of cuneiform literature in scientific and lexical texts.

PPAWA (449–50).

Susiana

Susiana was a region in south-western Iran, covering roughly the area of the modern province Khuzestan. Its history of settlement extends back to M8. In M6 and M5, its most important settlement was Chogha Mish, which was apparently abandoned in late M5 when the site of Susa was first occupied. Susa henceforth became the chief city in Susiana. It maintained this status, very largely, until the second half of M1 although already in late M4 (Susa II period) its supremacy was challenged for a time by the emergence of two other centres in the region, at Chogha Mish (once more) and Abu Fanduweh. In the final centuries of M3, Susiana became subject to the Akkadian and Ur III empires in succession. In M2, it was incorporated into the kingdom of Elam, and Susa became one of the royal Elamite capitals.

PPAWA (677–8).

14

The Amorites

The MAR.TU (i.e. the Amorites) who know no grain . . . no house nor town, the boors of the mountains. The MAR.TU who digs up truffles . . . who does not bend his knees (to cultivate the land), who eats raw meat, who has no house during his lifetime, who is not buried after his death.

(Sumerian text, trans.
E. Chiera, quoted in Roux 1980: 166)

Though there is much uncertainty about their identity and origin, the Amorites are commonly regarded as a branch of the north-west Semitic-speaking peoples, tribal nomadic groups in origin who inhabited parts of Syria and Palestine. (The Amorites of biblical tradition may have been only indirectly connected with the groups so designated in earlier historical sources.) Traditionally pastoralists, a number of these groups adopted a more settled urban way of life in the last centuries of M3 by moving to major urban centres like Ebla. Amorite names in the Ebla tablets of the period attest to their presence in the city. Qatna and Hamath on the Orontes river probably also acquired a significant Amorite element in their population at this time. By early M2, Qatna was ruled by an Amorite dynasty, becoming one of the most important Amorite kingdoms in Syria. It was often at enmity with the northern Syrian kingdom of Yamhad which had also become a major Amorite kingdom, ruled from its capital Aleppo. But while many Amorite groups rapidly adapted to and adopted a settled existence in cities which they often came to dominate, other groups maintained their traditional nomadic lifestyle and began spreading eastwards into Mesopotamia. Here they constantly menaced the cities and kingdoms of Sumer and Akkad in southern Mesopotamia. By the end of M3, they had overrun much of this region.

In northern Mesopotamia, the first great king of Assyria, Samsi-Addu (Akkadian Shamshi-Adad) (c. 1796–1775), was also the first of the great Amorite rulers. In Babylon, a dynasty of Amorite kings was established c. 1894. Its greatest ruler, Hammurabi (c. 1792–1750), was the fifth member of this dynasty. Yarim-Lim I (c. 1780–1765), ruler of the kingdom of Yamhad in northern Syria, was a third powerful king of Amorite descent who reigned in this period.

During the Middle Bronze Age, a confederation of Amorite tribal groups, attested in the archives of Mari, spread over large areas of Mesopotamia and northern Syria, especially in the region between Suhum and the borders of Yamhad. Their encampments were located principally along the Euphrates, with urban centres at Terqa and Tuttul. The Mari archives also attest to two regions of Amorite tribal occupation called Yamutbal. One was located in the east of northern Mesopotamia and centred upon the city Andarig. The other lay further to the south along the Tigris river. Its focus was the city Mashkan-Shapur (see map, p. 101).

By the middle of M2, the Amorites had largely merged with other population groups. However, their name lived on in the designation *Amurru*. In M3 and M2, this term applied to a large expanse

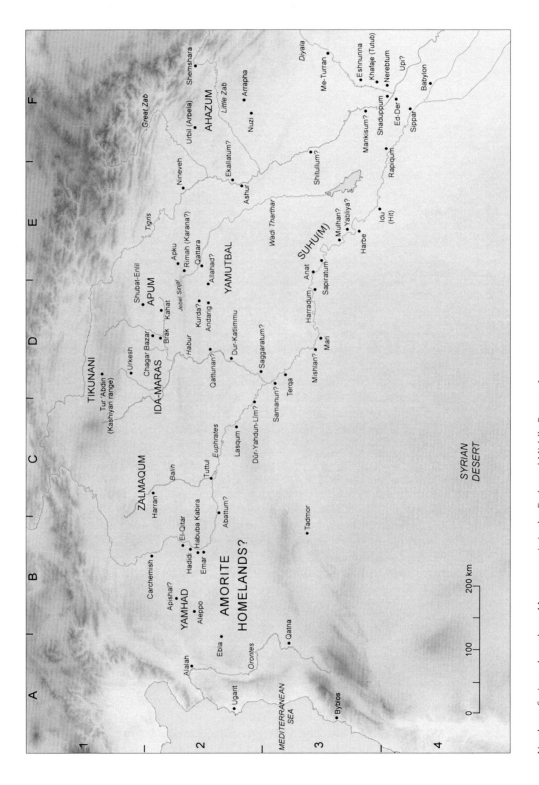

Northern Syria and northern Mesopotamia in the Early and Middle Bronze Ages

of territory extending through much of the region covered by modern Syria west of the Euphrates. But from C15 onwards, its use was restricted to the territory lying between the Orontes and the central Levantine coast.

Whiting (*CANE* 2: 1231–42); Buccellati (*OEANE* 1: 107–11); Van De Mieroop (2016: 111–12).

Ebla

Its origins dating back to mid M4, Ebla (Tell Mardikh) had by C24 reached the peak of its political and economic development, in what archaeologists call the Mardikh IIB1 phase. An imposing brick palace ('Palace G') dominated the city's acropolis. The surrounding lower city was fortified by a large earth-and-stone rampart penetrated by four gates. Prior to its excavation, which began in 1964, the city was known to us from a number of contemporary Mesopotamian texts. These include accounts of its conquests by the Akkadian kings Sargon and Naram-Sin, and economic texts from the Ur III dynasty. It later appears in texts from Alalah, dating to C17 and C15, and is listed among the con-

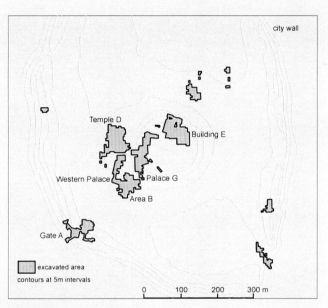

Ebla (after Roaf 1996: 87)

Figure 14.1   Ebla, Palace G. Photo courtesy J.N. Tubb.

quests in Syria and Palestine of the C15 pharaoh Tuthmosis III. Most important for Ebla's IIB1 phase was the discovery in Palace G of a large clay tablet archive. Some 2,500 documents were brought to light, many of them written in the local 'Eblaite' language, others in Sumerian. They indicate that Ebla was the most politically and commercially powerful kingdom of northern Syria in mid M3. More generally, the excavation of the city has proved extremely important to our understanding of the progress of urbanization in Syria in the later centuries of the Early Bronze Age.

Ebla was destroyed by the Akkadians at the end of its IIB1 phase. After being rebuilt on a

(continued)

(continued)

modest scale (IIB2), and then destroyed once more, c. 2000, it gained a new lease of life in the Middle Bronze Age (c. 2000–1800), when a new, grander city, designated as Mardikh IIIA, arose from the ashes of the old. Within a well-planned urban layout defended by a double fortification-wall, new sacred and secular buildings were constructed in the lower city, and large public buildings on the acropolis. There was further rebuilding and reconstruction in the following IIIB phase (c. 1800–1600), when the city was probably subject to the kingdom of Yamhad. But this phase ended abruptly in late C17 or early C16, when Ebla was again destroyed, this time probably by the Hittites. Its site was now largely abandoned, though there was some resettlement in the centuries that followed, with more substantial development in M1 BC, before the tell was abandoned during C2 BC. Other parts of the site continued to be sparsely occupied until M1 AD.

Milano (*CANE* 2: 1219–30); Matthiae *et al.* (*OEANE* 2: 180–6); Akkermans and Schwartz (2003: esp. 235–44, 292–303).

Part IV

The Middle Bronze Age
(continuing into the Late Bronze Age)

15

The Isin and Larsa dynasties

The southern Mesopotamian city Isin first rose to prominence at the end of M3 after the collapse of the Ur III empire c. 2004. Its rise was due to a man called Ishbi-Erra, a high-ranking official of the last Ur III king Ibbi-Sin and governor of the city of Mari. Ishbi-Erra extended his rule over much of the region where the Ur III dynasty had formerly held sway, and shifted the seat of his administration to Isin. Here, he became the founder of the First Isin dynasty. This lasted more than two centuries, through the reigns of Ishbi-Erra and his fourteen successors (c. 2017–1794). But throughout its existence, the Isin regime was constantly threatened by rival kings, particularly those of Larsa and Babylon. Already an important city during the Sumerian Early Dynastic period (c. 2900–2334), Larsa reached the height of its development in early M2 when, like Isin, it sought to fill the power vacuum left by the collapse of the Ur III empire. It was at this time ruled by a dynasty of fourteen successive kings, founded c. 2025 by a man called Naplanum, which held sway over Larsa and its surrounding region through the first quarter of M2. The city rose to particular prominence in the reign of its fifth king Gungunum (c. 1932–1906), who led Larsa into the first of a long series of conflicts with Isin (then ruled by Lipit-Ishtar), ending with the conquest of Isin by Larsa's king Rim-Sin c. 1794. Henceforth, Isin was incorporated into the kingdom of Larsa, and subsequently into the kingdom of Babylon when the Babylonian Hammurabi conquered Rim-Sin c. 1763. Along with other southern Mesopotamian cities, Larsa briefly regained its independence under another leader called Rim-Sin, during the reign of Hammurabi's successor Samsu-iluna. Rim-Sin was killed when the breakaway movements were crushed.

Through the Late Bronze Age, Isin remained under Babylonian rule, in the period when a line of Kassite kings held sway over southern Mesopotamia. An invasion of Babylonia by the Elamites from south-western Iran ended the Kassite regime c. 1155, and Isin *may* have regained its autonomy under a new ruling 'dynasty', referred to in a Babylonian King-List as the Second Dynasty of Isin. Most rulers of this eleven-member 'dynasty', which lasted from c. 1154 until 1026, seem not to have been related to each other. But its name suggests that the political and administrative centre of Babylonia may have shifted south from Babylon to Isin for a time. We do not, however, have any actual evidence for such a shift, and it seems that most of the members of the 'dynasty' ruled from Babylon. The most famous of its rulers was its fourth king Nebuchadnezzar I (1126–1105), who invaded Elam and sacked the city Susa.

Hrouda (*OEANE* 3: 186–7) (Isin); *PPAWA* (338–9) (Isin); *PPAWA* (410–11) (Larsa).

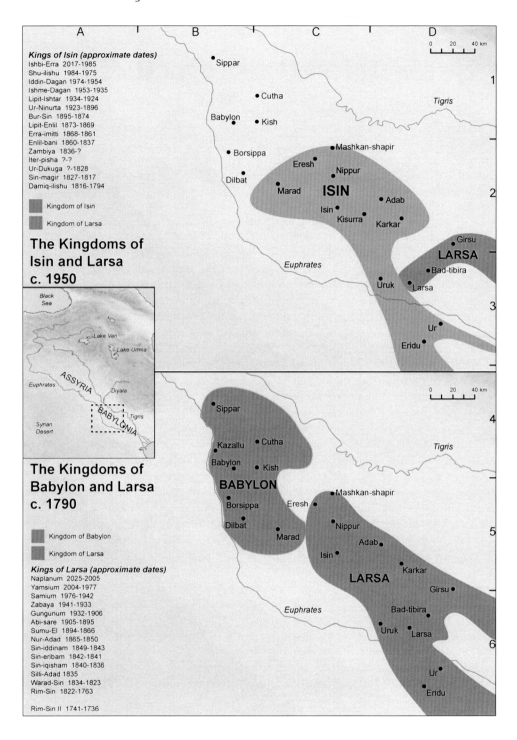

The kingdoms of Isin and Larsa (c. 1950) (after Roaf 1996: 109)

The kingdoms of Babylon and Larsa (1790) (after Roaf 1996: 109)

16

The Old Assyrian kingdom

The history of the Semitic-speaking people called the Assyrians spans some fourteen centuries, from the beginning of the Middle Bronze Age (c. 2000) until late C7 BC. During this period, the rulers of Assyria, whose heartland lay in northern Mesopotamia, built three of the Near Eastern world's most powerful kingdoms. These kingdoms provide our basis for dividing Assyrian history into three main phases: Old Assyrian (c. 2000–1763), Middle Assyrian (c. 1365–1076) and Neo-Assyrian (c. 911–610).

The first of these phases reached its full development in the reign of a king of Amorite stock called Samsi-Addu (Akkadian Shamshi-Adad). In 1796, this man seized power in the city of Ashur on the west bank of the Tigris. Later to become Assyria's chief religious and ceremonial centre, Ashur was initially, after the fall of the Ur III empire, a small independent city-state whose ruling dynasty was founded by a man of Akkadian stock called Puzur-Ashur. At the time of Samsi-Addu's coup, the Assyrian world consisted of no more than a collection of independent states of which Ashur was the most prominent. That changed dramatically under Samsi-Addu. He followed up his seizure of Ashur with a series of military campaigns which took him as far west as the Mediterranean coast. Most importantly, his military enterprises gave him control of the strategically valuable kingdom of Mari on the Euphrates. All the territories which he subjected between the Tigris and the Euphrates were consolidated into a united kingdom beneath his sway. It is only at this point in Assyria's history that a term like 'Assyrian Old Kingdom' might appropriately be used. However, modern scholars use the term 'Kingdom of Upper Mesopotamia' to refer to Samsi-Addu's realm.

To consolidate his authority over this realm, Samsi-Addu established viceregal centres at Mari, where he appointed his son Yasmah-Addu as viceroy, and in the city Ekallatum, which had served as his first capital and his base for his conquests. In Ekallatum he appointed his son Ishme-Dagan to the viceregal seat. The king himself took up residence in his newly established capital Shubat-Enlil (formerly Shehna, modern Tell Leilan). Commercial considerations no doubt provided one of the incentives for his military campaigns, for these campaigns gave him control over all the major trade-routes linking Ashur with Syria and eastern and central Anatolia. But though Samsi-Addu's kingdom flourished under his sovereignty, it rapidly began to disintegrate after his death c. 1775, surviving only for a dozen years before it fell to the Babylonian Hammurabi c. 1763.

Villard (*CANE* 2: 873–83); Radner (2015); Van De Mieroop (2016: 115–18).

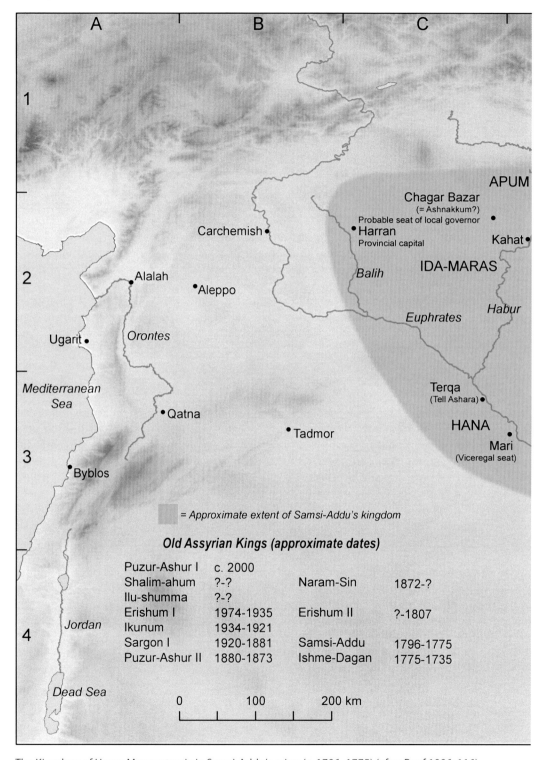

The Kingdom of Upper Mesopotamia in Samsi-Addu's reign (c. 1796–1775) (after Roaf 1996: 116)

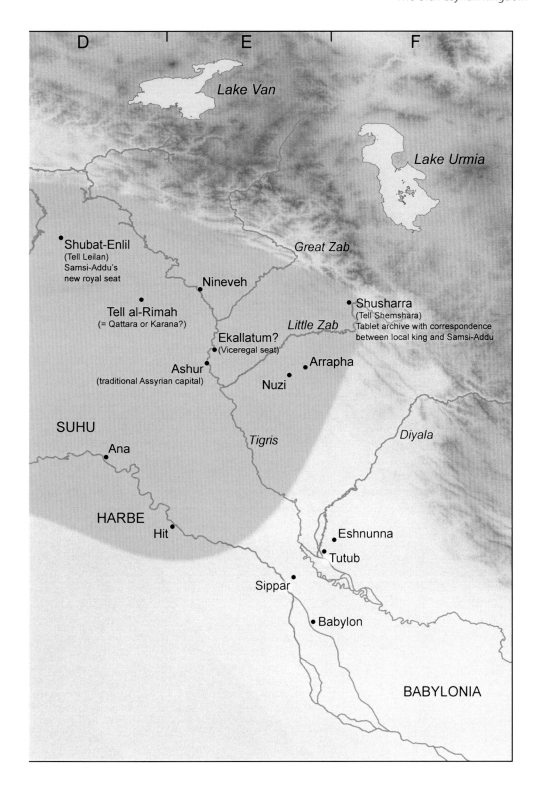

17

The Assyrian merchant colonies

From C20 to C18, during the Middle Bronze Age, Assyrian merchants conducted extensive trading operations in Anatolia by setting up merchant colonies along trade routes which linked the Assyrian city Ashur with the towns and kingdoms of northern and central Anatolia. Detailed records of their trading activities have been preserved on clay tablets in Assyrian cuneiform. These have been unearthed at several Anatolian sites, by far the greatest number at Kanesh (aka Nesa; modern Kültepe) which lay just south of the Kızıl Irmak r., 21 km east of modern Kayseri. More than 22,000 merchant documents have been recovered from the second of Kanesh's four major levels, and a further 420 from the succeeding level Ib. From these documents it is clear that Kanesh was the Anatolian headquarters of the trading network, and also the residence of one of the Anatolian kings. The settlement consisted of a 20 m high mound (c. 550 m in diameter), where the royal palace was located, and a lower city where the merchants dwelt. Information provided by the tablets indicates that there were at least twenty-one merchant colonies established between the Assyrian homeland and the five attested Anatolian kingdoms of the period. The more important colonies were called *kāru* (singular *kārum*), the lesser ones *wabaratum* (singular *wabartum*). So far only three have been identified, Kanesh, Hattus (on the site of the later Hittite capital Hattusa) and a settlement at modern Alişar (perhaps ancient Ankuwa). Tin, used in the manufacture of bronze, and high quality textiles were imported into the Anatolian kingdoms by donkey-caravans from Assyria – commercial ventures financed by consortia of Assyrian businessmen who established branch offices in the colonies often managed by family members. The imports were traded by the merchants for metals readily obtainable in Anatolia, especially silver and gold. The local rulers and the towns through which the caravans passed imposed heavy tolls and customs duties on the caravaneers, and there were severe penalties for those attempting to avoid these costs. Growing instability within and between the Anatolian kingdoms was almost certainly one of the main factors that ended the Assyrian colony period around mid C18.

Veenhof (*CANE* 2: 859–71); Bryce (2005: 21–40); Michel and Kulakoğlu (*OHAA*: 313–36, 1012–30); Atici *et al.* (2014).

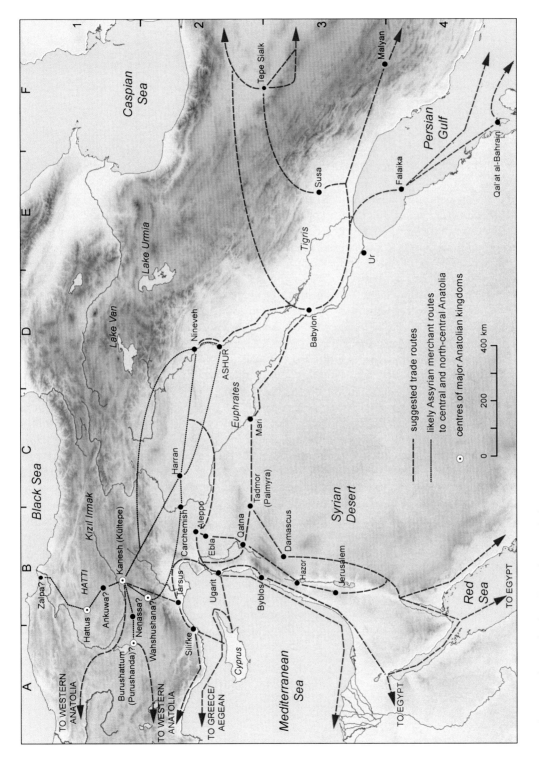

Trade routes during the Assyrian colony period

18

The Diyala region

The so-called Diyala region in eastern Mesopotamia is watered by the Diyala r., a tributary of the Tigris which it joins several kilometres downstream from Baghdad. Crossing the north-eastern part of the Mesopotamian alluvium, the river is fed by headwaters from the Zagros mts northeast of Baghdad. The region which it waters consists of three parts: the Upper, Middle and Lower Diyala. The third of these, which is watered by the river via irrigation canals, is particularly rich in archaeological finds, and the simple term Diyala is traditionally used to refer to this region. It lies south-west of the Hamrin range. Excavations in the Diyala conducted by the Oriental Institute of the University of Chicago between 1930 and 1938 focused on four major sites: Tell Asmar (Eshnunna), Khafajeh (Tutub, Dur Samsu-iluna), Ishchali (Nerebtum) and Tell Agrab. These sites spanned a total of seventeen centuries, from c. 3500 to 1800 – i.e. from the Late Uruk to the Old Babylonian period. Their excavation enabled the development of a long-range chronology for the Lower Diyala region, based especially on its ceramic sequence. Architectural remains of the sites from M3, especially temple remains, provided the basis for the definition of three phases: Early Dynastic I, II and III. However, scholars point out that this periodization reflects a local evolution and should not be applied too systematically to other regions.

In 1957 and 1958, T. Jacobsen, R. McC. Adams and F. Safar carried out extensive surveys of the Lower Diyala plain for the Diyala Basin Archaeological Project. The purpose of this project was to investigate the region's history of agriculture and irrigation over a period of more than 6,000 years. The surveys provided much important information about settlement patterns and canal systems in the region from the Ubaid period until C19. Increases in the number and size of settlements during the Jemdet Nasr and Early Dynastic periods (c. 3100–2334) point to steady population growth in these periods. Khafajeh, Tell Asmar and Tell Agrab developed as major urban centres, around which many other sites arose in a hierarchical settlement pattern. The surveyors noted that of ninety-six sites examined, ten were large towns (more than 10ha), nineteen were small towns (4–10ha) and sixty-seven were villages (less than 4ha). Settlement in the Akkadian period (c. 2334–2193) maintained its development along similar lines. The region is considered to have reached its political peak during the so-called Isin-Larsa period (c. 2000–mid C18), when Eshnunna, previously subject to the C21 Ur III dynasty, established its independence and became the major centre of the region. The Diyala prospered through the period of Eshnunna's dominance, but its *floruit* ended with the rise of the Old Babylonian kingdom under Hammurabi (c. 1792–1750).

Thursen (*OEANE* 2: 163–6).

Khafajeh (Dur-Samsu-iluna, Tutub)

A 216-ha complex consisting of four main settlement-mounds (A-D). The largest, Mound A, was occupied from the Late Uruk period until its abandonment c. 2300 during the Akkadian period. The excavation on the mound of a temple revealed an unbroken succession of levels from the Jemdet Nasr (late M4) through the Early Dynastic periods. The dominant building on it was an Early Dynastic Temple Oval, consisting of a temple on a raised platform, a courtyard, and two enclosing mudbrick walls, between which a large building was constructed. Remains from Mounds B and C, which probably formed a single settlement, date to the Old Babylonian period, perhaps continuing into the Kassite period. The settlement was built as a fortress-city by the Old Babylonian king Samsu-iluna (c. 1749-1712) and named Dur-Samsu-iluna ('Fort Samsu-iluna'). On mound D, which also dates to the Middle Bronze Age, the remains of a temple dedicated to the god Sin were uncovered.

Nerebtum (Ishchali)

Attested in Middle Bronze Age texts, Nerebtum was, in mid C19, among the cities which lost their independence to the kingdom of Eshnunna when Eshnunna's king Ipiq-Adad II extended his authority over the Diyala Valley. Nerebtum had till then been under the control of a local king called Sin-abushu. The city's principal deity had hitherto been the god Sin, but Ipiq-Adad re-dedicated Nerebtum to his own patron deity, the goddess Ishtar-Kititum, and built a temple for her worship in the city. Nerebtum was later seized by the Assyrian king Samsi-Addu. Later, its king Ibal-pi-El apparently regained control of it, but Nerebtum was among the cities in the region destroyed by the Elamites following their capture of Eshnunna in 1765.

Eshnunna (Tell Asmar).

From its origins in late M4 or early M3, Eshnunna developed into a major regional urban centre during the Early Dynastic period (c. 2900-2334). The city continued to flourish through the period of the Akkadian empire (c. 2334-2193), reaching its developmental peak and maximum size under the Ur III kings (C21) and in the following Isin-Larsa period (C20-18). During the first three centuries of M2, Eshnunna's kings became embroiled in conflicts with other rulers of the age including Assyrian, Babylonian, and Elamite rulers, partly due to its programme of aggressive territorial expansion. Its power was effectively destroyed in 1762 by the Babylonian king Hammurabi.

Tell Agrab

Survey has indicated that the earliest occupation of the site (anc. name unknown) dates from the Ubaid period. After its M3 heyday, Agrab was almost entirely abandoned late in the Early Dynastic period (c. 2900-2334), with brief and limited reoccupation in the Ur III and Larsa periods (late C22-18). Excavations uncovered the remains of a rectangular temple (84 x 62 m) with five building phases attributed to the Early Dynastic period. Further material remains from the site include a rampart of the Early Dynastic period, and two buildings of unknown purpose adjoining the city-wall on the west side of the settlement. The bricks of these buildings indicate a dating to the Isin-Larsa period (late C21-18).

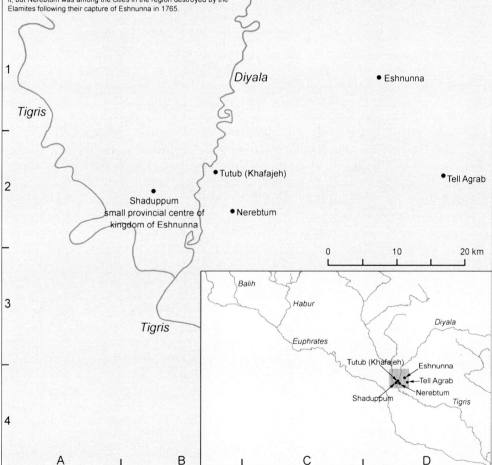

Main centres of the Diyala region

19

The Habur (Khabur) river region

The Habur is a tributary of the Euphrates with a large catchment area in northern Syria and northern Mesopotamia. This area is generally referred to in two parts, the Upper Habur (Habur Triangle) and the Lower Habur. The region is archaeologically significant because of the concentration within it of a number of important sites, including Tell Beydar, Tell Brak, Chagar Bazar, Tell Feheriyeh, Tell Halaf, Tell Hamoukar, Tell Leilan and Tell Mozan. In the Habur Triangle, the fertility of the soil combined with good annual rainfall facilitated a marked growth in the urbanization of the region in M3, and a relatively high level of prosperity in a number of centres like Tell Leilan and Tell Brak.

The end of M3 is thought to have witnessed a major collapse in settlement in the region, perhaps linked to the demise of the Akkadian empire. But the actual causes of this collapse are hotly disputed – climate change (drought) is one suggestion – as is its extent, since some sites, such as Tell Brak, were continuously occupied throughout the relevant centuries. Other sites, such as Tell Leilan, were resettled in early M2, with a period of decline later in the millennium. However, major settlements continued to develop and prosper there in the early Iron Age, including the city of Guzana (Tell Halaf), capital of the Aramaean kingdom Bit-Bahiani. In C8 and C7, the Habur region was incorporated into the Neo-Assyrian empire, and various major Assyrian settlements were established there, including the Assyrian fortress and administrative centre at Dur-Katlimmu (Tell Sheikh Hamad) on the lower Habur. The western part of the Habur triangle formed part of the province of Guzana, while the eastern part belonged to the province of Nasibina (Nusaybin).

Habur cities

Tell Brak (Nagar/Nawar) The history of this settlement-mound, now generally believed to be the site of the M3–2 city Nagar/Nawar, extends from the Ubaid period (M6–5) to the end of the Bronze Age. It became a major urban centre during the Uruk period (M4), and in the second half of this period developed extensive cultural and commercial contacts with the cities of southern Mesopotamia, Its most prominent architectural feature in this period was a tripartite 'Eye Temple', so called from the discovery in it of a number of small stone plaques with eye symbols. By mid M3, Tell Brak had probably become the most important political and economic centre in the Habur region, a status which it regained, after violent destruction c. 2300, under the Akkadian administration. The city was again destroyed at the end of the Akkadian period, c. 2193, but reoccupied soon after, when it probably became the capital of a Hurrian principality, most likely the kingdom of Urkesh and Nagar/Nawar. In the Late Bronze Age, it gained new prominence as a major centre of the kingdom of Mitanni. It apparently survived the Hittite conquest of Mitanni in the third quarter of C14, but its palace was destroyed the following century by the Assyrians. The site was finally abandoned early in C12.

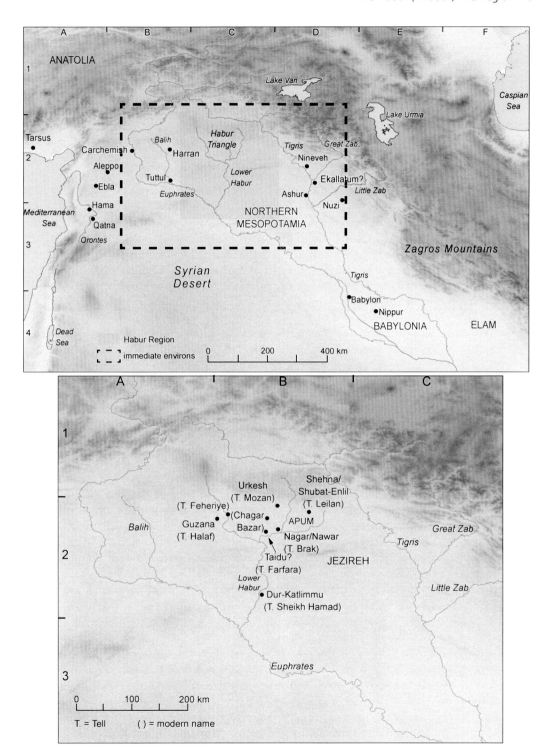

The Habur region and its environs

Chagar Bazar's history extends from the Halaf period (c. 6000–4500) to the middle of the Late Bronze Age. Its first major occupation phase dates to the Early Bronze Age, after a long period of abandonment. Material remains from the Early Bronze settlement include painted and incised pottery, bullae with seal impressions, and short Akkadian cuneiform inscriptions. Around 2000, the site was again abandoned, but came into prominence once more during the reign of the Assyrian king Samsi-Addu (c. 1796–1775). The settlement's mixed population at this time is reflected in the Hurrian, Akkadian and Amorite personal names attested in an archive of c. 100 tablets unearthed from a large building (a 'palace' or storehouse) of the period. The settlement was finally abandoned c. 1500.

Tell Feheriye (Sikanu, Sikkan) has eight occupation levels, extending from the Middle and Late Bronze Ages through the Iron Age, Hellenistic, Roman and Medieval periods. During the Late Bronze Age, it came first under Mitannian and then under Assyrian control. The latter appears to have ended in the second half of C11, with the expansion of Aramaean settlement through the Balih and Habur valleys. The settlement's ancient name Sikanu/Sikkan, first attested in an Ur III inscription of c. 2000 BC, remained current in the Iron Age. It has been suggested that Sikanu was the Mitannian capital Washshukkanni, whose site has yet to be conclusively identified. In 894, the city became a tributary of the Assyrian king Adad-nirari II.

Tell Halaf has two main periods of occupation – the Pottery Neolithic period characterized by a rich assemblage of decorated polychrome ceramic ware dating from mid M6 to M5, and a substantial several-layered Iron Age settlement extending from C12 to C7. Inscriptions indicate that the city in this period was called Guzana (biblical Gozan), and was the capital of the Aramaean state Bit-Bahiani. The city and its region were annexed by the Assyrians in C8.

Tell Leilan (Shehna, Shubat-Enlil) has six main occupation levels, extending from the Halaf period to the Middle Bronze Age (early M2). The region in which it lay was called Subir in M3 and Subartu in M2. Coming under Akkadian domination in C23, the city, then called Shehna, became a centre of the Akkadian imperial administration. It was subsequently abandoned and remained derelict until early C18 when the Assyrian king Samsi-Addu re-established it as his royal capital, with the name Shubat-Enlil. The many hundreds of cuneiform tablets unearthed from the throne-room of Samsi-Addu's palace include historical and administrative texts, treaties and letters, and a copy of the Sumerian King-List. Following Samsi-Addu's death, Shubat-Enlil came under the control of the rulers of the nearby land of Apum. Now commonly referred to by its original name Shehna, it became Apum's capital, and was caught up in the complex and constantly changing power structures and political relationships of the period, as recorded in letters from the Mari archive. Around 1728, the city was conquered and destroyed by the Babylonian king Samsu-iluna, who ended the reign of Apum's last king Yakun-ashar.

Tell Mozan (Urkesh) The history of the settlement extends from the beginning of M6 (Halaf period) to mid M2, with the most important occupational strata dating to the second half of M3. Throughout its Bronze Age phase, Urkesh was a major centre of Hurrian civilization. The settlement consists of two parts – a citadel mound extending over c. 18ha, and an outer city of c. 135ha. A temple and a palace, dating respectively to c. 2450 and 2200, were the most prominent features of the walled inner city on the mound. The settlement's obvious prosperity at this time was probably due very largely to its location at the hub of major trade routes, and its relative proximity to the copper mining region which lay to its north.

Settlement at **Tell Sheikh Hamad (Dur-Katlimmu)** covers the period from the Late Chalcolithic Age (late M4) to the early Islamic period. During the Middle Bronze Age, the site was expanded from a small village to a relatively large urban settlement (c. 15 ha), which included a citadel and lower city. In the Late Bronze Age, the city fell first under Mitannian, and subsequently under Assyrian control, becoming in C13 one of the regional centres of the Middle Assyrian empire. Important information about its administration in this period is provided by an archive of some 500 cuneiform tablets, unearthed in one of the wings of the governor's palace. This archive confirmed the city's Assyrian name Dur-Katlimmu, already known from other sources. By late C8, the city had grown substantially in size, becoming an important regional centre of the Neo-Assyrian empire. When the empire collapsed in 610, Dur-Katlimmu was among the Assyrian centres put to the torch by the Babylonian conquerors. But it was not totally destroyed. The site has produced important documentary evidence for the immediate post-Assyrian era, in the form of cuneiform tablets written in Assyrian but dated to 602–600, early in the reign of the Babylonian king Nebuchadnezzar II. Dur-Katlimmu once more flourished under Neo-Babylonian rule. It was occupied during the succeeding Persian, Hellenistic and Roman periods, but with a much reduced status.

Akkermans and Schwartz (2003: 259–62, 309–13, 346–50); individual entries in *PPA WA*.

20

The Old Babylonian kingdom

Babylonia is the name applied by scholars to ancient southern Mesopotamia. It extends from the area of Baghdad, where the Tigris and Euphrates rivers come close together, to the Persian Gulf. The name has been adopted from the region's most important ancient city Babylon. It refers primarily to the kingdom of which Babylon was the centre in M2 and the first half of M1 BC. The life-span of Babylon itself actually covers a much longer period, from mid M3 BC to C2 AD. Babylonia's history can be divided into several main phases: (a) the Middle Bronze Age kingdom ruled by an Amorite dynasty of which Hammurabi was the most important member; (b) the Late Bronze Age Kassite kingdom; and (c) the Neo-Babylonian kingdom, most notable for the reign of Nebuchadnezzar II. Between (b) and (c) there was a long interval to which it is difficult to assign a single label; it began in 1154, after the fall of the Kassite kingdom, with the emergence of the so-called Second Dynasty of Isin, and passed through a number of stages, including long periods of subjection to Assyria, before it ended with the rise of the Neo-Babylonian kingdom in 626. Through all these phases, Babylonia's and Babylon's histories are closely linked.

The Middle Bronze Age kingdom's rise to prominence began when an Amorite chieftain Sumu-abum paved the way for the establishment of the first royal dynasty at Babylon, founded by a man called Sumu-la-El c. 1880. Under Amorite rule, the

Figure 20.1 Sculpture atop Hammurabi's stele © Ivy Close Images/Alamy.

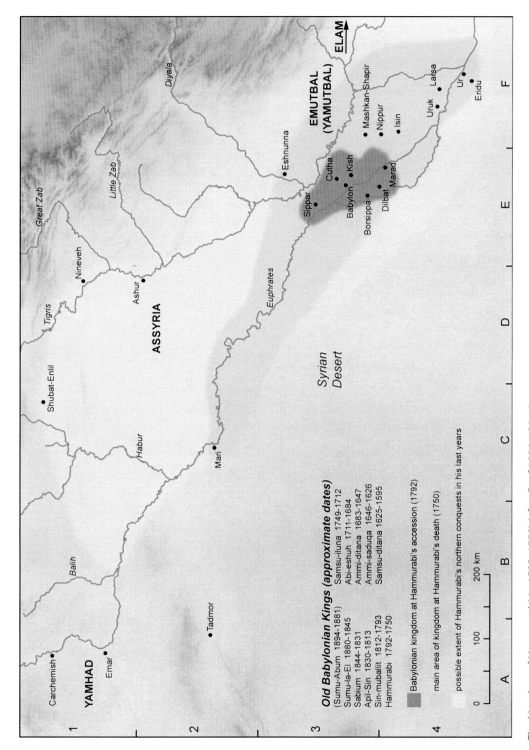

Old Babylonian Kings (approximate dates)

(Sumu-Abum 1894–1881)
Sumu-la-El 1880–1845
Sabium 1844–1831
Apil-Sin 1830–1813
Sin-muballit 1812–1793
Hammurabi 1792–1750

Samsu-iluna 1749–1712
Abi-eshuh 1711–1684
Ammi-ditana 1683–1647
Ammi-saduqa 1646–1626
Samsu-ditana 1625–1595

Babylonian kingdom at Hammurabi's accession (1792)

main area of kingdom at Hammurabi's death (1750)

possible extent of Hammurabi's northern conquests in his last years

The kingdom of Hammurabi (c. 1792–1750) (after Roaf 1996: 120–1)

kingdom reached its peak in the reign of its fifth king Hammurabi (c. 1792–1750), who made Babylon the centre of an empire which extended through the whole of southern and part of northern Mesopotamia. It included the last remnants of the Kingdom of Upper Mesopotamia which had earlier flourished under Hammurabi's former ally Samsi-Addu. To Babylonia's east, the kingdom of Elam posed a severe threat to Hammurabi's kingdom. But its aggression was effectively countered when Hammurabi formed an alliance with Zimri-Lim, king of Mari, and Yarim-Lim, king of Aleppo, and in combined military operations drove the Elamite invaders from his lands. Voluminous archives surviving from Hammurabi's reign, including hundreds of letters addressed to officials and foreign rulers, attest to the king's high level of administrative and diplomatic skills and activities. But he is best known for his so-called 'code of laws', the most famous surviving example of which appears on a 2 m high diorite stele now in the Louvre. Though harsh in some of the penalties they impose for a wide range of offences, the laws reflect the king's role as protector of his people and upholder of peace and justice within his realm.

Sasson (*CANE* 2: 901–15); Roth (1997: 71–142 (Hammurabi's Laws)); Leick (2003: 30–43); Van De Mieroop (2005, 2016: 118–27); Charpin (2012).

21

Mari

The history of Mari (Tell Hariri), located on the west bank of the middle Euphrates, extends from the beginning of M3 BC until its destruction by Hammurabi c. 1762. There was some later occupation of the site down to the last centuries of M1 BC. Excavations by a succession of French teams from 1933 onwards have identified the chief phases in Mari's history; these date successively to the Sumerian Early Dynastic, Akkadian, Ur III and Old Assyrian periods, and a brief period of independence following the last of these. By mid M3, Mari had become a wealthy city, due no doubt to its central position in a fertile strip of land along the Euphrates, and its involvement in the international trading operations that passed between Babylonia and Syria. Towards the millennium's end, it was subject to a line of rulers constituting the so-called Shakkanakku dynasty. Their regime was marked by extensive building operations in the city, including a new palace, which was regularly restored, re-developed and enlarged. The dynasty ended at a time and in circumstances unknown to us. After a period of obscurity, Mari again came into prominence with the accession of a king called Yahdun-Lim (c. 1810–1794), who held sway over a substantial amount of territory in the middle Euphrates region, up to the mouth of the Balih river. Conflict broke out with Mari's western neighbour, the kingdom of Yamhad. But shortly after Yahdun-Lim's death, Mari came under the control of the Assyrian king Samsi-Addu, who incorporated Mariote territory into his own kingdom and installed one of his sons, Yasmah-Addu, as viceroy there.

When Samsi-Addu's kingdom began to disintegrate shortly after his death, Zimri-Lim, a member of the former ruler Yahdun-Lim's family,

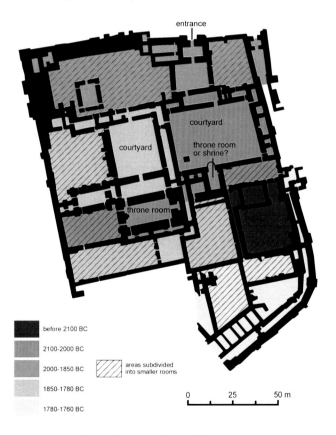

The palace of Mari (after Roaf 1996: 119)

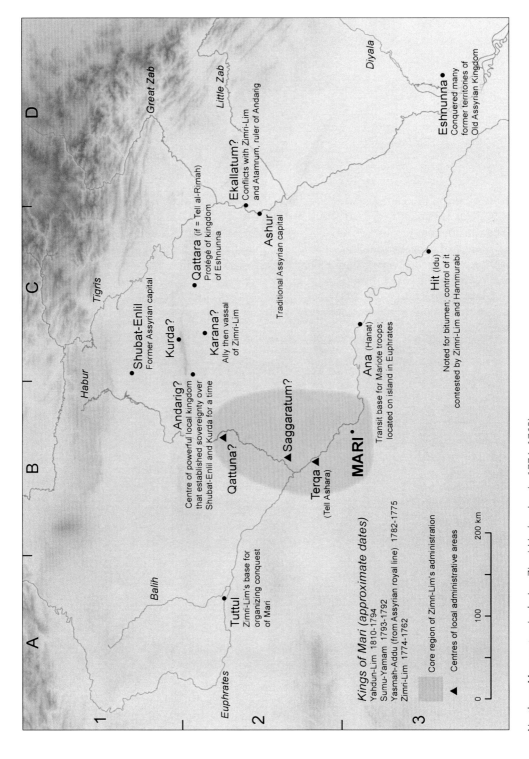

Northern Mesopotamia during Zimri-Lim's reign (c. 1774–1762)

Kings of Mari (approximate dates)
Yahdun-Lim 1810–1794
Sumu-Yamam 1793–1792
Yasmah-Addu (from Assyrian royal line) 1782–1775
Zimri-Lim 1774–1762

Core region of Zimri-Lim's administration

▲ Centres of local administrative areas

regained control of Mari and ruled there for thirteen years (c. 1774–1762). This was arguably the peak period in Mari's history, a period when Mari wielded considerable political influence in Near Eastern affairs, and amassed considerable wealth, which enabled Zimri-Lim to complete the great palace-complex on a scale of unprecedented size and splendour. It all ended abruptly c. 1762, when the Babylonian king Hammurabi attacked and occupied the city, plundered the palace, and later burnt all the city's monumental buildings. Mari never recovered from his onslaught. But enough of it has survived to enable us to recreate a fairly clear picture of what it was like in its original splendour. And we learn much about its daily affairs, its cultural and commercial activities, its alliances, and its fluctuating political and military fortunes from the discovery of both private and public archives in the city. More than 22,000 clay tablets containing this information have been unearthed, mostly in and around the great palace.

Margueron (*CANE* 2: 885–99, *OEANE* 3: 413–17); Akkermans and Schwartz (2003: esp. 262–7, 313–17); Heimpel (2003).

22

The cities and kingdoms of Syria in the Middle and Late Bronze Ages

During the Middle and Late Bronze Ages, the region we have broadly defined as ancient Syria, encompassing the territories between the Euphrates and the Mediterranean coast (see p. 44), was occupied by a large number of cities and small kingdoms. The most important of these, listed below in a rough north–south progression, are:

Carchemish (*Karkamish, Jerablus*) first appears among the cities subject to the king of Ebla in the second half of M3. In C18, it was ruled by a local dynasty which enjoyed peaceful trading relations with Mari. Subsequently, it became a subject-state of the kingdom of Yamhad. Following Yamhad's conquest by the Hittites in early C16, Carchemish was incorporated into the kingdom of Mitanni, and remained under Mitannian control until captured by the Hittites in 1327. Henceforth, it became a viceregal seat of the Hittite empire, and maintained that status, under the direct rule of a member of the Hittite royal family, until the end of the Bronze Age. In the succeeding Iron Age, Carchemish was one of the most important centres of the Neo-Hittite world.

Mukish First mentioned in tablets of the Ur III period (C21), Mukish was in C16 incorporated into the kingdom of Aleppo, but later became subject to the Mitannian king Parrattarna when he established his rule over Aleppo (C15). In mid C14, Mukish was among the lands conquered by the Hittite king Suppiluliuma I during his so-called one-year Syrian war (late 1340s) against Mitanni. An anti-Hittite alliance which it joined in an attempt to break away from Hittite sovereignty was crushed by a Hittite expeditionary force. Suppiluliuma thereupon handed over a substantial part of its territory to his loyal subject-ally Niqmaddu II, king of Ugarit.

Yamhad At the peak of its power in C18 and C17 BC, Yamhad held sway over some twenty subject states between the Euphrates and the Orontes rivers. Its dominance over northern Syria continued until the reign of Yarim-Lim III in the second half of C17. In this period, the Hittite king Hattusili I conducted a series of campaigns against the city-states subject or allied to Yamhad. He succeeded in capturing and destroying a number of these states, but failed to take the royal capital Aleppo (Halab/Halap in Hittite texts), which was finally captured and sacked by his successor Mursili I c. 1595. Its destruction brought the kingdom of Yamhad to an end.

Alalah (*Tell Atchana*) Alalah's seventeen levels of settlement indicate that the city's history extended through the Middle and Late Bronze Ages, with evidence also of Chalcolithic and Early Bronze Age occupation. The most important periods of its history are represented archaeologically by levels VII and IV, dating respectively to C17 and C15. Both levels have produced tablet archives. The (almost 200) tablets discovered in level VII indicate that Alalah was subject then to the Yamhadite king Yarim-Lim III. In his first campaign against Yamhad, the Hittite king Hattusili I (c. 1650–1620) led

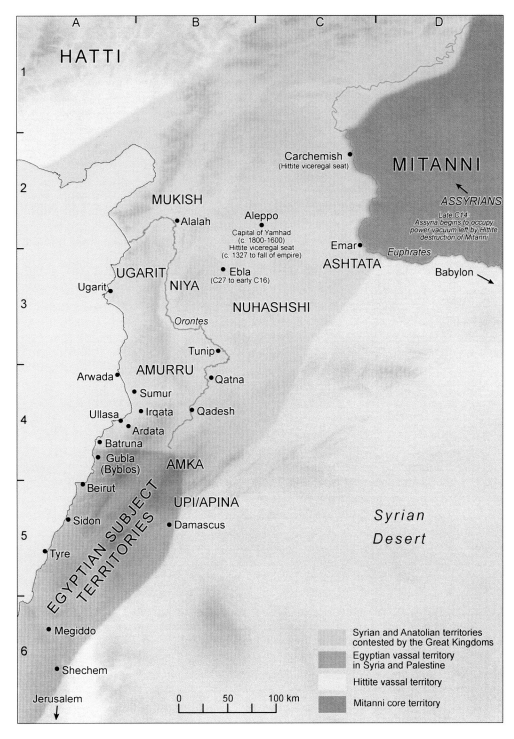

Syria, south-eastern Anatolia, and north-western Mesopotamia in the 2nd millennium BC

Figure 22.1 The citadel of Aleppo today. Photo courtesy J.N. Tubb.

his troops against Alalah and destroyed it. The city was rebuilt, but later became subject in C15 to the Mitannian king Parrattarna. It was to this period in its history that the famous Idrimi episode belongs (see pp. 125–6). Level IV ended with another destruction of the city. Subsequently, the Hittites rebuilt and fortified it, but it was again destroyed in late C14, and never reoccupied.

Aleppo Probably not long after its destruction by the Hittite king Mursili I c. 1595, Aleppo was rebuilt and regained its independence. It maintained this into the following century (and in fact expanded its territory to include a number of nearby states), until it was conquered by the Mitannian king Parrattarna. It was later among the Mitannian dependencies that fell to the Hittite king Suppiluliuma, and became one of the two Hittite viceregal centres which he established in Syria. In M1, it became part of the Aramaean kingdom Bit-Agusi. The city was politically insignificant now, but remained an important cult-centre (as in the Late Bronze Age) where the storm god Adad was worshipped.

Emar (***Meskene***) was located at the junction of major land- and river-routes, on the west bank of the middle Euphrates. Its site is now partially covered by Lake Assad, created by the construction of the Tabqa Dam in the 1970s. Excavations were carried out between 1972 and 1978, and were resumed in 1996, following the development of the dam and lake, to examine those areas of the site left clear of the water. Previously, texts found at Ebla, Mari, Nuzi and Ugarit made it clear that Emar had, by early M2, become a major commercial centre, providing an important focus for the economic and commercial activities of Mesopotamia and northern Syria. The excavations revealed part of the Early and Middle Bronze Age levels. But the most extensively excavated phase of the city's history belongs to the Late Bronze Age. In this period, the Hittites built a new city, which became capital of the Hittite subject-kingdom Ashtata. Immediate jurisdiction over Emar was in the hands of the Hittite viceroy at Carchemish. The Late Bronze Age excavations have uncovered a palace, residential quarters, and four temples. They also brought to light approximately 800 cuneiform tablets and fragments (see p. 55). The city was destroyed in early C12 during the upheavals at the end of the Late Bronze Age.

Niya (***Nii***) was one of the Syrian lands that in C16 were absorbed by the expanding kingdom of Aleppo. After a short period of independence, it became a subject-state of Mitanni and subsequently fell to the Hittite Suppiluliuma.

The ***Nuhashshi Lands*** are first attested in C18 Mari texts, which indicate that at this time the northern part of them belonged to the kingdom of Yamhad, the southern part to the territory of Qatna. In C15, Nuhashshi was among the lands conquered by the pharaoh Tuthmosis III. Later Hittite texts referring to the 'kings of Nuhashshi' indicate that the region was then (if not before) divided among a number of principalities or small kingdoms. By mid C14, Nuhashshi had become subject to Mitanni. Before his 'one-year Syrian war' against Mitanni, Suppiluliuma concluded an alliance with one of the Nuhashshi kings, but the region as a whole apparently remained hostile to Hatti until Suppiluliuma conquered Mitanni and imposed his sovereignty over all its northern Syrian principalities. Subsequently, Nuhashshi rebelled unsuccessfully against Suppiluliuma's second successor Mursili II (c. 1321–1295). It figures later as the place of exile King Hattusili III chose for his nephew Urhi-Teshub after seizing the Hittite throne from him.

Tunip Seized by Tuthmosis III during his Syrian campaigns, Tunip had become by the Amarna period (mid C14) one of Egypt's three major strongholds in the north (the other two were Sumur and Ullassa). By the end of the period, it had probably become subject or allied to Hatti.

Amurru As noted earlier (pp. 81–3), the name Amurru was restricted in the Late Bronze Age to the territory lying between the Orontes and the central Levantine coast. This territory was incorporated into the Egyptian empire in C15 by Tuthmosis III. But its attachment to Egypt remained tenuous. It was a wild and anarchic region, inhabited by semi-nomadic groups called the Habiru. In mid C14, a local leader called Abdi-Ashirta united these groups under his command, and while claiming allegiance to the pharaoh (Amenhotep III?), used them to plunder many of Egypt's subject-territories in the region, before his career ended in capture by the Egyptian authorities. But de facto leadership of the country was inherited by his son Aziru who like his father attacked and plundered neighbouring states while maintaining a semblance of loyalty to the pharaoh (now Amenhotep IV/Akhenaten). Finally Aziru proclaimed allegiance to the Hittite Suppiluliuma. Thereafter, control of Amurru was disputed by Hittite and Egyptian kings until the Hittites firmly established their authority over it in the aftermath of the Qadesh engagements (see pp. 139–41).

Qatna (***Mishrifeh***) We have noted (p. 81) that early in M2 Qatna was ruled by an Amorite dynasty and became one of the most important Amorite kingdoms in Syria. By late C16, however, it had fallen to the Mitannian empire, and subsequently during the reigns of the pharaohs Tuthmosis I and Tuthmosis III was subject to Egypt. The following century (C14) saw its conquest by the Hittite Suppiluliuma. But its king at the time, Akizzi, broke from Hittite control and declared allegiance to the pharaoh Akhenaten – until action against his kingdom by pro-Hittite states in the region probably forced him to accept Hittite overlordship once more. Qatna was destroyed in the Hittite empire's final years, but it was resettled in the Iron Age, apparently by Aramaeans, and enjoyed a flourishing existence as a trading centre during the Neo-Babylonian period (C6).

   German excavations conducted in 2002 in the city's palace uncovered a hoard of sixty-seven tablets and fragments. Also discovered was an underground shaft leading to a royal tomb, which contained a main chamber and three side-chambers. Two identical seated 'ancestor-statues' made of basalt flanked the tomb-entrance. The tomb's burials were still intact. Most were found in the main chamber, which appears to have been used also for ceremonial feasts.

Amka (***Amqa***, ***Amki***) Located in the Biqaʻ Valley on the northern frontier of Egyptian subject territory, Amka was caught up in the contests between Egypt and Hatti for the control of the Syrian states to which both kingdoms laid claim. During Akhenaten's reign, word was brought to Egypt that Hittite troops had captured cities in the land of Amka. Subsequently, in the death-year of Akhenaten's successor Tutankhamun (1327), a Hittite force attacked the land, allegedly in retaliation for an Egyptian attack on Qadesh, now under Hittite control. The Hittite assault on Amka violated an earlier treaty drawn up between Hatti and Egypt (the so-called Kurustama treaty), and was seen to be one of the causes of a god-inflicted plague that allegedly devastated the Hittite homeland for twenty years.

   See *PPAWA* entries for more details on the above cities and countries.

Ugarit

Ugarit (Ras Shamra) (after Yon 2006: vi)

Located on a 50 km stretch of the northern coast of Syria, Ugarit became one of the most important and wealthiest kingdoms of the Syro-Palestinian region in the Late Bronze Age. It derived its wealth from a number of sources – rich timberlands, fertile steppes and plains that produced a flourishing cattle industry and a wide range of agricultural goods, including grain, wine, oil and flax. Ugarit was also the centre of thriving manufacturing industries, where the arts of bronzesmiths and goldsmiths prospered and a wide range of linen and woollen goods were produced for export. The small finds unearthed in the city – jewellery, weapons, figurines, gold bowls, faience and alabaster vases – reflect the high level of local craftsmanship and the extensive foreign commercial and cultural contacts which Ugarit enjoyed. Its location was of considerable strategic significance, providing as it did a major link between the Mediterranean world and the lands stretching to the Euphrates and beyond. Through Ugarit's territory passed some of the most important land-routes of Syria, north to Anatolia and east through Aleppo to Mesopotamia.

Substantial remains survive of the kingdom's capital, also called Ugarit. Its dominant building was a royal palace, covering an area of c. 10,000 square metres and including one or more upper storeys, accessed by a dozen staircases. The palace contained luxuriously appointed private apartments, which in one area opened on to a large garden. Other parts of the palace were used for administrative and official purposes. The whole complex was walled off from the rest of the city, which contained blocks of houses of varying size, generally built along narrow winding streets. In several of these houses as well as in the palace, a number of tablet archives have come to light (see p. 57). They provide us with one of our most valuable sources of information on international relations in the Late Bronze Age.

In the contest between the Great Kingdoms of the age for supremacy over Syria, Ugarit became an ally and then a vassal state of the Hittite empire in mid C14. It was destroyed during the upheavals at the end of the Bronze Age, and never rebuilt.

Yon (2006); Burns (2009: 297–301).

Figure 22.2 Postern Gate, Ugarit. Photo by Trevor Bryce.

Part V

The Late Bronze Age
(continuing into the Iron Age)

23

The major Late Bronze Age kingdoms

During the Late Bronze Age, the Near Eastern world was dominated by five major powers. First, Hatti (the kingdom of the Hittites), whose power-base lay in north-central Anatolia, Mitanni, formed from a Hurrian confederation of states, whose power-base lay in northern Mesopotamia, Babylon, whose kingdom extended through southern Mesopotamia, in the region now commonly called Babylonia, and Egypt in the land of the Nile. After the Hittites destroyed the Mitannian empire in the second half of C14, Assyria replaced Mitanni as one of the Great Kingdoms of the age. Correspondence between the rulers of these kingdoms was exchanged through diplomatic missions on a regular basis. In this correspondence, the Great Kings address each other as 'My Brother', and expressions of love and devotion regularly preface the business section of their letters (often acrimonious in their suspicions and complaints). There were remarkably few wars between the Great Kings during the half-millennium of Late Bronze Age history. (Most notable among them were those that culminated in the Hittite destruction of Mitanni, the Hittite–Egyptian conflicts at Qadesh and the Hittite–Assyrian engagement at Nihriya in northern Mesopotamia.) The relative peace between the great powers, though often strained, was probably due in large measure to the fact that their rulers regularly talked to each other, via their diplomatic missions.

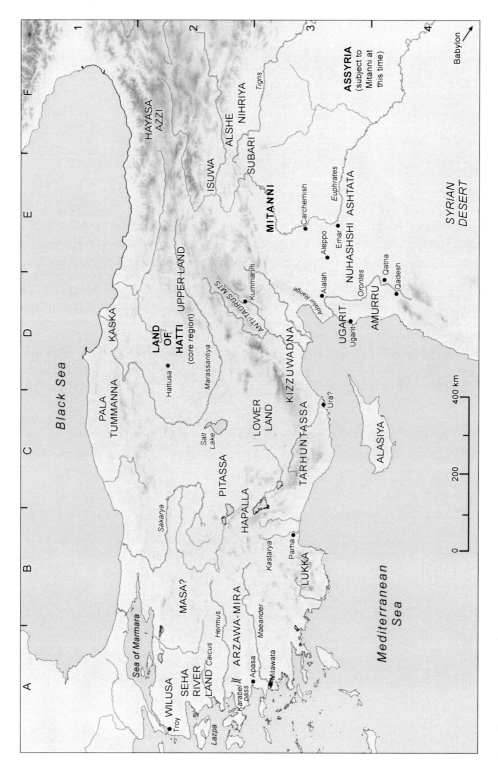

Late Bronze Age Anatolia, northern Syria, and northern Mesopotamia (mid 14th cent.)

24

The Hittites

'Hittite' is the name applied by modern scholars to the Late Bronze Age peoples who inhabited the land called Hatti in north-central Anatolia. The name arose out of the assumption, first made by C19 scholars, that the people so called were linked with the Hittites attested in biblical sources.

The Bronze Age kingdom of Hatti was founded probably early in C17 by a king called Labarna, who established a royal dynasty which, with a few brief interruptions, lasted until at least the early decades of the Iron Age. Labarna and his royal successors were members of one of three Indo-European groups who probably entered Anatolia during M3 BC. The other groups we call Palaians

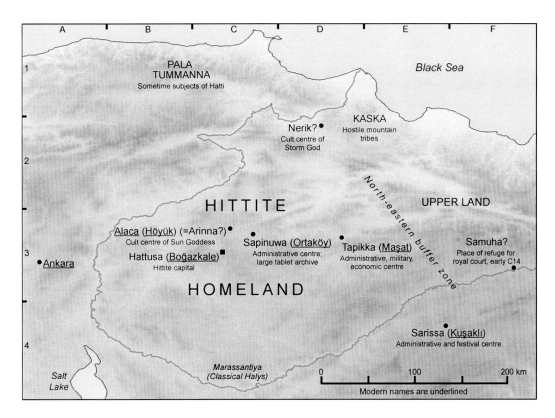

The Hittite homeland

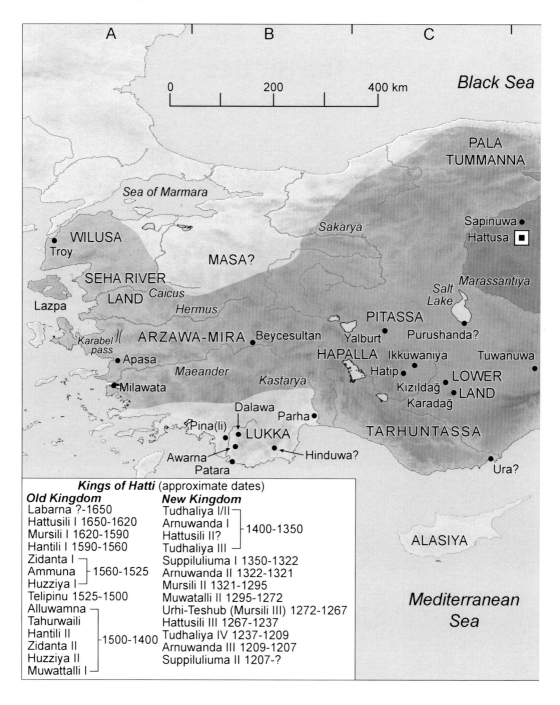

Kings of Hatti (approximate dates)

Old Kingdom	New Kingdom
Labarna ?-1650	Tudhaliya I/II ┐
Hattusili I 1650-1620	Arnuwanda I ├ 1400-1350
Mursili I 1620-1590	Hattusili II? │
Hantili I 1590-1560	Tudhaliya III ┘
Zidanta I ┐	Suppiluliuma I 1350-1322
Ammuna ├ 1560-1525	Arnuwanda II 1322-1321
Huzziya I ┘	Mursili II 1321-1295
Telipinu 1525-1500	Muwatalli II 1295-1272
Alluwamna ┐	Urhi-Teshub (Mursili III) 1272-1267
Tahurwaili │	Hattusili III 1267-1237
Hantili II ├ 1500-1400	Tudhaliya IV 1237-1209
Zidanta II │	Arnuwanda III 1209-1207
Huzziya II │	Suppiluliuma II 1207-?
Muwattalli I ┘	

The Hittite empire (late 14th–13th cent.)

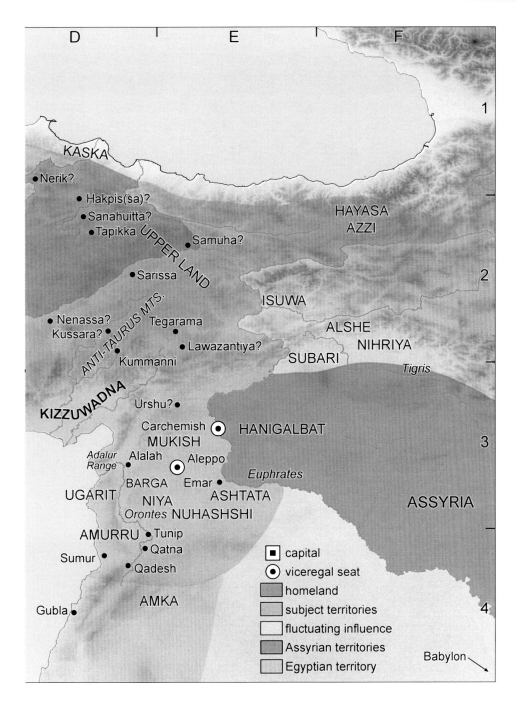

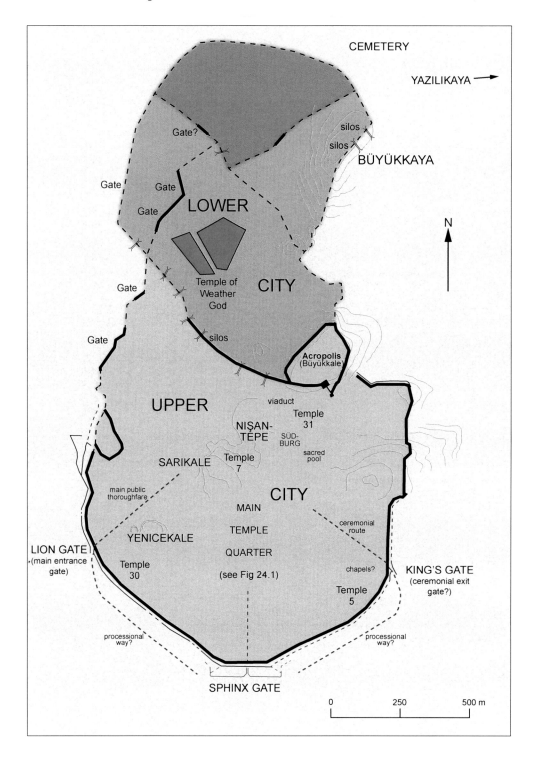

Hattusa

and Luwians after the languages they used. The kingdom over which Labarna ruled was originally small, but in a series of military campaigns he expanded its territories until he held sway over a region extending south from the Marassantiya river (Classical Halys, modern Kızıl Irmak) to the Mediterranean Sea. His grandson(?) and successor Hattusili I consolidated his conquests, and was probably responsible for resettling the abandoned site called Hattus, making it the royal Hittite capital Hattusa.

Hattusa lay within the Marassantiya river basin, in the region now commonly called the Hittite homeland. The name Hatti, used by the Hittites themselves, preserves the

Figure 24.1 Part of the main temple quarter, Hattusa. Photo by Trevor Bryce.

original pre-Indo-European name of the region. From his capital, Hattusili embarked on campaigns which took his armies westwards into the Arzawa lands, and south-eastwards across the Taurus mountains into Syria. His military enterprises in the south-east brought him into conflict with the northern Syrian kingdom of Yamhad, and with the Hurrian peoples, later to unite into the kingdom of Mitanni. The campaigns against Yamhad were successfully completed by his grandson and successor Mursili I who sacked its capital Aleppo, and then led his troops along the Euphrates to Babylon, which he captured and destroyed (c. 1595).

In the second half of C14, the kingdom of Hatti reached its peak of power and influence in the Near East. This was in the reign of Suppiluliuma I (c. 1350–1322), who destroyed the kingdom of Mitanni and expanded his own empire, which now stretched from Anatolia's Aegean coast eastwards to the Euphrates, and southwards through Syria to the frontiers of Damascus. But Hatti's territorial claims in Syria led to increasing tensions with Egypt, which contested sovereignty with it over a number of the Syrian principalities. A showdown between the forces of the Hittite king Muwattalli II and those of the pharaoh Ramesses II in 1274 at Qadesh on the Orontes (after an earlier confrontation there between Muwattalli and Ramesses' father Seti I, which Seti won) ended in stalemate, though in the long term the Hittites acquired control over all the contested territories. A treaty was subsequently drawn up (in 1259)

Figure 24.2 The walls of Hattusa. Photo by Trevor Bryce.

between Ramesses and Muwattalli's brother and second successor Hattusili III, which formally ended hostilities between Hatti and Egypt. Relations between the two kingdoms remained peaceful for the rest of the Late Bronze Age.

We have noted that the Hittite ruling class was of Indo-European origin. But already in its early years this particular Indo-European group may well have been a minority in the kingdom, its royal dynasty holding sway over a predominantly indigenous population called Hattians. And in later years its proportions must have progressively diminished as the homeland's population was swelled by deportees brought back as spoils of conquest from military campaigns abroad. A large number of these deportees came from Luwian-speaking regions, like the western Arzawa lands. By the time of the empire's collapse, Luwian speakers may have formed the majority of the homeland population, and indeed of the populations of western, central and southern Anatolia. This may well explain why Hittite kings in the last century of the kingdom used the Luwian language, written in its hieroglyphic form (there was also a cuneiform version of the language), on their public monuments. For their chancery records, however, they retained their own language, which they called Nesite (after the city of Nesa just south of the Marassantiya river where the royal dynasty's ancestors may have ruled), written in a cuneiform script. Akkadian, the Late Bronze Age international language of diplomacy, was used for diplomatic communications with foreign kings and with the Hittite kings' Syrian vassal rulers.

Administratively, the Hittite empire consisted of (a) core territory, the land within the Marassantiya basin which we have called the Hittite homeland, (b) a number of vassal states spread over many parts of Anatolia and northern Syria, and (c) from Suppiluliuma I's reign onwards, two viceregal kingdoms in northern Syria, one at Carchemish, the other at Aleppo; these were ruled by close members of the king's family, generally his sons. The vassal states were administered by local rulers, bound by treaties to the Great King. By and large, the vassal rulers remained loyal to their treaty obligations. But there were some notable exceptions, especially as the empire entered its final years. The Hittite kingdom collapsed in early C12, amid the general upheavals which brought many Bronze Age states and cities to an end. The formal end of the empire came when the last Hittite king, Suppiluliyama (Suppiluliuma II), abandoned his capital, leaving it to be pillaged and destroyed by marauders and enemy forces.

Bryce (2002, 2005, *AANE*: 722–39); Collins (2007); Seeher, Beal, Glatz, van den Hout and Mielke (*OHAA*: 376–92, 579–603, 877–99, 900–13, 1031–54, respectively).

25

Arzawa and the Luwians

Arzawa

Arzawa (early variant Arzawiya) is the name applied in Hittite texts to a region encompassing much of western and south-western Anatolia. It is sometimes used as a generic term for the region as a whole, and sometimes as a designation for a group of up to five local kingdoms which collectively made up the 'Arzawa lands'. The original nucleus of these lands was probably a specific kingdom called Arzawa, now referred to as 'Arzawa Minor' or 'Arzawa Proper' to distinguish it from the rest of the Arzawa group. Initially, 'Arzawa Minor' may have exercised some form of political or military hegemony over the whole Arzawa complex. It occupied a region extending inland from the central Aegean coast, perhaps in part along the Maeander river valley, and was ruled from its capital Apasa, which lay on or near the site of Classical Ephesus. The other lands belonging to the Arzawa complex were Mira (with its extension Kuwaliya), Seha River Land, Wilusa and Hapalla. The first three occupied much of the western sector of Anatolia, from the Maeander valley northwards to the Troad; Hapalla lay further east, towards the territory called the Lower Land in Hittite texts.

Mira probably became the largest of the Arzawa states when the Hittite king Mursili II conquered and depopulated its neighbour Arzawa Minor (c. 1320), then ruled by one of the Hittites' most persistent enemies Uhhaziti, and (very likely) handed

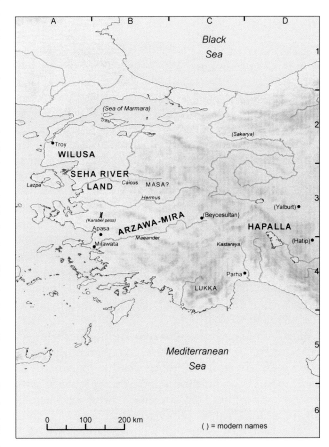

The Arzawa lands

Figure 25.1 The Karabel monument. Photo by Mr Necdet Düzen.

over its territory to Mira. A well-known relief sculpture with Luwian hieroglyphic inscription carved in the Karabel pass near Izmir has recently been identified with a C13 king of Mira called Tarkasnawa (see p. 56). The monument may well have lain on the boundary between Mira and Seha River Land. Wilusa almost certainly lay to the north of the latter, thus in the Troad. Most scholars believe that it is to be identified with the kingdom called Troy in Classical sources, referred to in Homer's *Iliad* by the alternative names (W)Ilios and Troia. From the reign of Mursili II onwards, the Arzawa lands became vassal states of the Hittite empire.

The Luwians

The Luwians were one of three Indo-European speaking peoples who migrated into the Anatolian peninsula from a homeland perhaps north of the Black Sea, and probably during M3 BC. Luwian-speaking peoples dispersed widely through the Anatolian peninsula during M2, perhaps from a core region in central Anatolia, settling particularly in large areas of western and southern Anatolia. In the west, they may have been the principal population group of the Arzawa lands. In the south, they made up a large part of the populations of the Lukka Lands, Tarhuntassa and Kizzuwadna.

They are known to us primarily from inscriptions in their language, represented in both cuneiform and hieroglyphic scripts. The former appear in several hundred passages, primarily of a religious and ritual character, which are incorporated into Hittite texts and are identified by the term *luwili* ('in the language of Luwiya'). The actual name 'Luwiya' is attested only in very early versions of the Hittite laws, where it is replaced by 'Arzawa' in subsequent versions. Hieroglyphic inscriptions appear (a) on seal impressions, often combined with cuneiform inscriptions, (b) as graffiti on the paving stones and orthostats of the Temple of the Storm God at Hattusa, and on a number of bowls and other small metal objects, and (c) as monumental inscriptions on rock-faces and built stone surfaces. Most of the monumental inscriptions have been found within the Hittite homeland, but are otherwise widely distributed throughout Anatolia.

Following the collapse of the Hittite empire, the Hittite cuneiform script and language disappeared. But the Luwian hieroglyphic tradition was preserved, becoming one of the most important distinguishing features of the Neo-Hittite kingdoms which emerged in south-eastern Anatolia and northern Syria during the Iron Age. It was adopted by the rulers of the Neo-Hittite kingdoms as it had been by their Bronze Age Hittite counterparts for use on their public monuments, and at least in some cases for their administrative records. Whether or not the survival of this tradition represents an influx of Luwian refugees from the Anatolian peninsula into northern Syria after the fall of the Hittite empire remains debatable.

Melchert (2003); Bryce and Yakubovich (*OHAA*: 363–75, 534–47).

26
The Hurrians and Mitanni (Mittani)

The Hurrians

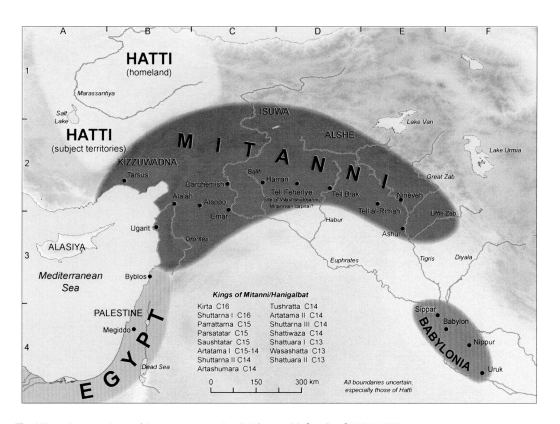

The Mitannian empire and its contemporaries (15th cent.) (after Roaf 1996: 134)

The Hurrians were a large group of peoples, of uncertain origin, who from late M3 onwards had begun to spread through northern Mesopotamia, northern Syria, and eastern Anatolia. The Kura-Araxes region in Transcaucasia and eastern Anatolia has been proposed as their original homeland. Hurrian states are first attested in C23, as subjects of the Akkadian king Naram-Sin. After the Akkadian's empire's fall c. 2193, Hurrian-speaking groups established a number of small

123

principalities through northern and eastern Mesopotamia. Later, Hurrians appear among the traders in eastern and central Anatolia during the Middle Bronze Age Assyrian Colony period. By the end of C16, a number of small states with predominantly Hurrian populations had been amalgamated into a single political federation called the kingdom of Mitanni, which became one of the Great Kingdoms of the Late Bronze Age. Already before the formation of this kingdom, the Hurrians were involved in bitter conflict with the Hittites for control over northern Syria and eastern Anatolia. It was only when the Hittite king Suppiluliuma I destroyed the kingdom of Mitanni during the second half of C14 that Hittite–Hurrian conflicts ended.

Many elements of Hurrian culture survived and flourished in the Hittite world after the Hurrians had ceased to be a political force in the Near East. Hurrian deities and religious practices were adopted with particular enthusiasm in C13 by the Hittite king Hattusili III and his Hurrian queen Puduhepa, and subsequently by Hattusili's son and successor Tudhaliya IV – as illustrated by the reliefs and inscriptions of the Hittite rock sanctuary at Yazılıkaya near Hattusa. And Hurrian mythological tales became embedded in Hittite literary tradition, notably the Kumarbi epic. In southern Anatolia, the state of Kizzuwadna (Kizzuwatna) was probably created under Hurrian influence in C16, and contained a substantial Hurrian element in its population. The Hurrians spoke a language, preserved primarily in cuneiform inscriptions, which is unrelated to any other language known to us, with the possible exception of Urartian.

Mitanni (Mittani)

As we have noted, the kingdom of Mitanni was formed by the end of C16 from a number of small predominantly Hurrian states in upper Mesopotamia. The Egyptians and Canaanites called it Naharina or Naharima. In C15, Mitanni became one of the four Great Kingdoms of the Near Eastern world (the others at that time were Hatti, Babylon and Egypt). From their capital Washshukkanni, the kings of Mitanni held sway over a large range of territories extending from northern Mesopotamia through northern Syria and parts of eastern Anatolia. (Washshukkanni has yet to be located with certainty though it is commonly thought to be the site of Tell Feheriye in the Habur triangle.) An elite class of warriors called the *maryannu* provided an important basis of the kingdom's military might.

Mitanni's aggressive programme of territorial expansion west of the Euphrates brought it into conflict with both Hatti and Egypt. The contests between Mitanni and Egypt were finally resolved when an agreement was reached early in C14 between the Mitannian king Artatama and the pharaoh Tuthmosis IV over a division of Syrian territory between them: the lands of northern Syria were acknowledged as Mitannian possessions, and much of southern and part of coastal Syria were confirmed as Egyptian subject territory. That set the stage for a showdown between the Mitannian king Tushratta and his Hittite counterpart Suppiluliuma. In the 1340s, the final contest between the two powers began. It resulted eventually in victory for Suppiluliuma, and the destruction of Mitanni, whose last stronghold Carchemish fell to Suppiluliuma in 1327. Tushratta was later assassinated, and his son Shattiwaza subsequently installed as a Hittite ally and puppet ruler of the kingdom of Hanigalbat, the much reduced successor of the Great Kingdom of Mitanni.

Wilhelm (1989); *CANE* (2: 1243–54).

27

The adventures of Idrimi

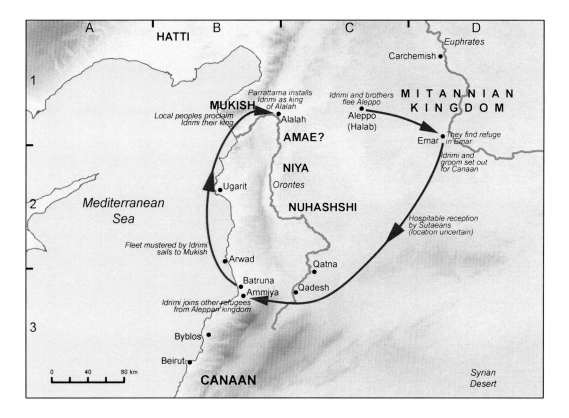

Idrimi's quest (after Rainey and Notley 2006: 62)

The statue of Idrimi, now in the British Museum, was unearthed by Leonard Woolley during excavations at Tell Atchana (ancient Alalah). It dates to Alalah level IV in archaeological terms (C15). This phase of Alalah was destroyed by the Hittites, who subsequently rebuilt the city (level III). The statue itself was damaged, but preserved, in pieces, and finally deposited in the precincts of Alalah's main temple.

Figure 27.1 Idrimi, king of Alalah
© World History Archive/
Alamy.

An Akkadian cuneiform inscription, 104 lines long, is carved across the front of the statue and provides us with an *alleged* autobiographical account of Idrimi's adventures. His story begins in Aleppo when some unspecified hostile action took place, perhaps the violent overthrow of his father, King Ilim-ilimma. Idrimi and his brothers fled the city, eventually finding refuge in Emar, their mother's home-town. But Idrimi grew restless in exile, and resolved to reclaim his father's throne for himself. Word reached him that a number of his father's former subjects had rejected the new regime in Aleppo and were now living in a city called Ammiya, in the region of Canaan. So he set out for Ammiya across the Syrian wilderness, and after an encounter with the Sutaeans, bedouin tribesmen who proved friendly, he reached his destination. Once there, he began preparing for his return to Aleppo, his followers from Aleppo and neighbouring regions boosted by troops of the landless outlaws called Habiru. Aleppo was now subject to the Mitannian king Parrattarna, and Idrimi allegedly spent seven years preparing for his return to reclaim his father's throne. Finally, he set sail for the north, making a landfall probably near the mouth of the Orontes. But he soon realized he had no chance of defeating Parrattarna in a military confrontation, and so negotiated a peace deal with him. In accordance with its terms, he was installed as king, not of Aleppo, but of Alalah, and as the vassal of Parrattarna. He apparently remained loyal to his Mitannian allegiance for the rest of his career.

Greenstein (*CANE* 4: 2423–8).

28

The Middle Assyrian empire

In the first half of the Late Bronze Age, Assyria became a vassal state of Mitanni. But the disintegration of the Mitannian kingdom (caused by the Hittites) between c. 1340 and 1327 paved the way for an Assyrian resurgence during the reign of Ashur-uballit (c. 1365–1330). In effect the founder of what we call the Middle Assyrian kingdom, Ashur-uballit, rapidly filled the power vacuum east of the Euphrates left by Mitanni's colllapse, and then looked to expanding his territories west of the Euphrates and south into Babylonia. An Assyrian invasion across the river threatened Hittite vassal states in northern Syria and ultimately Egyptian subject territories in southern Syria and Palestine. The threat never materialized. But Babylonia suffered invasion by Assyria on at least two occasions, firstly under the command of Ashur-uballit and subsequently by a later Assyrian king Tukulti-Ninurta I (c. 1244–1208). Babylon was twice conquered, and on the second occasion incorporated by Tukulti-Ninurta into his subject territories. This king also resoundingly defeated a Hittite army led by Tudhaliya IV, in the so-called battle of Nihriya in northern Mesopotamia. But in the end Tukulti-Ninurta's ambitious military enterprises overstretched his kingdom's resources, and he was assassinated by disaffected subjects after suffering a series of military defeats. Babylon subsequently regained its independence, and once more, the kingdom of Assyria was in decline.

But it proved resilient. It survived the catastrophes that ended many Bronze Age kingdoms and cities, and in the reign of Tiglath-Pileser I (c. 1114–1076), still retained control over a substantial part of northern Mesopotamia. Indeed, Tiglath-pileser extended considerably the earlier boundaries of Assyrian enterprise by leading an expedition across the Euphrates to the Mediterranean coast. His reign, however, proved little more than a temporary bounce in the kingdom's fortunes. After his death, Assyria entered upon one-and-a-half centuries of relative weakness, its territory being reduced, by the beginning of M1, to a narrow strip of land stretching 150 km along the Tigris.

Radner (2015); Van De Mieroop (2016: 190–5).

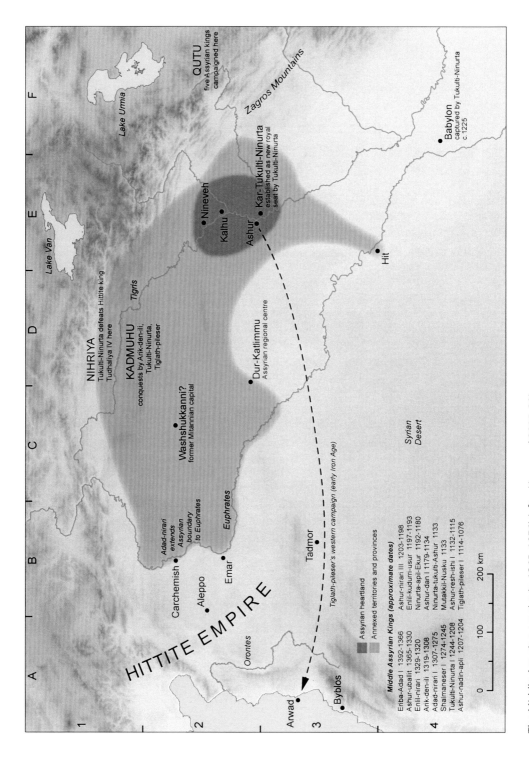

The Middle Assyrian empire (c. 1365–1076) (after Haywood 2005: 39)

29

Kassite Babylonia

Soon after Hammurabi's death, the Old Babylonian kingdom began to contract. This was due to a number of factors, including rebellions within the subject territories, further invasions by the Elamites, and the occupation of Babylonia, as far north as Nippur, by a new dynasty called the 'Sealand' from the marshlands of southern Mesopotamia. But the kingdom lingered on until it was abruptly terminated, c. 1595, by the Hittite king Mursili I, who sacked and destroyed Babylon, ending the reign of the last Amorite king Samsu-ditana. Mursili's victory paved the way for the rise of a Kassite dynasty in Babylonia. First attested in texts from Hammurabi's reign, the Kassites were immigrants to Babylonia, perhaps from an original homeland in the Zagros Mountains. They settled peacefully in their new land, after some initial hostilities with its existing inhabitants, and by the time of the Hittite conquest, a group of them were becoming a major political force within Babylonia. Following their conquest of the 'Sealanders', they established a ruling dynasty, under which the Babylonian kingdom once again became a major international power. Its administrative seat was shifted from Babylon to a new site Dur-Kurigalzu (modern Aqar Quf). But the Kassites took care to preserve and nurture the cultural traditions of Hammurabi's Babylon, and the former capital remained Babylonia's cultural and religious centre. Indeed under Kassite patronage, the arts and sciences flourished in Babylonia as never before. Akkadian in its Babylonian dialect became the international language of diplomacy, used widely throughout the Near East. Kassite rulers belonged to the elite group of Great Kings of the Near East, a status they shared with the pharaohs of Egypt, and the rulers of Hatti and Assyria. But disputes and conflicts with their northern neighbour Assyria led to at least two Assyrian invasions of their kingdom and eventually subjection to Assyrian rule by Tukulti-Ninurta I (c. 1244–1208). Fifteen years after Tukulti-Ninurta's death, the Kassites regained their independence – but for a few decades only. Their kingdom fell finally to the Elamites c. 1155.

Sommerfeld (*CANE* 2: 917–30); Leick (2003: 43–61); Arnold (2004: 61–73); Van De Mieroop (2016: 183–90).

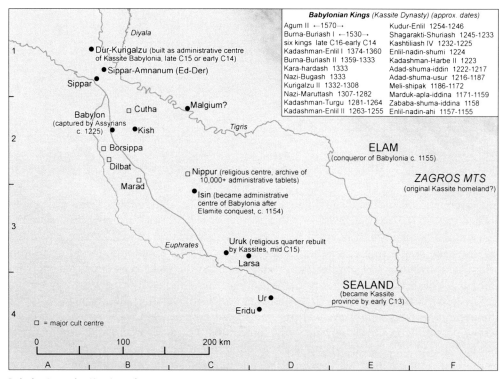

Babylonia under Kassite rule

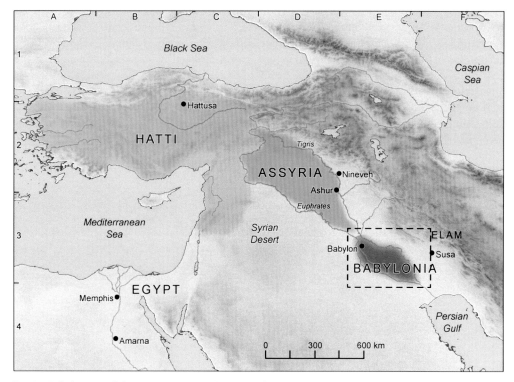

Kassite Babylonia and the contemporary 'Great Kingdoms'

30

Middle and New Kingdom Egypt

A few years after the death of the last significant Old Kingdom ruler Pepi II, Egypt entered a period of disunity and anarchy. Spanning about a century (c. 2160–2055), it is commonly known as the First Intermediate period. A new, more stable era succeeded it, the period called the Middle Kingdom. This lasted until c. 1650, and was followed by a further period of weakness and instability, designated as the Second Intermediate period (c. 1650–1550). A feature of it was the appearance of a line of kings called the Hyksos, who established their capital at Avaris in the eastern Delta. They had emerged from northern hordes of Syro-Palestinian origin who had invaded Egypt a century or so earlier. The Hyksos were finally driven from Egypt by a local leader called Ahmose who captured Avaris and became c. 1550 founder of the Egyptian New Kingdom. Thebes in Upper Egypt had been the centre from which resistance against the foreigners had been organized. Ahmose was the first ruler of the famous 18th Dynasty, whose most illustrious member Tuthmosis III (1479–1425) firmly established his kingdom as a major international power by a series of military campaigns through Palestine and Syria, in the wake of those conducted by his royal predecessors, one of whom, Tuthmosis I (1504–1492) had led his forces to the banks of the Euphrates.

Egypt's expeditions into Syria and Palestine inevitably led to contests with Mitanni and Hatti for control over these regions. At the time of the Hittite conquest of Mitanni, Egypt's throne was occupied by the so-called 'heretic pharaoh' Amenhotep IV (1352–1336), son and successor of Amenhotep III, who renamed himself Akhenaten after the Sun God Aten to whose worship he devoted himself exclusively. In honour of his god, he built a new capital called Akhetaten 'Horizon of Aten' (modern el-Amarna) in middle Egypt, shifting the royal seat from the traditional capital Thebes. Akhenaten's 'heretic' religion was abandoned shortly after his death, but the pharaoh's alleged neglect of his country's affairs had left the kingdom in a weak, divided state, and severely reduced its influence on the international scene. The sudden death of his second successor, the boy-king Tutankhamun, brought the 18th Dynasty to an end.

But Egypt gained a new lease of life with the rise of a new ruling family, the 19th (Ramesside) Dynasty, founded by Ramesses I (1295–1294). Its second and third rulers, Seti I and his son Ramesses II, restored Egypt's prosperity and built their kingdom once more into a major international political and military power. Tensions with the Hittites persisted and indeed increased as both Seti and Ramesses conducted aggressive new campaigns in Syria and Palestine. These brought them into conflict with the Hittites in two major battles at Qadesh on the Orontes (see below). Henceforth relations between the two kingdoms, formalized by a peace treaty in 1259, were generally peaceful.

During the crises which engulfed the Aegean and Near Eastern worlds in early C12, many Late Bronze Age centres of power were destroyed, including the Hittite kingdom. Egypt too suffered

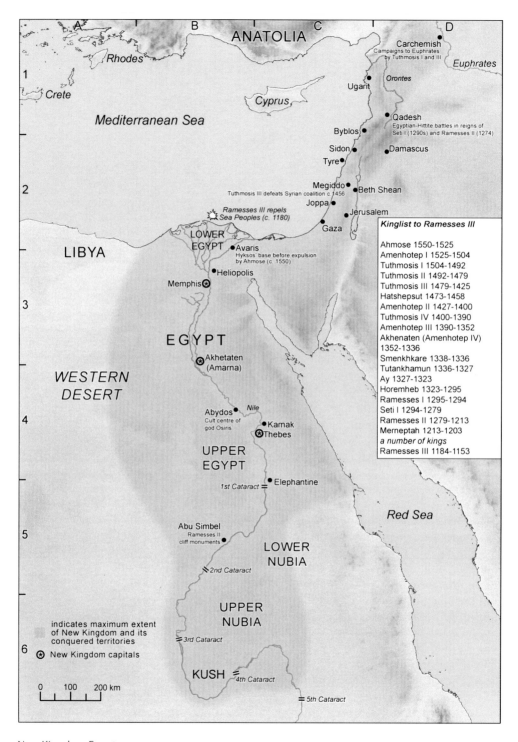

New Kingdom Egypt

The following labels appear on the map:

A B C D

ANATOLIA

Rhodes

1

Crete

Mediterranean Sea

Cyprus

Ugarit

Carchemish
Campaigns to Euphrates
by Tuthmosis I and III

Euphrates

Orontes

Qadesh
Egyptian-Hittite battles in reigns of
Seti I (1290s) and Ramesses II (1274)

Byblos

Sidon

Damascus

Tyre

Megiddo
Beth Shean

Tuthmosis III defeats Syrian coalition c. 1456

Joppa

Jerusalem

*Ramesses III repels
Sea Peoples (c. 1180)*

Gaza

LOWER
EGYPT

Avaris
Hyksos' base before expulsion
by Ahmose (c. 1550)

LIBYA

Heliopolis

Memphis

EGYPT

Akhetaten
(Amarna)

WESTERN
DESERT

Abydos
Cult centre of
god Osiris

Nile

Karnak
Thebes

UPPER
EGYPT

1st Cataract   Elephantine

Red Sea

Abu Simbel
Ramesses II
cliff monuments

LOWER
NUBIA

2nd Cataract

UPPER
NUBIA

indicates maximum extent
of New Kingdom and its
conquered territories

New Kingdom capitals

3rd Cataract

KUSH   4th Cataract

0   100   200 km

5th Cataract

Kinglist to Ramesses III

Ahmose 1550-1525
Amenhotep I 1525-1504
Tuthmosis I 1504-1492
Tuthmosis II 1492-1479
Tuthmosis III 1479-1425
Hatshepsut 1473-1458
Amenhotep II 1427-1400
Tuthmosis IV 1400-1390
Amenhotep III 1390-1352
Akhenaten (Amenhotep IV)
1352-1336
Smenkhkare 1338-1336
Tutankhamun 1336-1327
Ay 1327-1323
Horemheb 1323-1295
Ramesses I 1295-1294
Seti I 1294-1279
Ramesses II 1279-1213
Merneptah 1213-1203
a number of kings
Ramesses III 1184-1153

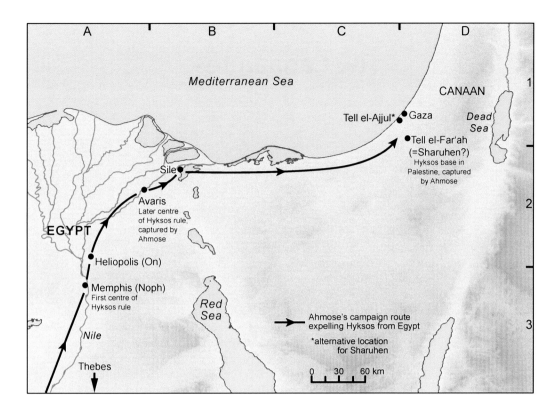

Ahmose's expulsion of the Hyksos

from the chaotic conditions at the end of the Bronze Age, made worse by political squabbles and faction strife within the kingdom. Inevitably, this took its toll on Egypt's international standing. By the end of C12, it had withdrawn from all political and military involvement in the Syro-Palestine region, thereby losing its status as a major international power.

Chapters by various authors in Shaw (2000: 148–329).

31

The Canaanites

In its broadest sense, we use the term 'Canaanite' to refer to the ancient peoples and cultures of the Levant, up to the last decades of C4 BC. But the peoples so called were divided into a number of tribal groups, city-states and kingdoms, each of which developed its own political and social structures, and a number of its own distinctive cultural traits. They identified themselves, and were almost always identified by others, not as Canaanites but by the names of the specific tribal and political units to which they belonged. This explains why in the ancient sources 'Canaanite' is rarely used as a generic designation for them, outside the Bible. The first clearly attested use of the term occurs in the C18 archives of Mari on the Euphrates, and there are occasional references to Canaan and Canaanites in later Bronze Age texts; for example, Canaanites were among the prisoners-of-war deported to Egypt by the C15 pharaoh Amenhotep II, and in the following century, Canaan appears several times in the Amarna letters. But the rarity of such references reflects the lack of perception, either by the Canaanites themselves or by their contemporaries, of a common identity which linked all Canaanites together – until they figure in Old Testament sources as the pre-Israelite occupants of 'the Promised Land'.

Canaan's strategic location at an important meeting-place between the Near Eastern, Egyptian, and Mediterranean worlds gave it excellent access to trade contacts with these worlds. This provided the stimulus, in the Early Bronze Age, for the development of a number of flourishing urban communities throughout Canaanite territory. In the Middle Bronze Age, these became the centres of city-states and kingdoms. Many were massively fortified, like Akko, Ashkelon, Dan, Dor, Gezer, Hazor, Lachish and Megiddo. The gold hoards unearthed in Tell el-Ajjul, located a few kilometres south-west of Gaza, provide some of the finest examples of Canaanite craftsmanship in the Middle Bronze IIB-C period (c. 1750–1550), sometimes called the golden age of Canaanite culture.

Egyptian campaigns in Syria and Palestine in late C16 and C15, culminating in Tuthmosis III's victory over a coalition of Canaanite and Syrian forces at Megiddo, reduced many of the Canaanite cities and kingdoms to Egyptian vassal status. But other great powers of the day, notably Mitanni and Hatti, also sought to extend their sovereignty over Canaanite territory.

The upheavals at the end of the Bronze Age led to major changes in the nature and patterns of settlement in the Canaanite region, with the collapse of the Hittite empire and the gradual withdrawal of Egypt, completed by late C12, from Syria-Palestine. Deprived of the stability and protection which their overlords had (to a reasonable degree) afforded them, a number of the Canaanite settlements were abandoned. Other major centres continued to survive and prosper, though some of them too disappeared eventually, when many of their inhabitants took to the hills. In this transitional period between the Bronze and Iron Ages, Old Testament tradition distinguishes three major groups in Palestine – the Philistines along the southern coast, the Canaanites on the plains and the Israelites in the hills. Though in biblical tradition, the Canaanites were

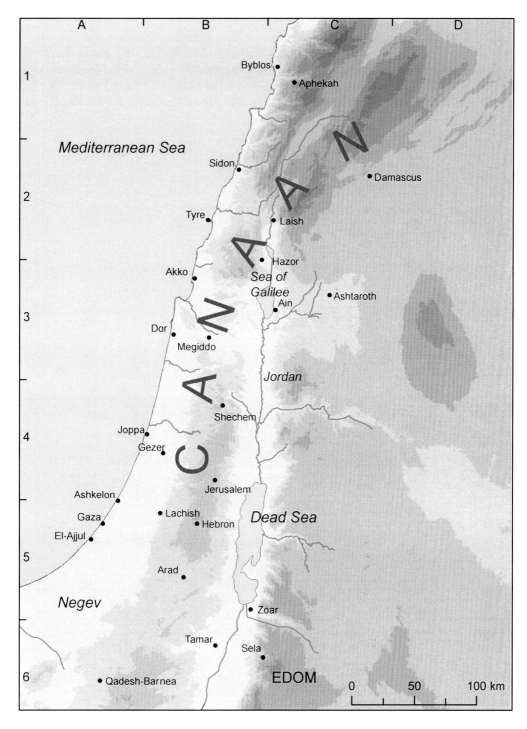

Canaan

displaced by the Israelites, some scholars have suggested that the latter were simply a sub-group of the former, who initially abandoned their cities on the plains and the coast, and resettled in the Palestinian hill-country. In any case, Canaanite culture survived for many more generations, particularly through the medium of the people called Phoenicians by the Greeks. The Phoenicians were in effect the Canaanites' M1 successors, continuing many of the mercantile and artistic traditions which had brought prosperity and distinction to the cities of Canaan in the Middle and Late Bronze Ages.

Tubb (1998).

32

The Syro-Palestinian states attested in the Amarna letters

Egypt's Syrian and Palestinian vassal rulers and their kingdoms feature prominently in the correspondence of the mid C14 Amarna archive. The archive contains a large number of letters written (a) by the vassals to the reigning pharaoh, either Amenhotep III or his successor Amenhotep IV (Akhenaten) (a few Amarna letters also date to the reigns of Akhenaten's successors Smenkhkare and Tutankhamun), (b) by the pharaoh to them, (c) to the pharaoh about them, by other vassals and Egyptian officials, as well as (d) correspondence between the pharaoh and his foreign peers. Collectively, the letters provide a rich source of information on the volatile political and military situation in Syria and Palestine during the period of their composition, including details about the activities and interests of two other great powers in the region – Hatti and Mitanni. A number of themes recur throughout the vassal letters: urgent requests to the pharaoh for military or other assistance to meet a current crisis, complaints about the activities of a predatory neighbour, or of a corrupt Egyptian official, reports on collusion between a treacherous subject-ruler and an external enemy menacing Egypt's frontiers, assurances that the pharaoh's orders have been or will be faithfully carried out, or excuses for failing to carry them out.

Moran (1992); Cohen and Westbrook (2000).

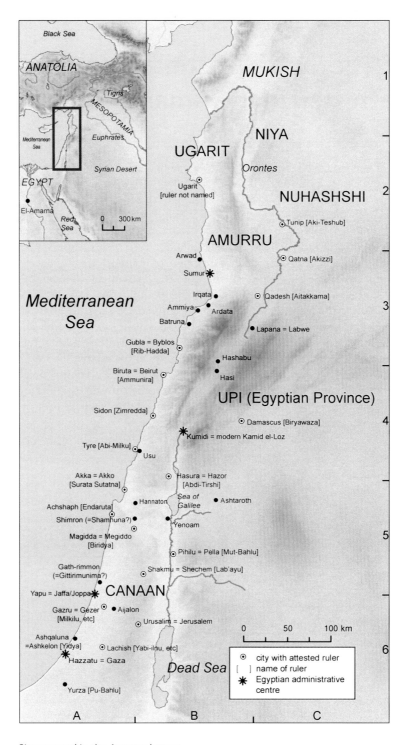

Sites named in the Amarna letters

33

Hittites and Egyptians in conflict

Qadesh (Kinza, modern Tell Nebi Mend) first appears in written records as an ally of Mitanni. It joined a coalition of Syro-Palestinian states that opposed and was defeated by the pharaoh Tuthmosis III at the battle of Megiddo (1479), and was incorporated into Egyptian subject-territory. Later, the city became embroiled in territorial disputes between Egypt and Hatti. This led eventually to open conflict when Seti I (1294–1279) confronted the Hittite king Muwattalli II in a contest for possession of Qadesh and Amurru. The battle, fought near Qadesh, resulted in a decisive Egyptian victory, and Amurru and Qadesh reverted to Egyptian control. Yet this was merely a prelude to a second battle of Qadesh fought between Seti's son and successor Ramesses II and Muwattalli in 1274.

Ramesses recruited four military divisions for the engagement, each named after an Egyptian god – from Thebes the army of Amun, from Heliopolis of Re, from Memphis of Ptah, and probably from Tanis the army of Sutekh. At the head of the Amun division, the pharaoh led his assembled troops from his capital Pi-Ramesse into the northern lands. But as they marched northwards, the divisions became widely separated from each other, with the pharaoh's Amun division advancing far ahead of the others. Deceived by two bogus Hittite defectors into believing that the entire Hittite army was far to the north, Ramesses crossed a ford on the Orontes south of Qadesh, and started setting up his camp to the north-west of the city. But while doing so, he learned that Muwattalli's army was in a concealed position on the other side of Qadesh, poised to attack. The pharaoh sent urgent orders to the Re and Ptah divisions to proceed post-haste to Qadesh to help the Amun division meet the attack. The Sutekh division was too far behind to be of any assistance. The Re division rushed north as quickly as possible. But as it crossed the Orontes, it was caught by the charge of the Hittite army and broke apart. Its troops fled in panic to the camp still being set up by Ramesses – with the Hittite chariotry in hot pursuit. A rout looked inevitable. But Ramesses' army was saved from annihilation by an apparent breakdown in discipline among the Hittite troops who

Figure 33.1 Hittite warriors at Qadesh (Temple of Luxor, Egypt). Photo by Trevor Bryce.

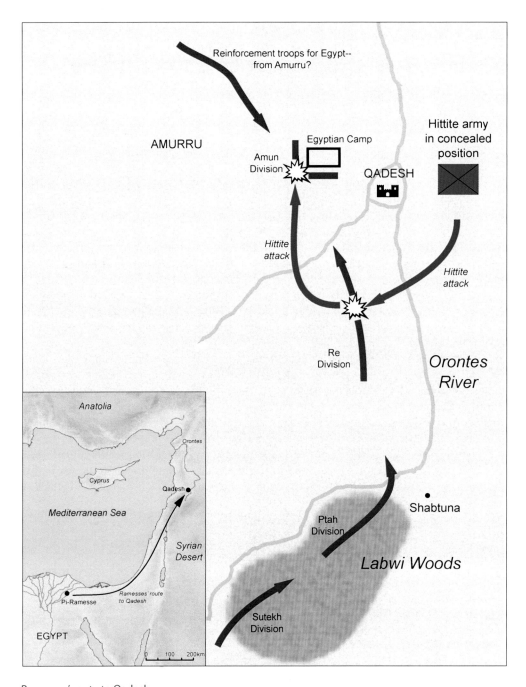

Ramesses' route to Qadesh

The Hittite attack at Qadesh (after Kitchen 1982: 52)

had set about looting the Egyptian camp before the victory was secured, and by the timely arrival of reinforcements from the west, perhaps a contingent from Amurru. Early the following day, Ramesses attacked the Hittites once more. Muwattalli's forces held firm against the onslaught, though they were unable to launch a successful counter-attack. The contest thus ended in a stale-mate, with neither side emerging as its winner. In the long term, however, the Hittites could justifiably be regarded as the victors in the contest. For they regained the disputed territories Qadesh and Amurru, and retained them until the end of the empire.

Kitchen (1982); Spalinger (2005: 209–34).

34
Troy

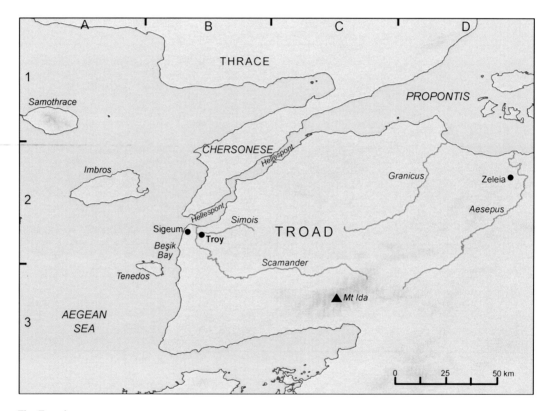

The Troad

The site identified as Troy, setting for the Trojan War in Greek legendary tradition, is located in north-western Anatolia, in the region of the Classical Troad. It lay on the Asian side of the strait called the Dardanelles, Classical Hellespont, on the mound now known as Hisarlık (Turkish 'fortress'). Settlement there extended almost without interruption from the beginning of M3 BC through much of M1 AD, as established by three main series of excavations: (1) seven campaigns by Heinrich Schliemann between 1871 and 1890, followed by two further campaigns by Schliemann's associate Wilhelm Dörpfeld (1893 and 1894); (2) campaigns by Carl Blegen on behalf of the University of Cincinnati, 1932 to 1938; (3) campaigns by teams from the University

142

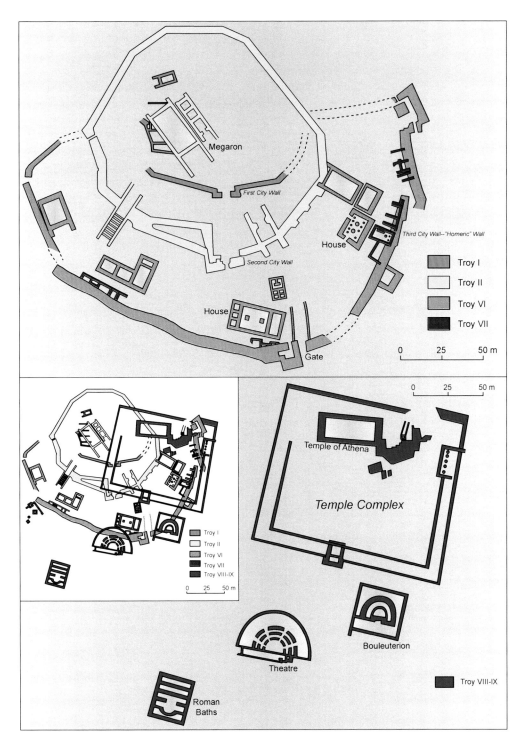

Citadel of Troy, major levels

of Tübingen, led initially by Manfred Korfmann, from 1988 onwards. By the end of his final season, Schliemann had identified nine major levels on the mound, each of which was divided into a number of sub-levels (more than forty) with a total height of over 20 m.

The settlement reached its first peak in the Troy II period, c. 2600–2350, as reflected in the impressive stone fortifications, the monumental ramp, and what is left of the residential architecture of this period. Schliemann wrongly concluded that this was the level of Homeric Troy, the city of King Priam. His alleged discovery in the city-wall of a large cache of objects, many made of precious materials, reinforced his belief. After the destruction of Troy II by fire, a sequence of three relatively undistinguished levels followed (III to V). The last of these was again destroyed by fire, and was succeeded by the Late Bronze Age city Troy VI, extending from c. 1750/1700 to 1280, by far the most impressive of Troy's Bronze Age cities. Its final sub-level, VIh, is now regarded as the most likely candidate for the city of the alleged Trojan War. In the course of his excavations, Korfmann identified a substantial lower settlement, dating to the Late Bronze Age and now almost entirely covered by later Roman remains. It extended to the south and east of the citadel, giving Late Bronze Age Troy, with citadel and lower settlement combined, a total area of c. 200,000 square metres, according to Korfmann. This city, with its peripheral territories, is almost certainly to be identified with the north-western Hittite vassal kingdom called Wilusa in Hittite texts and its adjacent territory Taruisa. Most scholars equate Wilusa and Taruisa with Homer's (W)Ilios and Troia, used as alternative names for Troy in the *Iliad*.

Following its destruction c. 1280, by earthquake or human agency or a combination of both, Troy VIh was succeeded by Troy VIIa (sometimes called Troy VIi), with no perceptible break in its population or basic culture. But the citadel was now crowded with smaller, humbler structures, indicative of significant material decline in this level, which was also destroyed by fire. Following two further sub-levels, VIIb1 and VIIb2 (c. 1180–1110), occupation of the site appears to have been greatly reduced, though Troy was not entirely abandoned (Troy VIIb3; c. 1110–950). It was subsequently settled by Greeks during C8. The name Ilion, used of the settlement throughout M1 (Troy VIII), may date back to this period.

Figure 34.1 The sloping walls of Troy VI. Photo by Trevor Bryce.

For a number of centuries Ilion remained a relatively obscure backwater, until it gained a new lease of life in the Hellenistic period (late C4 – early C1 BC), initially in fulfilment of the wishes of Alexander the Great who had made a pilgrimage to the site in 334. This level was destroyed in 85 BC by the Roman commander Fimbria. But under Roman imperial sponsorship, particularly that of the emperor Augustus, Troy rose once more, and flourished as New Ilium (Troy IX), before it sank slowly into obscurity in the Byzantine period.

Latacz (2004); Bryce (2006); Bryce and Jablonka (*OHBAA*: 475–82, 849–61); Cline (2013).

35

Ahhiyawa

The identification of the land called Ahhiyawa in Late Bronze Age Hittite texts has been much debated since the 1920s, when the Swiss scholar Emil Forrer equated it with the Mycenaean Greek world. Forrer argued that Ahhiyawa was the Hittite name for the land of the Achaians, one of three names Homer uses for the Greeks in his *Iliad*. (He otherwise calls them Argives and Danaans.) Though Forrer's proposal generated much scepticism among his peers (and sometimes outright rejection), most scholars now accept the validity of it. On this basis, Ahhiyawa appears to be used in Hittite texts (a) as a general ethno-geographical designation encompassing all areas of Mycenaean settlement, both in mainland Greece and overseas; (b) to designate a specific Mycenaean kingdom, at least one of whose rulers corresponded with his Hittite counterpart; (c) to designate this kingdom in a broader sense, including the territories attached to it as political and military dependencies. Mycenae may have been the the kingdom in question, the nucleus of the Ahhiyawan/Mycenaean world, as suggested both by its archetypal status in Mycenaean archaeology as well as by the pre-eminence of its legendary king Agamemnon in the Trojan War tradition. But other possibilities, notably Thebes, have been proposed.

In the so-called Tawagalawa letter, written by a C13 Hittite king (probably Hattusili III) to a king of Ahhiyawa, the author addresses his correspondent as 'My Brother', and accords him the title 'Great King'. This places him within the exclusive 'club' of the Great Kings of the Near Eastern world. The recognition thus bestowed by the Hittite upon his Ahhiyawan 'brother' may have been somewhat exaggerated, for the sake of winning his co-operation in attempting to sort out political and military problems in western Anatolia. But it does to serve to illustrate what is evident from other Hittite texts – that an Ahhiyawan kingdom was politically and militarily involved in Near Eastern affairs, particularly western Anatolian affairs, during the Late Bronze Age. Its presence there is already attested in C15, and becomes most intensive two centuries later. By the early years of C13, an Ahhiyawan king had established sovereignty over Milawata (aka Millawanda, Classical Miletus), and thence sought to extend his influence further afield in western Anatolia, often through the agency of anti-Hittite insurrectionists in the region. Ahhiyawan intervention in western Anatolia clearly threatened the Hittites' control of their western vassal states. But the threat appears to have ended in late C13, when Ahhiyawa lost possession of Milawata and ceased to have an effective presence on the Anatolian mainland. This is a likely conclusion to be drawn from the surviving draft of a treaty drawn up between the current Hittite king Tudhaliya IV and one of his Syrian vassals Shaushgamuwa. The treaty contains a list of the Great Kings of the time, from which a reference originally inserted to the king of Ahhiyawa has been struck out.

Subsequently, a group called 'Hiyawa-men', located in the Lukka lands in south-western Anatolia, are mentioned in two texts dating to the reign of the last Hittite king Suppiluliuma II (c. 1207–). It is possible that 'Hiyawa' is an apharesized form of 'Ahhiyawa' (aphaeresis designates the loss of a syllable or letter at the beginning of a word). If so, the context of these documents *may* indicate that the Hiyawa-men were Mycenaean warriors preparing to enter the Hittite defence forces in southern Anatolia as mercenaries.

Beckman *et al.* (2011).

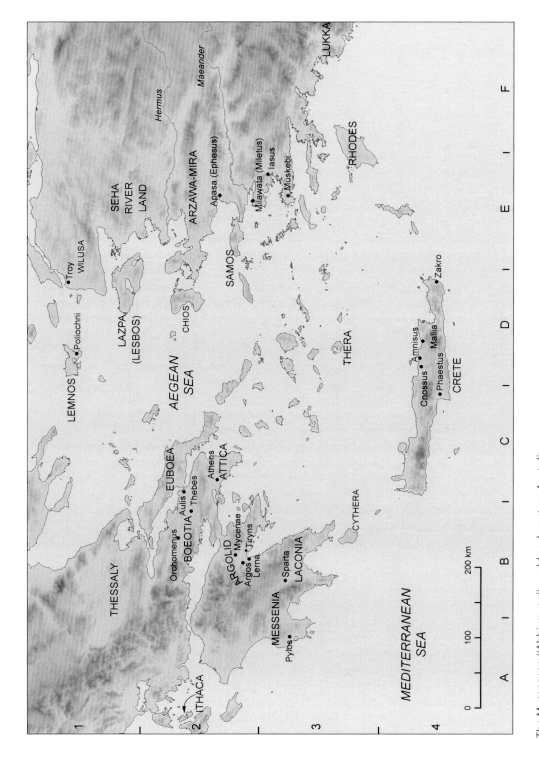

The Mycenaean ('Ahhiyawan') world and western Anatolia

36
Bronze Age Cyprus

Covering an area of 9,251 km², Cyprus is the third largest island in the Mediterranean, its most prominent topographical features being (a) the Troodos mountain massif in the central-western region, (b) the fertile Mesaoria plain lying to its north-east, and (c) the Kyrenia mountain range which dominates the island's northern littoral. Well located within the ancient international trading network which linked Egypt and the Aegean and Near Eastern worlds, Cyprus through much of its history enjoyed close cultural and commercial ties with the civilizations of these worlds, from the late Middle Bronze Age onwards. This is well illustrated by the large deposits of Cypriot goods discovered in numerous overseas sites, and by the many imported products found in Cyprus. The

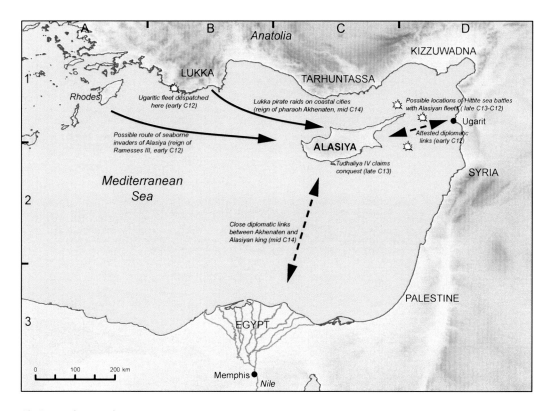

Alasiya under attack

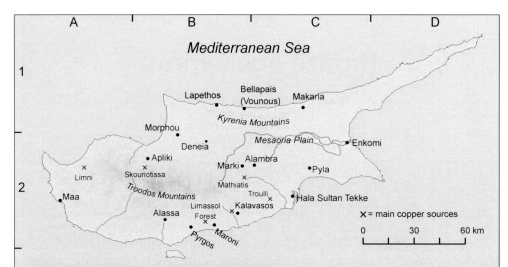

Alambra: Early and Middle Bronze Age settlement and cemetery.

Alassa: Late Bronze Age settlement in the lower foothills of the Troodos Range, perhaps managing the production and transportation of copper from the mines of the region to the coast.

Apliki: A major Late Bronze Age copper-mining and smelting centre.

Bellapais: Early and Middle Bronze Age cemetery from which 164 tomb-complexes were uncovered, containing more than 200 burials accompanied by a wide range of tomb-gifts.

Deneia: Bronze and Iron Age site in the Ovgos valley, probably associated with agricultural and mining activities. Extensive burial grounds have been unearthed nearby.

Enkomi: Late Bronze Age city, whose substantial wealth may have derived from its copper industry, as indicated by its many copper-smelting installations. A large quantity of Mycenaean pottery indicates trading contacts with the Mycenaean world.

Hala Sultan Tekke: One of the largest towns in Late Bronze Age Cyprus, its wealth no doubt due to its copper-production and craft industries in precious and semi-precious materials.

Kalavasos (Ayios Dhimitrios): Dating back to the Neolithic period, the settlement reached the peak of its development in C13 when it was almost certainly a centre for copper production and copper trading activities.

Lapethos: Bronze and Iron Age settlement which reached its peak in the Middle Bronze Age. Over 250 Early and Middle Bronze Age burials were excavated, with substantial quantities of bronze weapons and other implements suggestive of a large-scale local metallurgical industry.

Maa: Late C13 and C12 fortified settlement, whose excavations provide evidence for olive-oil and metallurgical production and storage.

Makaria (Moulos): Site located on the Moulos headland of northern Cyprus. Pottery-sherds indicate settlement during the Late Bronze Age. The settlement apparently survived until the Byzantine period, but was gradually abandoned after the Arab invasions of 647.

Marki: Early and Middle Bronze Age settlement and cemetery complex probably built to take advantage of nearby copper sources. Its inhabitants also engaged in agriculture and animal husbandry and the production of pottery and textiles for local use.

Maroni: Late Bronze Age settlement in the Maroni valley, with evidence of olive oil processing, cereal grinding, large-scale storage of staples, metalworking, weaving, and writing.

Morphou: Excavations have uncovered pottery workshops, houses, and rich chamber-tombs of Late Bronze Age date. The settlement decreased in importance after C13, finally being abandoned c. 700 BC.

Pyla: Late C13 fortified site, identified either as one of the earliest settlements established by Aegean colonists in Cyprus, or as a local stronghold for securing movement of goods, in particular metals, between coastal towns and the hinterland. It was occupied for only 25-30 years.

Pyrgos: Early and Middle Bronze Age settlement containing a large Middle Bronze Age industrial and storage area, and cemeteries of both periods.

Cyprus: main Bronze Age sites

island was noted for its substantial deposits of copper ore, a principal component of the cargoes of Late Bronze Age merchant-vessels which plied their trade through the ports of the Eastern Mediterranean and Aegean lands. Timber also played an important role in the island's economy, both for local building activities as well as for export.

Cyprus is almost certainly to be identified with the land called Alasiya in Late Bronze Age Egyptian and Hittite texts. A number of these texts make clear that the island's excellent strategic location made it vulnerable to attacks by pirates and other seaborne enemies. On a more peaceful note, letters exchanged between the pharaoh and the king of Alasiya in mid C14 (the letters are among those found in the Amarna archive) indicate a close relationship between the two rulers. The Cypriots had their own writing system, the so-called Cypro-Minoan script, but these letters are written in Akkadian, the Late Bronze Age international language of diplomacy. From them, we learn that Alasiya supplied Egypt with copper, under the guise of 'gifts' from its king, in exchange for silver supplied by the pharaoh. From mid C14 until early C12, Alasiya was subject to attacks by groups of sea raiders, as attested in Egyptian records. Also, the third-last and last kings of the Hittite empire, Tudhaliya IV and Suppiluliuma II respectively, claimed to have conquered the island.

Muhly (*OEANE* 2: 89–94); Steel (2004, *OHBAA*: 804–19).

37

The Sea Peoples

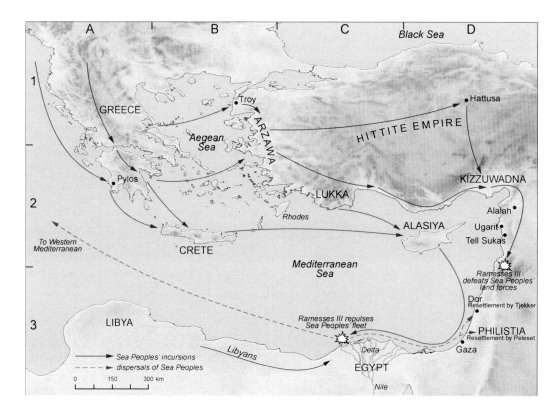

Suggested routes of the Sea Peoples

Early in C12, large groups of peoples swept through and devastated many parts of the Near Eastern world, from Anatolia to Cyprus and across much of Syria and Palestine, before they were finally defeated and repelled on the Egyptian coast by Ramesses III (1184–1153). Though commonly known as 'Sea Peoples', from Egyptian references to them as peoples from the sea, their invasions clearly involved extensive operations on land as well as by sea. Some of the groups had already attacked the Egyptian Delta in the reign of Merneptah (1213–1203). They included groups called Sherden, Shekelesh, Ekwesh, Lukka and Teresh. But their attacks on Egypt in Merneptah's reign were merely a prelude to the comprehensive onslaughts on the eastern Mediterranean countries

Figure 37.1 Sea Peoples, Temple of Ramesses III, Medinet Habu. Photo courtesy of the Oriental Institute, University of Chicago.

in Ramesses' time. On the walls of his temple at Medinet Habu, Ramesses records the trail of devastation left by these marauders. He reports that they formed a confederation consisting of peoples called the Peleset, Tjekker, Shekelesh, Denyen and Weshesh. But their invasions were not merely military operations. They involved large masses of people, including families and all their portable possessions, who were seeking new lands to settle. Very likely many of them had been displaced from their original homelands in the widespread upheavals associated with the end of the Late Bronze Age. They were probably as much the victims as the perpetrators of these upheavals, being forced to take on a marauding aspect in their search for new homelands.

The historical veracity of the above account, based on Ramesses' record, is regarded by some scholars as highly questionable. Many scholars take the view that Ramesses' description of the so-called Sea Peoples' invasions is a conflation into a single episode of a number of clashes with groups of foreign forces, extending over many decades, at least back to the reign of Merneptah. It is suggested, for example, that Ramesses was merely repeating Merneptah's battle accounts, and claimed earlier victories for himself (see Van De Mieroop, 2016: 208). Archaeological evidence also provides some significant inconsistencies with the Egyptian written record. The map accompanying this section reflects a conventional reconstruction of the movements of the 'invaders', and may require considerable revision in light of ongoing research into the ethnic, political, and cultural changes that took place in the Near Eastern and Aegean worlds during the early post-Bronze Age era.

Sandars (1985); Oren (2000); Cline (2014); Van De Mieroop (2016: 203–10).

38

The Middle Elamite and Neo-Elamite periods

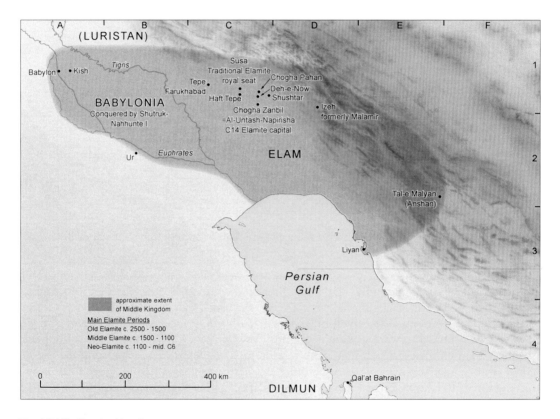

The Middle Elamite kingdom

Following the end of the *sukkalmah* dynasty, Elam reached a new peak in its development, in the so-called Middle Elamite period (c. 1500–1100), during the reign of a king called Untash-Napirisha (c. 1340–1300), whose ancestry linked him with the Kassite regime of Babylonia. Untash-Napirisha's reign has been referred to as an artistic golden age, one which witnessed a cultural renaissance and religious revolution, reflected in the king's building of a splendid new religious centre called Al-Untash-Napirisha. The extensive remains of this complex, covering c. 100 ha, occupy the site now known as Chogha Zanbil. Despite marriage- and blood-links between the Elamite and Kassite royal dynasties, the kingdoms were frequently at war with each other. Matters came to a head when the C12 Elamite king Shutruk-Nahhunte I invaded Babylonia, capturing many of its cities and installing one of his sons on the throne of Babylon. A Kassite king Enlil-nadin-ahi (c. 1157–1155) was subsequently appointed to the throne by the Elamites, as their subject-vassal. But his reign ended abruptly when he rebelled against his overlords, was defeated in battle by them, and exiled to Susa. This marked the end of Kassite rule in Babylonia. But hostilities with Elam were continued by the rulers of the

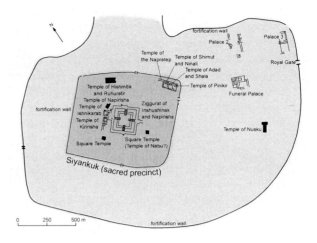

Al-Untash-Napirisha (Chogha Zanbil) (after Roaf 1996: 143)

Second Dynasty of Isin (see p. 87), culminating in a major defeat of the Elamite kingdom at the hands of Nebuchadnezzar I, fourth ruler of the dynasty. Nebuchadnezzar went on to sack Susa.

Figure 38.1 Chogha Zanbil (anc. Al-Untash-Napirisha). Photo courtesy of D.T. Potts.

Conflicts with the Mesopotamian states persisted through the following and final phase of Elam's existence, known as the Neo-Elamite period (c. 1100–mid C6). For most of this period, Elam's political and military involvement in the broader Near Eastern world was a relatively insignificant one, with occasional periods of renewed vigour and a final brief resurgence of Elamite power in late C8 and early C7, during the reigns of Shutruk-Nahhunte II (c. 716–699) and his brother and successor Hallushu (c. 699–693). But c. 653, the Elamite king Te-Umman was killed during a campaign into his country by the Assyrian king Ashurbanipal, and eight years later, the Assyrians sacked the Elamite capital Susa, forcing the last known Elamite king Humban-haltash III to flee for his life. He was subsequently captured by local tribesmen and handed over to Ashurbanipal. Later, Elam appears among the subject states of the Persian empire listed in the inscriptions of Darius I (522–486), which report several Elamite uprisings at the beginning of his reign. The rebellions were crushed, effectively sealing the end of Elam as a political entity.

A corpus of 'Middle Elamite' documents, dating to C13 and C12, includes votive texts, best represented by the hundreds inscribed on mud bricks, and a small number of administrative texts. The former reflect a large number of construction projects in this period. 'Late Elamite' inscriptions, dating to the reigns of Shutruk-Nahhunte II and Hallushu, belong to the final florescence of the Elamite kingdom and are the most varied in content of all Elamite texts. They include votive texts, inscriptions carved on rock surfaces, business contracts, a small number of letters, and a couple of literary texts. The Elamite language survived through the period of the Persian empire (559–330), when Persian kings used it in their monumental inscriptions – notably Darius I, whose famous trilingual inscription at Bisitun was written in Old Persian, Babylonian and Elamite – and as a chancery language in administrative documents. But it probably rapidly died out as a spoken language, along with all other traces of the Elamite civilization, except for a few references in documents of the Hellenistic period.

Potts (1999: 188–308, *OHIH*: 37–56); Henrickson (*OEANE* 2: 232–5); *PPAWA* (221–4); Álvarez-Mon (*AANE*: 750–6); Van De Mieroop (2016: 195–200).

Part VI

The Iron Age

39

The age of iron

The period now commonly referred to as the Iron Age followed the collapse of the Late Bronze Age civilizations and the political and social upheavals that accompanied it. Scholars differ on the dates they assign to the Iron Age, but as a rough guide, the period covered will here be dated from late C12 to the end of C7 BC, when the Neo-Assyrian empire fell. During this and later periods, iron was widely used in the manufacture of tools, weapons and other artefacts (though bronze continued in use as well). The period also saw major changes in the geopolitical character of many parts of the Near Eastern world, with the development of a number of new cities and kingdoms, like the so-called Neo-Hittite kingdoms, and the appearance of new population groups, or the reappearance of existing population groups of the region under a hitherto unattested name, most notably the Aramaeans. A number of cities with a Bronze Age pedigree rose again in the new age, like Sidon, Tyre, Byblos and Dor, some becoming major political and commercial centres. All these states and cities had the good fortune of being able to develop free from interference by any major power seeking to impose its dominance over them – until the early decades of C9, when Assyria once more set its sights on conquests west of the Euphrates.

The Aramaeans

The Aramaeans, large population groups first attested in our Iron Age sources, spread widely through the Near Eastern world, particularly Syria and Mesopotamia, and spoke a West Semitic language called Aramaic. They were once thought to have been tribal pastoral peoples who immigrated into Syria and northern Mesopotamia, perhaps from the fringes of the Syrian Desert. But many scholars now believe that they were descendants of the West Semitic populations, like the Amorites, who already occupied parts of Syria in M2. The earliest references we have to them occur in texts of the Assyrian king Tiglath-pileser I (1114–1076), who claims to have conducted twenty-eight campaigns across the Euphrates against them and an associated tribal people called the Ahlamu. Though they may originally have been predatory nomadic or semi-nomadic desert-dwellers, many of the Aramaean groups had by the end of M2 adopted a more settled way of life. This led to the emergence of a number of Aramaean states, particularly in areas of Mesopotamia, Syria and eastern Anatolia. Some of the more important Aramaean states were Bit-Zamani, Bit-Bahiani, Bit-Adini, Bit-Agusi, Aram-Damascus and Sam'al. The prefix 'Bit' ('House (of)') reflects the likely tribal origins of these states.

Eventually, all the Aramaean states became subject territories of the Neo-Assyrian empire. They never established any kind of political federation, but some of them from time to time formed military alliances in partnership with other states, including the Neo-Hittite kingdoms, with the objective of breaking free from their Assyrian overlordship. Though this they failed to achieve,

The Iron Age kingdoms of northern Syria and south-eastern Anatolia

they nonetheless enjoyed a relatively prosperous existence as Assyrian tributaries and subjects, provided they paid their overlord his dues. Even so, resistance movements continued in many of them. But their uprisings were ruthlessly put down. By the end of C8, all had been dismantled and destroyed by their Assyrian conquerors. Their territories were absorbed within the Assyrian provincial administration, and a large proportion of their inhabitants were deported, for resettlement elsewhere in the Assyrian realm.

The Aramaeans were thus widely dispersed throughout the regions where Assyria held sway, as far east as the lands beyond the Tigris. An important consequence of this dispersal was that it contributed substantially to the expansion of Aramaean influence in the Near East. By this process, Aramaic, written in an alphabetic script taken over from the Phoenicians, replaced Akkadian as the international language of diplomacy in the Near Eastern world.

Dion (*CANE* 2: 1281–94); Lipiński (2000).

Damascus

Occupation of the site of Damascus dates back at least to the Middle Bronze Age, but the city is first attested in written records among the principalities captured by the pharaoh Tuthmosis III at the battle of Megiddo in 1479. It remained under Egyptian control for the rest of the Late Bronze Age. Letters from the mid C14 Amarna archive indicate its involvement in the disputes and conflicts among Egypt's Syrian and Palestinian vassals during Akhenaten's reign.

Probably in C10 BC, Damascus became the capital of one of the most important Aramaean states in the Levant, called Aram or Aram-Damascus. Biblical sources report a number of conflicts in which it engaged with the Israelites from C10 onwards. In 853, and on several later occasions, it played a leading role in the anti-Assyrian coalition that confronted the forces of the Assyrian king Shalmaneser III at the battle of Qarqar on the Orontes. Shalmaneser finally crushed the allied forces in 845. But Damascus subsequently rallied, and despite further Assyrian campaigns against it, retained its independence, building under its king Hazael (mid C9–803?) a 'mini-empire' which incorporated large parts of Palestine, Israel and Philistia. Its conflicts with Assyria continued, however, through the reigns of a succession of Damascene and Assyrian kings until it was incorporated into the Assyrian provincial system by Tiglath-pileser III (c. 732 BC).

Because of its valuable strategic location on the major trade-routes of the region, Damascus played an important role in the commercial activities of the Levant through the Assyrian, Babylonian and Persian Achaemenid periods. Under Achaemenid rule it probably became the capital of the satrapy of Syria (called *Ebirnari* in Babylonian, or *'Abr Nahra* in Aramaic, meaning '(the satrapy) beyond the river (Euphrates)'), and headquarters of the Persian forces in Syria. After Alexander's conquests of the region in 333, Damascus enjoyed a new lease of life as the site of a Macedonian colony. It later became part of the Seleucid empire until captured and briefly held by the Nabataeans early in C1 BC. It was subsequently annexed to Rome by Pompey the Great in 64 BC.

Lipiński (2000: 347–407); Burns (2009: 94–140).

40

The Neo-Hittite kingdoms

In the early Iron Age, a number of kingdoms emerged or developed afresh in south-eastern Anatolia and northern Syria following the collapse of the Hittite empire. They are commonly referred to as the Neo-Hittite kingdoms, since they preserved a number of Hittite cultural traditions, including elements of Hittite religion, architecture and iconography. Most notably, the rulers of the Neo-Hittite states, and elite members of their administrations, used the Luwian hieroglyphic script and language for the records they inscribed on public monuments. These were dedicatory or commemorative in nature, and sometimes contained an outline of their author's building and military achievements. A small group of economic texts and letters written in Luwian hieroglyphs on lead strips have also come to light. The former were found at the site now called Kululu, just south of the Halys r., the latter in the Assyrian city Ashur (their original provenance is unknown). Luwian had become the most widely spoken language of the Hittite empire, and in the empire's final century was regularly used by Hittite kings for recording their achievements on public monuments. Its status as the language of royalty was preserved in the Neo-Hittite kingdoms. Many of the rulers of these kingdoms bore the names of Late Bronze Age Hittite kings, like Suppiluliuma, Muwattalli and Hattusili.

The most prominent of the Neo-Hittite states was Carchemish, located on the west bank of the Euphrates and formerly a viceregal centre of the Hittite empire. It appears to have been unaffected by the catastrophes that afflicted most of the other centres of Late Bronze Age civilization, and after the fall of the Hittite empire may for a time have exercised some form of hegemony over the empire's south-eastern remnants. Its first Neo-Hittite king Kuzi-Teshub, son of the last known Hittite imperial viceroy, appears to have assumed the title 'Great King', after the royal line at Hattusa had ended. Other Neo-Hittite kingdoms that emerged in C12, or later, included (a) Malatya (Assyrian Melid) and Kummuh which lay north of Carchemish, (b) Gurgum in the Anti-Taurus region, (c) Walistin (formerly Palistin) (Assyrian Pat(t)in, Unqi) and Hamath in western Syria, (d) Masuwari (Assyrian Til Barsip) on the east bank of the Euphrates, (e) the kingdoms of Tabal which lay south of the Halys r., and (f) Hilakku and Adanawa (Hiyawa, Assyrian Que) in the region of later Cilicia on the eastern Mediterranean coast.

The name Hatti was also preserved in Iron Age Assyrian, Hebrew and Urartian texts. It seems to have been confined largely to northern Syria in these texts, covering the territories of many of the Neo-Hittite kingdoms, but also several Aramaean states located west of the Euphrates, most notably Bit-Agusi and Sam'al. Some scholars believe that the Neo-Hittite states evolved from refugee populations who fled western and central Anatolia during the early C12 upheavals, seeking new lands to settle in the south-east. It is possible that the peoples of the Neo-Hittite kingdoms contained Anatolian refugee components. But many of the inhabitants of these kingdoms may

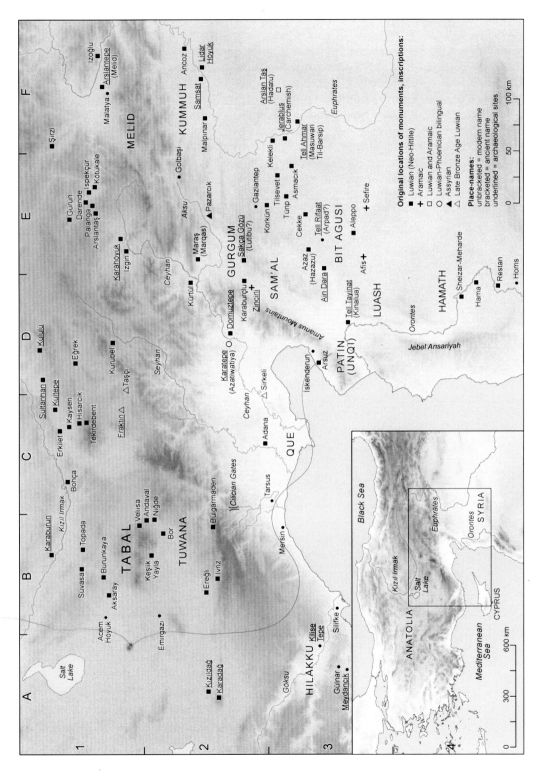

The region of the Neo-Hittite states

have been descendants of already established population groups rather than new immigrants from devastated homelands in the west. That of course leaves open the question of why the Luwian language and hieroglyphic script were adopted by the administrative elites of these kingdoms, and raises the possibility that they may have had connections of one kind or another with the old Hittite ruling class.

During C9, the Neo-Hittite kingdoms along with other cities, tribal states and kingdoms west of the Euphrates, became tributaries of Assyria. Though many sought to break free from Assyrian overlordship, sometimes forming military coalitions with other local states for this purpose, none succeeded. And in the last half of C8, from the reign of the Assyrian king Tiglath-pileser III onwards, the Neo-Hittite states progressively lost their local-kingdom status, and effectively their identity, as they were absorbed into the Assyrian provincial administration. The last of the kingdoms fell to the Assyrian Sargon II between 717 and 708, though rulers in Tabal and Melid regained their independence for a time in the following century.

Bryce (2012).

41

Tabal, Hilakku and Que (Adanawa/Hiyawa)

Tabal

In the early Iron Age, the region called Tabal in Neo-Assyrian texts was occupied by a number of mainly small independent kingdoms. The Assyrian king Shalmaneser III claims to have received gifts from twenty (or twenty-four) of their rulers during his expedition to their lands c. 837 BC. A century later, five kings from the region were listed among the tributaries of Tiglath-pileser III: Wassurme (Luwian Wasusarmas), Ushhiti, Urballa (Luwian Warpalawas), Tuhamme and Uirime. They were the rulers, respectively, of the kingdoms of Tabal, Atuna, Tuwana (Assyrian Tuhana), Ishtuanda and Hupishna. In a broad sense, the Assyrians may have applied the term Tabal to all the kingdoms that lay within these territories. But in a specific political sense, the term appears to have been used, prior to the reign of Sargon II, exclusively of the northernmost of these kingdoms, over which Wasusarmas had held sway. His was almost certainly the largest of the Tabalic kingdoms, and probably incorporated a number of the small principalities to which Shalmaneser had referred. Its capital *may* have been located on the site of modern Kululu, which lies 30 km north-east of Kayseri. Tiglath-pileser's second successor, Sargon II, claims to have 'widened the land' of Tabal, expanding it, probably, to the northern border of Hilakku (see below). The enlarged kingdom was now called Bit-Burutash. Later in Sargon's reign, c. 713, Bit-Burutash along with Hilakku were placed under an Assyrian governor – the first clear indication we have of direct Assyrian rule being imposed in this region. But Assyrian sovereignty was shortlived, almost certainly coming to an end in 705 when Sargon undertook an expedition to the region, and was probably killed there, perhaps while fighting the Cimmerians.

Hilakku

The kingdom of Hilakku, attested in Neo-Assyrian sources, extended over much of the territory of Classical Cilicia Tracheia/Aspera ('Rough Cilicia'). Along with its eastern neighbour Que, it constantly resisted attempts by Assyrian kings to impose their sovereignty upon it. In 858, both kingdoms sent contingents to join an alliance of northern Syrian states against Shalmaneser III. They were eventually absorbed into the Assyrian provincial system in the reign of Shalmaneser V (726–722) or his successor Sargon II. But the spirit of rebellion remained strong within them, flaring afresh after Sargon's death. Hilakku repeatedly resisted Assyrian attempts to dominate it, and although Esarhaddon, Sargon's second successor, claimed to have subdued its rebellious population, the land had regained its freedom by the reign of Esarhaddon's successor Ashurbanipal (668–630/27). In Neo-Babylonian texts, the kingdom called Pirindu can be equated largely, if not

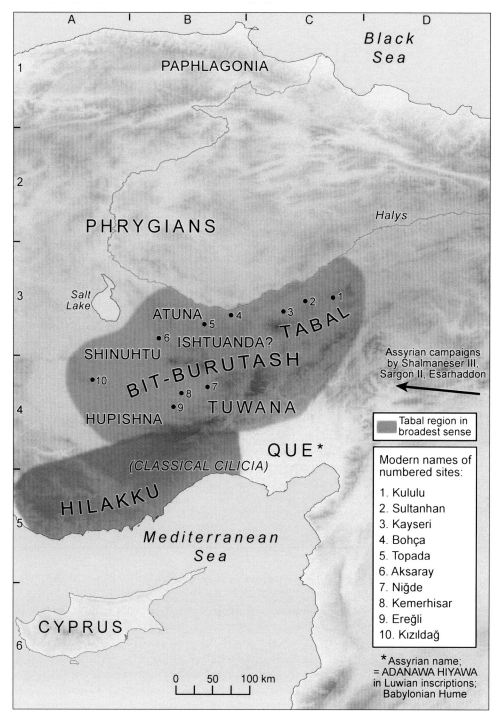

The kingdoms of Tabal, Hilakku and Que

entirely, with the former Hilakku. These texts too indicate ongoing rebellions by the rulers of the land against their foreign overlords.

Que

Que, the Assyrian name for the kingdom known as Adanawa and Hiyawa in Luwian texts, extended over much of the Cilician plain and (originally) the mountainous region to the north-east of it. We have noted its participation in an anti-Assyrian alliance which fought Shalmaneser III in 853. The alliance was defeated, but Que escaped retaliation until 839, when Shalmaneser conducted an expedition into it and captured a number of its cities. In 833, 832 and 831, he led further expeditions into the land, the third of which was followed by a temporary end to Assyrian military enterprises in Anatolia. Around 800, Que joined other states in another anti-Assyrian uprising, but Assyrian control of it had been firmly restored by the last decades of C8. In Esarhaddon's reign (680–669) it became an Assyrian province. In the following century, the Babylonians undertook several expeditions into the land, which they called Hume, and which the Babylonian king Nebuchadnezzar II (604–562) claimed amongst his Anatolian conquests.

Bryce (2012: 141–62).

42

The Neo-Assyrian empire

Ashur-dan II (934–912) is generally regarded as the founder of the Neo-Assyrian kingdom. With his reign began the final, the most illustrious and the most bloodthirsty phase in Assyria's history. His programme of renewed imperial expansion was enthusiastically embraced by his son Adad-nirari II (911–891), whose campaigns in Babylonia and against the Aramaeans in the Tigris Valley laid the foundations for further military enterprises abroad. Expansion westwards across the Euphrates through Syria and Palestine to the Mediterranean coast was undertaken by Adad-nirari's grandson Ashurnasirpal II (883–859), and subsequently on a much more comprehensive scale by Ashurnasirpal's son and successor Shalmaneser III (858–824). Assyrian kings also conducted numerous campaigns to the north, east and south-east of their homeland, against both rebellious subject states and foreign powers, the latter including Babylonia, Elam and the territorially aggressive kingdom of Urartu.

Figure 42.1 Tiglath-pileser III, from Nimrud. Picture from History/Bridgeman Images.

In 745, the seizure of the throne by a usurper Tiglath-pileser III (745–727) marked the beginning of a vigorous new stage in the kingdom's development. One of the main features of Tiglath-pileser's reign was his programme of territorial absorption, which imposed direct Assyrian rule over many of the tributary states in the regions where he campaigned. The former semi-autonomous cities and states were incorporated within the Assyrian provincial administration and placed under the authority of Assyrian governors. Often, their populations were deported and resettled in distant parts of the Assyrian realm, to be replaced by settlers brought from other parts of it. Tiglath-pileser's policies were vigorously pursued by the king's second successor Sargon II (721–705), who incorporated

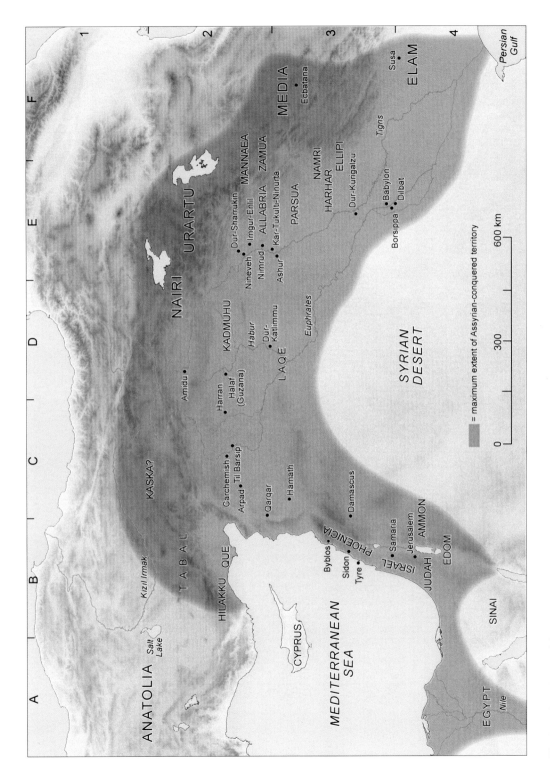

The Neo-Assyrian world

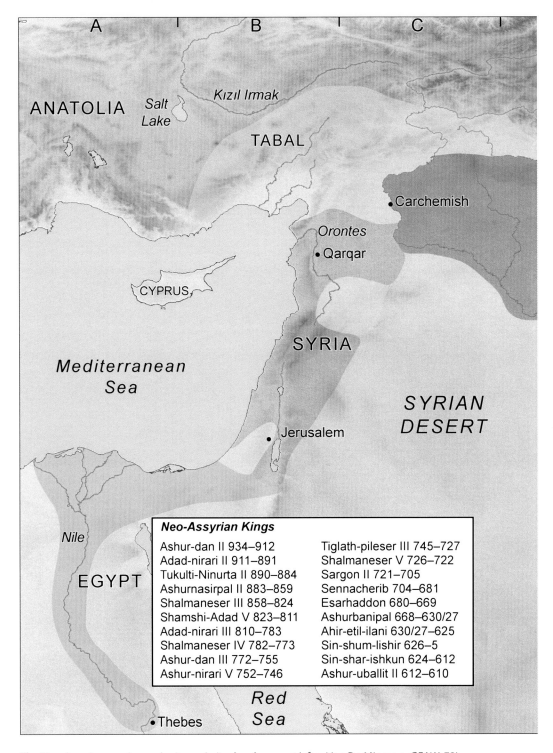

The Neo-Assyrian empire: main stages in its development (after Van De Mieroop, *GEAW*: 73)

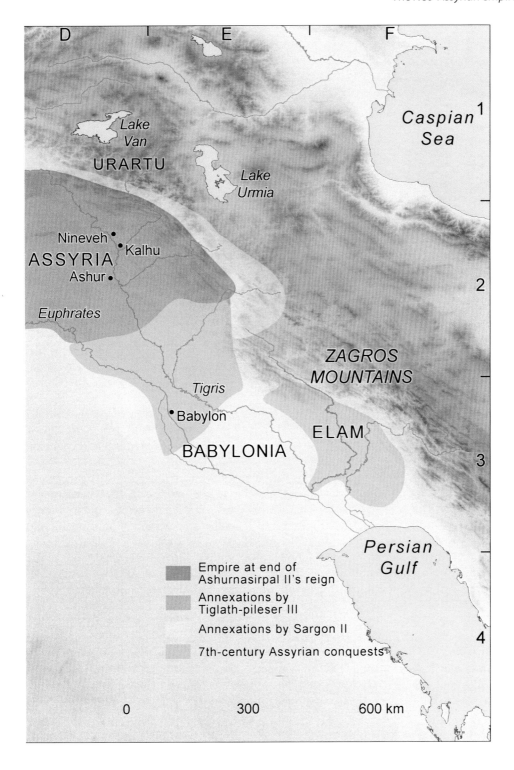

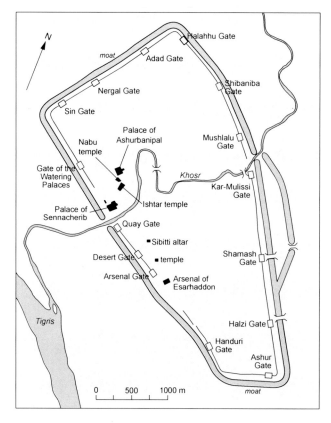

Nineveh (after Roaf 1996: 186)

the remaining western tributaries into the provincial system. Other features of Sargon's career include his decisive victory over the Urartian king Rusa I during his invasion of Urartian territory in 714, and his unexpected peace accord with another of his arch-enemies, the Phrygian king Mita (Greek Midas). Sargon's son and successor Sennacherib (704–681) also campaigned widely throughout the Near Eastern lands, particularly in the Zagros mountain region and other parts of Iran, in Syria and Palestine in the west, and in Babylonia in the south. His own son and successor Esarhaddon (680–669) added further to the lands subject to the Assyrian crown by extending Assyrian sovereignty to Egypt. But it was under Esarhaddon's son Ashurbanipal (668–630/27) that the Neo-Assyrian empire reached its greatest territorial limits. It now extended from Elam in the east to central-southern Anatolia in the west, and from the upper Euphrates in the north to Egypt in the south-west.

This proved too much. By now the empire had grown beyond the capacity of its rulers to administer and defend it. In the reigns of the last Assyrian kings, and already in Ashurbanipal's reign, its existence was threatened by an ever-increasing array of external enemies and by widening political unrest within the homeland. The empire fell finally to a coalition of Babylonians and Medes, following a Median invasion of Assyria in 615, and in 612 the capture and destruction by Babylonian and Median forces of Assyria's administrative capital Nineveh. By year's end, all the chief cities of the Assyrian homeland had been destroyed. The last remaining Assyrian stronghold, Harran in north-western Mesopotamia, fell to the Babylonian and Median armies in 610.

Grayson (*CANE* 2: 959–68); Van De Mieroop (*GEAW*: 70–97); Pedde and Parker (*AANE*: 851–76); Radner (2015).

Note: The outer limits of the shaded area on the map on p. 167 include territories through which Assyrian armies *may* have campaigned without imposing lasting authority over them. But these limits are conjectural. The shaded areas on the map on pp. 168–9 include areas where Assyrian authority was imposed, often in the wake of military conquest.

Battle of Qarqar (853)

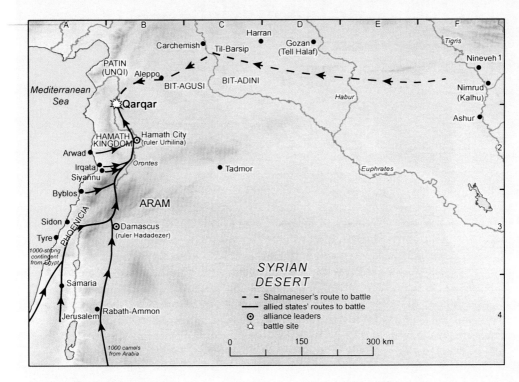

Routes leading to Qarqar

Qarqar lay on the Orontes river within the kingdom of Hamath. In 853, it was the site of a battle fought between Shalmaneser III and a coalition of anti-Assyrian states. Shalmaneser claims that an alliance of twelve kings had been formed against him, in which the Hamathite king Urhilina (Assyrian Irhuleni) played a leading role. Other coalition leaders included Hadad-ezer (Adad-idri), king of Damascus, and Ahab, king of Israel. Though Shalmaneser claimed victory in the battle, capturing and destroying Qarqar itself, the outcome of the conflict seems to have been inconclusive, for in later years (849, 848, 845), the king was forced to engage in further conflicts with the same alliance.

Excavations carried out at Tell Qarqur in the Orontes valley indicate that a significant Iron Age site was located there. It may be the historically attested Qarqar, but a firm identification has yet to be established.

PPAWA (576).

43

The Phoenicians

Phoenicia was the Classical name for a region in the Levant whose cities flourished in the Iron Age and later centuries of M1 BC. It extended from the coast inland to the Jebel Ansariyah and Lebanon ranges, and through the coastal regions to the south as far as the northern part of modern Israel. Derived from the Greek word *phoinix*, 'crimson-red' or 'purple', its name may have been prompted by the Phoenicians' copper-coloured hair and skin; more likely, it arose from the famous purple dye extracted from the murex shellfish found off the region's coast. In any case, 'Phoenicia' was not a native name. If the 'Phoenicians' ever thought of themselves as having a common identity, they would probably have called themselves Canaanites, after their Bronze Age ancestors in the region. Their language was in fact a later version of Canaanite. Phoenicia was never united politically, but consisted of a number of independent city-states, the most prominent of which were Sidon, Tyre and Byblos. And like their Bronze Age predecessors, these small principalities came under the sway of the successive great powers of their period – Assyria, Babylonia, Persia and Macedon.

The Phoenician cities were highly prosperous for most of their existence – and thus a valuable source of revenue to their overlords, due mainly to their international mercantile operations. Timber and the extremely valuable purple dye were among their most important products, along with a range of high-quality manufactured goods fashioned from ivory, wood, stone, metal, wool and linen. These products were exported to many overseas destinations by Phoenician merchantmen, who brought back in exchange a wide assortment of exotic items, including ivory, ebony, precious stones, spices, aromatic substances, gold and silver, and various commodity metals. Their trading expeditions in search of these products, especially silver which was widely used as a medium of exchange, took them far into the western world, to western Italy, western Sicily, Sardinia, southern Spain and the coast of Africa. From C8 onwards, they established a number of settlements in the western Mediterranean, to develop and extend their commercial enterprises. Mostly, these settlements were temporary encampments, promptly abandoned once the local resources they were set up to exploit were exhausted. But some settlements, in Spain, Sicily and north Africa, became permanent Phoenician colonies. Carthage in Tunisia was the most successful of the Phoenician colonial enterprises. Founded in late C9 by settlers from Tyre (according to tradition), it became one of the great political, commercial and military powers of the western world.

The Phoenician language, like its Canaanite precedessor, is a Semitic tongue, known to us from c. 6,000 inscriptions (mainly commemorative, votive, and funerary ones, which are of very limited historical value), scattered throughout the lands where the Phoenicians had trading contacts and established settlements, as far west as Spain and Tunisia. These inscriptions are written in what is commonly called an alphabetic script, consisting of twenty-two symbols. The script was transmitted to the Greek world, perhaps by merchant-travellers, and became the basis of the Greek alphabet – and thus the ancestor of alphabets widely used throughout the world today.

Lipiński (*CANE* 2: 1321–33); Markoe (2000).

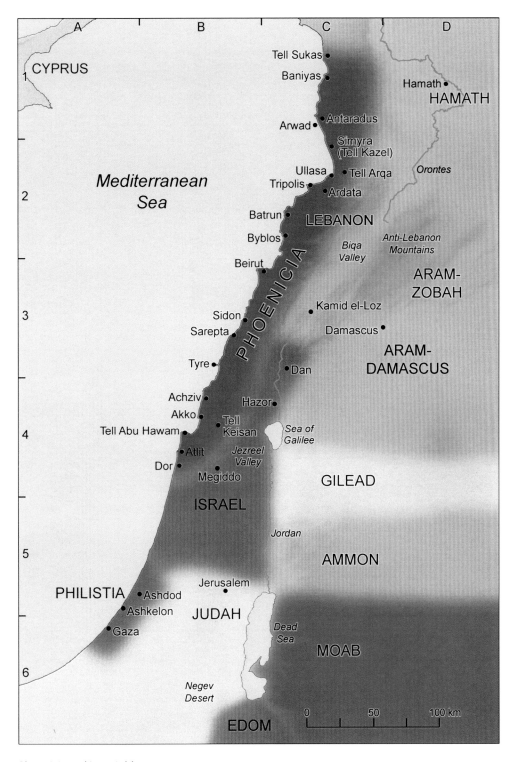

Phoenicia and its neighbours

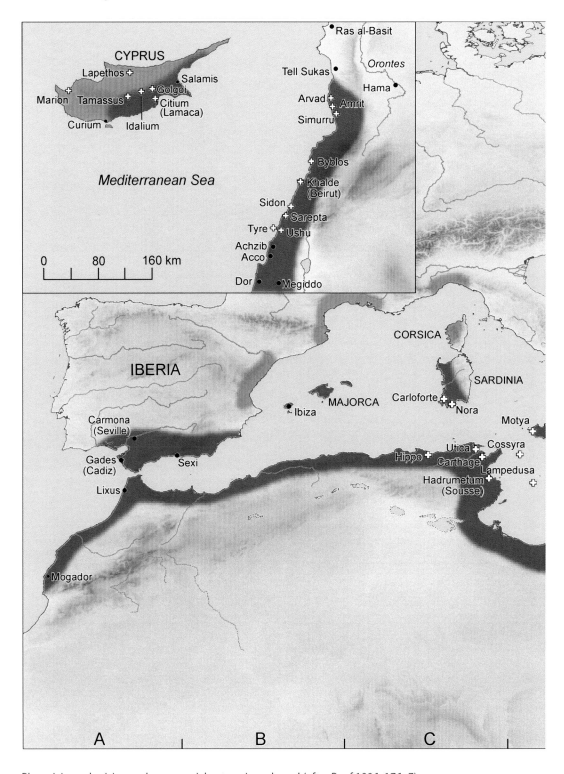

Phoenician colonizing and commercial enterprises abroad (after Roaf 1996: 176–7)

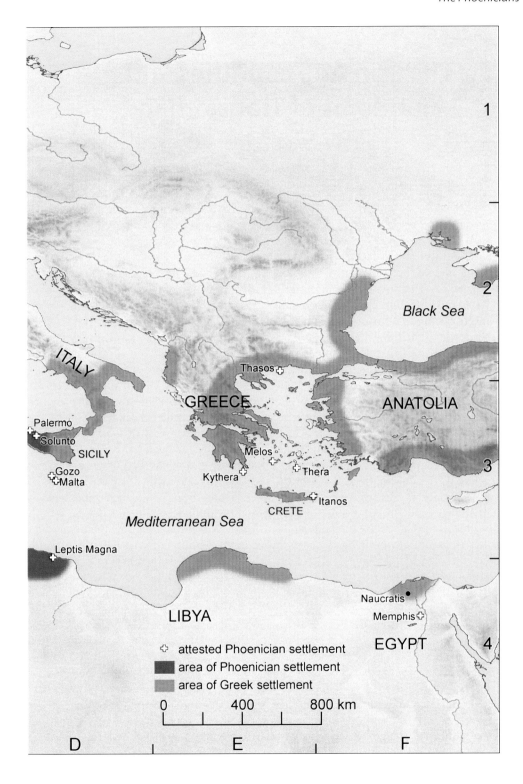

44

The Iron Age countries and kingdoms of Transjordan

Transjordan is a modern name which in its literal sense applies to the region referred to in biblical texts as 'beyond the Jordan river', reflecting the perspective of those peoples who lived between the river and the Mediterranean. However, the term is generally used in a broader sense to encompass the lands located on the high plateau both east of the river and further south to the head of the Gulf of 'Aqaba, covering the territory of today's Hashemite Kingdom of Jordan. A number of small tribal states and kingdoms arose in this region during the Iron Age, as attested in both biblical sources and contemporary historical texts.

The northernmost of these was the mountain land of *Gilead*. Occupying a strategically important position on the King's Highway, which linked Damascus with the Gulf of 'Aqaba, Gilead came under Israelite control during the Israelites' conquest of the region, according to biblical tradition, and remained subject to Israel until it fell to the Assyrian king Tiglath-pileser III c. 732. At that time, many of its inhabitants were deported to Assyria. Gilead became a separate province under Persian rule (C6–4). In the Hellenistic period, the region was called Galaaditis.

The Iron Age kingdom *Ammon* lay south of Gilead, to the north-east of the Dead Sea. Its chief city Rabbath-Ammon occupied the site of the modern Jordanian capital Amman. Arising from a number of settlements that first appeared towards the end of the Late Bronze Age, the kingdom reached its full development between C8 and C6. This is illustrated by the remains of Rabbath-Ammon's once impressive acropolis and lower city, and the nearby walled settlements of Tell el Umeiri and Hesban. The Ammonites appear frequently in Old Testament sources, as both enemies and subjects of the Israelites. And from Neo-Assyrian records, we know the names of a number of their kings, one of whom, Ba'asa, participated in the coalition of Syro-Palestinian states that confronted the army of Shalmaneser III at Qarqar in 853. Like other members of the defeated coalition, Ammon was subject to Assyria for much of the Neo-Assyrian period. Subsequently, in C6, it was a vassal of the Neo-Babylonian empire. It retained a reasonably high degree of autonomy during this period under its own kings. But when Babylon fell to the Persians in 539, the kingdom came to an end, and its territory and cities were absorbed into the Persian provincial administrative system.

The kingdom of *Moab* lay on the plateau east of the Dead Sea between Ammon and Edom. Biblical tradition makes Abraham's nephew Lot the ancestor of the Moabite people. But the first historical reference we have to the land dates to the reign of the pharaoh Ramesses II (1279–1213) who conducted campaigns in both Moab and Edom. These campaigns belong to the last century of the Late Bronze Age. From the end of this era onwards, there appears to have been a marked increase in the number of settlements in Moab, hitherto only sparsely populated. But an actual kingdom of Moab may not have been established until late M2 or early M1. Old Testament tradition reports that Moab was conquered in early C10 by the Israelite king David, after its earlier

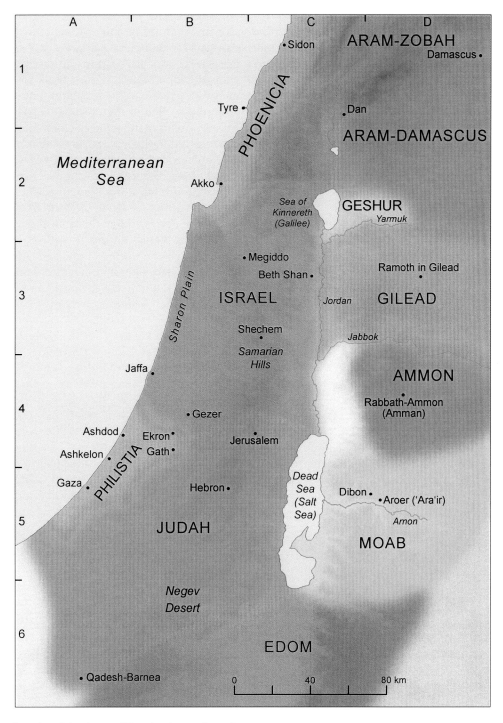

Iron Age Palestine and Transjordan: main regions

Figure 44.1 Mesha stele (aka Moabite stone). Photo by CM Dixon/Print Collector/Getty Images.

inconclusive conflicts with David's predecessor Saul. But the following century, its king Mesha regained its independence. Moab flourished under Mesha's rule. We learn this particularly from the discovery in Moab's capital Dibon of an inscribed black basalt stele, commonly referred to as the Moabite stone. Its 34-line inscription, written in the Moabite language, celebrates Mesha's building and military achievements (*CS* II: 137–8), including his success in establishing his kingdom's independence from Israel. It provides one of the best known instances where contemporary historical sources and biblical tradition coincide, for Mesha was already known as a king of Moab from 2 Kings 3:4. Later, Moab was among the lands reduced to Assyrian subject status during Tiglath-pileser III's western campaigns between 734 and 732. After the fall of Assyria, Moab, like other Transjordanian states, became subject to the Neo-Babylonian and the Persian empires. In the Hellenistic period, it came under Nabataean control.

The land called **Edom** lay south of the Dead Sea. Its name comes from a Semitic word meaning 'red' or 'ruddy', reflecting the colour of the local sandstone mountains. The Edomites were a Semitic-speaking people who probably settled in the region in C14, perhaps earlier. But they are first attested in late C13, in the records of the pharaoh Merneptah (1213–1203), who granted Edomite nomadic groups access to the pasture-lands of the eastern Egyptian Delta. Thereafter Edomites appear frequently in Old Testament sources. These report that they were conquered by the Israelite king David early in C10, but re-established their independence when they rebelled against the Judaean king Jehoram (c. 849–842). In C8 and C7, Edom was subject to Assyria. But the demands Assyria imposed upon it were probably not burdensome, for Edom appears to have flourished under Assyrian rule, due partly, perhaps, to the wealth it derived from its copper resources. The kingdom was destroyed by the Babylonians c. 550.

Contributions by various scholars in *OEANE* (1: 103–7) (Ammon); *OEANE* (2: 189–91) (Edom); *OEANE* (4: 38–41) (Moab); *OEANE* (5: 226–43) (Transjordan).

Israel in the 1st millennium BC

Our earliest reference to Israel appears in an inscription on a granite stele of the pharaoh Merneptah (1213–1203), discovered in Merneptah's mortuary temple in Thebes, chief city of upper Egypt. The inscription lists the 'people of Israel' among the pharaoh's Asiatic conquests, thus attesting the Israelites' existence as an identifiable ethnic group by the last decades of the Late Bronze Age. But Israel as a nation-state seems not to have developed until the very end of M2. Or so we may conclude from Old Testament tradition and chronology, according to which a united kingdom of Israel was established by Saul, who reigned c. 1020–1000. Saul's reign ended with his suicide after he was decisively defeated by the Philistines. He was succeeded by David, from the land of Judah in the south of the kingdom, who continued his predecessor's conflicts with the Philistines with

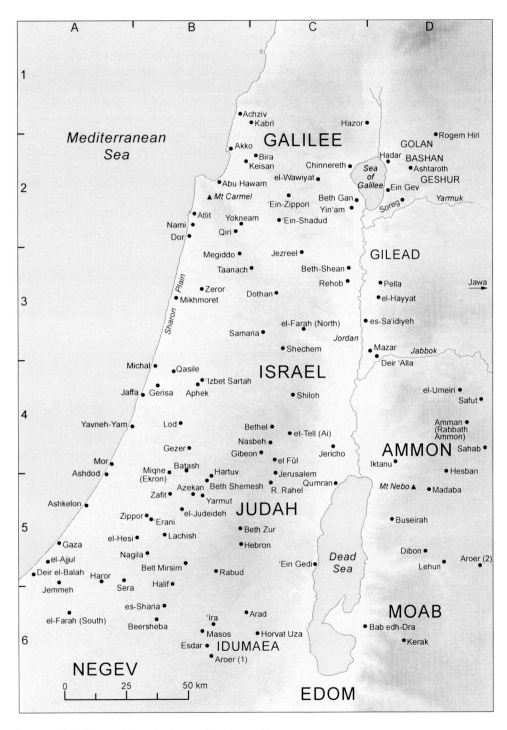

Iron Age Palestine and Transjordan: main cities and towns

considerable success. By the end of his reign, David had effectively destroyed their military power. But his greatest achievement was his establishment of Jerusalem as a new capital of Israel. Under the reign of his son and successor Solomon (c. 960–922), Israel reached a high level of cultural and commercial development, due largely to the king's promotion of close cultural and commercial links with foreign countries, which greatly boosted his kingdom's prosperity, and endowed the royal court at Jerusalem with a cosmopolitan character far removed from the ascetic lifestyle of the king's predecessors. But throughout his reign, tensions were mounting between the northern and southern tribes of Israel. These finally erupted into open conflict on his death, leading to the establishment of two separate kingdoms – Israel in the north, with its capital at Samaria, and Judah in the south, with Jerusalem its capital.

This reconstruction of early Israelite history is based entirely on Old Testament sources, and many scholars are sceptical about the historical validity of a united Israelite kingdom at this time, or indeed about the biblical account of Israel's early history in general, in the absence of contemporary archaeological or written evidence to support it. It is not until the reign of Omri (c. 876–869), allegedly the sixth king of Israel, that the biblical record begins to be confirmed by external sources. It was only in Omri's reign, some scholars argue, that a united Israelite kingdom was created, with Samaria its capital. Omri founded a dynasty whose second member Ahab joined the anti-Assyrian coalition defeated by Shalmaneser at Qarqar in 853. The united kingdom ended with the death of Jehoram (Joram), last member of the Omride dynasty, c. 842 (though there is doubt about the length and dates of the dynasty).

Subsequently, Israel became subject to Assyria, its king Joash being listed among the Syro-Palestinian tributaries of Adad-nirari III (810–783). A later Assyrian king Tiglath-pileser III (745–727) made extensive conquests in the land, and under his successor Shalmaneser V (726–722) or successor-but-one, Sargon II (721–705), the kingdom of Israel ended with the Assyrian destruction of its capital Samaria, which had rebelled against its overlord. Judah survived, as a tributary of Assyria. After the fall of Assyria in late C7, it became a vassal of Egypt. But in 586, the Babylonian king Nebuchadnezzar II captured and ordered the destruction of its capital Jerusalem, and (allegedly) deported almost all its population to Babylonia. Thus began the period of the Israelite 'exile', which ended in 539 when the Persian king Cyrus II conquered Babylon, and in the following year, allowed the Israelites living in exile to return to their homeland.

McCarter (*HCBD*: 466–70); Fritz (*OEANE* 3: 192–7).

45

The Philistines

Scholars generally agree that after the dispersal of the Sea Peoples, one group of them, the Peleset, perhaps a people of Aegean origin, finally settled in south-western Palestine, on that part of the southern coastal plain of Palestine which came to be called Philistia. The Peleset re-emerged in Old Testament tradition as the Philistines, about the same time as the Canaanites occupied the inland plains, and the Israelites the hill-country beyond. Five main cities, the so-called Philistine Pentapolis, provided the focal points of Philistine civilization. They were Ashdod, Ashkelon, Ekron, Gaza and Gath. Contrary to the negative impressions given by biblical sources, the Philistines were a highly cultured people, with advanced architectural, engineering, technological and craft skills. And their urban-based civilization was supported by a flourishing agricultural industry.

To judge from Old Testament sources, the Philistines came into conflict with the Israelites fairly early in their history as they sought to expand their territory eastwards, at the same time as the hill-country Israelites began expanding their territories westwards. The wars between Israelites and Philistines culminated in the defeat of the latter by the Israelite king David early in C10, though sporadic conflict between Israelites and Philistines continued until the last decades of C8. This at least is the information provided by our biblical sources – for which we have yet to find confirmation from independent sources. Like other kingdoms, countries, and city-states of Syria and Palestine, Philistia came under the control of the Great Kingdoms of the

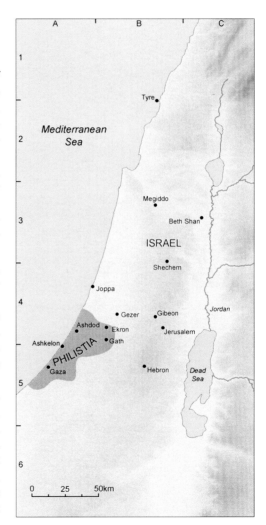

Philistia and its neighbours

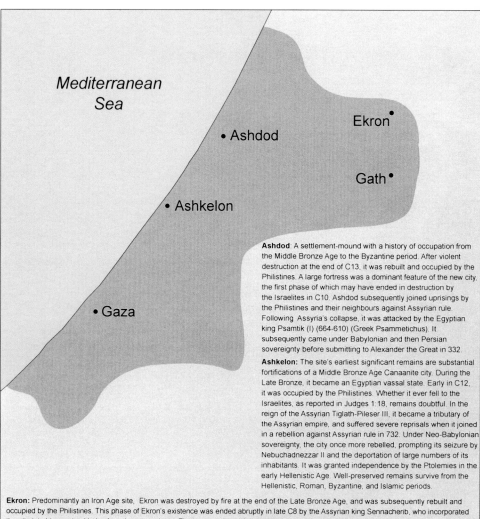

Mediterranean Sea

• Ashdod

Ekron•

Gath•

• Ashkelon

• Gaza

Ashdod: A settlement-mound with a history of occupation from the Middle Bronze Age to the Byzantine period. After violent destruction at the end of C13, it was rebuilt and occupied by the Philistines. A large fortress was a dominant feature of the new city, the first phase of which may have ended in destruction by the Israelites in C10. Ashdod subsequently joined uprisings by the Philistines and their neighbours against Assyrian rule. Following Assyria's collapse, it was attacked by the Egyptian king Psamtik (I) (664-610) (Greek Psammetichus). It subsequently came under Babylonian and then Persian sovereignty before submitting to Alexander the Great in 332.

Ashkelon: The site's earliest significant remains are substantial fortifications of a Middle Bronze Age Canaanite city. During the Late Bronze, it became an Egyptian vassal state. Early in C12, it was occupied by the Philistines. Whether it ever fell to the Israelites, as reported in Judges 1:18, remains doubtful. In the reign of the Assyrian Tiglath-Pileser III, it became a tributary of the Assyrian empire, and suffered severe reprisals when it joined in a rebellion against Assyrian rule in 732. Under Neo-Babylonian sovereignty, the city once more rebelled, prompting its seizure by Nebuchadnezzar II and the deportation of large numbers of its inhabitants. It was granted independence by the Ptolemies in the early Hellenistic Age. Well-preserved remains survive from the Hellenistic, Roman, Byzantine, and Islamic periods.

Ekron: Predominantly an Iron Age site, Ekron was destroyed by fire at the end of the Late Bronze Age, and was subsequently rebuilt and occupied by the Philistines. This phase of Ekron's existence was ended abruptly in late C8 by the Assyrian king Sennacherib, who incorporated the city into his empire. Under Assyrian sovereignty, Ekron was substantially redeveloped, now reaching its maximum size. It was later subject to Egypt, and was destroyed by the Babylonians in 603.

Gath: Iron Age city, frequently referred to in Old Testament sources – e.g. as the home of the Philistine champion Goliath, and as the city to which the Ark of the Covenant was sent. According to 2 Kings 12:17, Gath was attacked and captured by Hazael, king of Aram-Damascus in the second half of C9, prior to his attack upon Jerusalem. Around 712, the city was conquered by the Assyrian king Sargon II. Gath's location has not yet been firmly established, though most scholars now equate it with mod. Tel Zafit/Tell es-Safi.

Gaza: Cult centre of the Philistine god Dagon. It fell to the Assyrian Tiglath-pileser III in 734, the Judaean king Hezekiah several decades later; and the pharaoh Necho II in 609. During the Persian Achaemenid period, Gaza was an important royal fortress. In 332, it was conquered by Alexander the Great. Following his death, it first came under the control of the Ptolemies, serving as the northern outpost of their empire, but was captured by the Seleucid king Antiochus III in 198. It was a flourishing city under Roman rule and continued to be so in the Byzantine period.

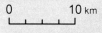

0   10 km

The Philistine Pentapolis

Figure 45.1 Philistines among Sea Peoples captured by Ramesses III. J.T. Vintage/Bridgeman Images.

age, who imposed their rule over a wide range of territories west of the Euphrates. Between C9 and C6, the Philistines were in succession subjects of the Assyrian, Egyptian and Babylonian empires.

Mattingly (*HCBD*: 846–9); Laughlin (2006: 235–42).

46
1st millennium BC Anatolia

Following the collapse of the Late Bronze Age civilizations, a number of new cities and kingdoms emerged throughout Anatolia. Most notable among these was the kingdom of Urartu in the east and the kingdoms of Phrygia and Lydia in the west. Also, from late M2 onwards, the Anatolian coastal regions and their hinterlands were settled by numerous Greek peoples, immigrants for the most part from the Greek mainland or Aegean islands. The pages that follow contain more details of these new peoples and kingdoms. We have already dealt with the contemporary Neo-Hittite kingdoms that emerged in Tabal in the south-eastern sector of the Anatolian peninsula, and the kingdoms of Hilakku and Que along the coast.

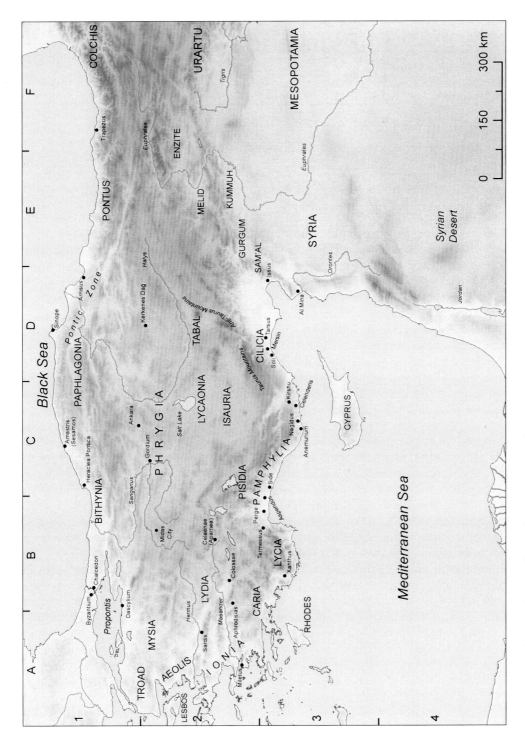

Countries, kingdoms and cities of 1st millennium BC Anatolia

47

Phrygia and Lydia

Phrygia

Centred on the city of Gordium, 100 km west of Ankara, the kingdom of Phrygia evolved in western Anatolia during the early centuries of M1. In Greek tradition, the Phrygians were a western people who migrated into central Anatolia from homelands in Macedonia and Thrace during the upheavals at the end of the Late Bronze Age – though Homer lists them among Troy's allies in the Trojan War. But a number of scholars have attributed the kingdom's development to an amalgamation of these 'western' Phrygians with an immigrant group into central Anatolia from the east, called the Mushki in Assyrian texts; the latter were a conglomeration of aggressive tribal groups, perhaps originating in the Armenian highlands. If such a union did take place, it may have been the achievement of a king called Midas in Greek, commonly identified with the Mushki leader Mita, attested in records of the Assyrian king Sargon II in the last decades of C8. But there is no scholarly consensus on this. The fact that Greek sources never refer to the Mushki, nor Assyrian ones to the Phrygians, has lent support to the argument that there were in fact two separate major kingdoms in central Anatolia at this time, perhaps arising as much, or more, from indigenous population elements as from immigrant groups. Fresh doubts have also been raised about Phrygian chronology, by the excavators of Gordium. At all events, the territories over which the rulers of Phrygia held sway at the peak of their power constituted one of the largest kingdoms of the Iron Age world. Eastwards, its subject lands extended towards the Euphrates, southwards into the region later known as Cappadocia, and westwards as far as the Aegean Sea. The kingdom seems to have been abruptly terminated early in C7 by an invading Cimmerian force. But a number of Phrygian settlements, including Gordium, recovered from the invasions, and after the final withdrawal of the invaders in late C7 or early C6, regained some of their former prosperity as small principalities subject to the kings of Lydia.

The burial tumuli and sculptured rock façades, particularly those found at Gordium, provide the most notable surviving features of Phrygia's material civilization. Phrygian graves were typically wooden, flat-roofed chambers built into rectangular pits sunk into the ground, and then covered with mounds (tumuli) of rocks and earth. Gordium's cemetery contained c. 140 of these burial structures, which range in date from C8 to the Hellenistic period. The largest, still 53 m high (even after erosion) and almost 300 m in diameter, covers a wooden burial chamber with gabled roof. Within it were found the remains of a man in his sixties, laid out on a bier. The tomb, and the body within it, belong, it has been proposed, to Midas' father Gordius.

The Phrygian language, written in an alphabetic script, is a member of the Indo-European language family. Our knowledge of it comes from two groups of inscriptions, now only partly

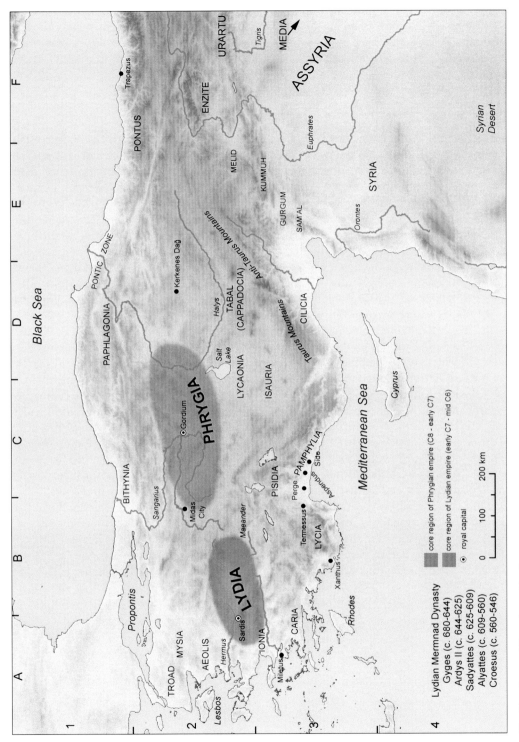

The kingdoms of Phrygia and Lydia

Lydian Mermnad Dynasty
Gyges (c. 680–644)
Ardys II (c. 644–625)
Sadyattes (c. 625–609)
Alyattes (c. 609–560)
Croesus (c. 560–546)

core region of Phrygian empire (C8 - early C7)
core region of Lydian empire (early C7 - mid C6)
royal capital

intelligible. Those of the first group are found mainly on the façades of rock-cut monuments dating from C8 to C3 BC; the second group dates to C2 and C3 AD, and consists mainly of curse formulae.

Sams (*CANE* 2: 1147–59); Roller and Voigt (*OHAA*: 560–78, 1069–94); Roosevelt (*AANE*: 896–907).

Lydia

Around 685 BC, the Lydian king Candaules was assassinated by his bodyguard Gyges, who established in Lydia a new line of kings known as the Mermnad dynasty. From his capital Sardis, Gyges embarked on a programme of territorial expansion, continued by his successors, which made Lydia the dominant power in western Anatolia after the fall of Phrygia. The Greeks along the Aegean coast were among the peoples incorporated into the Lydian empire. But Lydia's existence was long threatened by the Cimmerians, destroyers of the Phrygian kingdom. After some forty years on the throne, Gyges himself was killed in a Cimmerian onslaught, which devastated part of the royal capital Sardis (c. 644). Lydia survived the onslaught, and continued its conflicts with the invaders until the reign of Alyattes (c. 609–560), fourth ruler of the Mermnad dynasty, who eventually drove them from his lands.

Alyattes' kingdom was also threatened by another major enemy – the westward expanding kingdom of the Medes, whose heartland lay in the Zagros mountains. Five years of conflict between the Medes and the Lydians culminated in the so-called 'battle of the eclipse', fought between Alyattes and the Median king Cyaxares on the banks of the Halys river. The outcome was a treaty between the two kings, which established the border between their kingdoms along the river's banks. In the reign of the last Mermnad king Croesus (c. 560–546), Lydia faced a formidable new enemy from the east – the kingdom of Persia, founded by Cyrus II c. 559 BC. Like Cyaxares, Cyrus embarked on a vigorous westward expansion of his territories, which eventually brought him into Lydian-controlled territory in the Halys region. After an inconclusive confrontation with Cyrus' army east of the river in the spring of 546 (the so-called battle of Pteria), Croesus withdrew his forces to the west, rapidly pursued by the Persians. The final showdown took place in a pitched battle outside Sardis. Croesus was decisively defeated, and taken prisoner. His kingdom was incorporated into the Persian empire, and Sardis became Persia's chief administrative centre in the west.

Much of Lydia's wealth was derived from the precious metals, especially silver and gold, that were mined from the kingdom's soils and rivers. In C6, the Lydians invented coined money – an invention that rapidly spread to the Greek world. The Lydian language survives in approximately sixty-four inscriptions, dating from C6 to C4 and found mostly on grave steles in Sardis. The language used in these inscriptions belongs to the Indo-European language family, but is still only partly intelligible.

Greenewalt (*CANE* 2: 1173–83, *OHAA*: 1112–30); Roosevelt (*AANE*: 897–907).

48

Urartu

The kingdom of Urartu arose in the highland regions of eastern Anatolia, around the core region of Lake Van. During C8 and C7 BC, it developed into one of the most powerful Near Eastern states, its rulers the equals and often bitter enemies of their western neighbours, the Great Kings of Assyria. 'Urartu' is in fact an Assyrian name. The Urartians themselves called their country 'Biainili', from which the name Van is derived. Their kingdom was created in C9 out of a number of small independent principalities by Sarduri I (c. 832–825), who established a royal dynasty in the city of Tushpa (modern Van), which he made the capital of his fledgling kingdom. Sarduri and his successors, notably Ishpuini, Minua and Argishti I (his son, grandson and great-grandson respectively), embarked on campaigns of territorial expansion which carried Urartu's frontiers northwards to the Araxes river and into Armenia, south-eastwards to the shores of Lake Urmia, and south-westwards towards the Tigris. Inevitably, the kingdom's ever-expanding territorial ambitions led to conflict with Assyria. With variable outcomes. One of the lowest points in Urartu's fortunes came in 714, when the Assyrian king Sargon II crossed its borders (during his famous 'Eighth Campaign'), and decisively defeated the army led against him by the Urartian king Rusa I. Rusa survived the conflict, but in the same year, he suffered a further disaster when his forces were routed by the Cimmerians. He committed suicide soon after.

But his kingdom quickly recovered. Fresh campaigns were undertaken by the new king Argishti II (c. 713–679) who led an expedition further to the north-east than any of his predecessors. And Argishti's successor Rusa II (c. 678–654), eager to impress his subjects, allies and enemies with the material might and splendour of his kingdom, undertook an ambitious building programme throughout the land, constructing massive new fortified centres at the sites now called Ayanis, Adilcevaz, Karmir Blur and Bastam. Built on towering outcrops of rock, the kingdom's great fortress-cities were strategically located to control the plains and valleys which lay between the rugged highland ranges. Within these fortresses were located Urartu's temples, palaces and administrative centres, and the warehouses which stored the produce of the plains. Large-scale irrigation works, consisting of great canals and dams, ensured that the kingdom's foodlands remained highly productive. The greatest of the irrigation works was an aqueduct and canal built by King Minua, which watered the plain of Van.

Written information about, and found within, the Urartian kingdom, is provided by both Assyrian and Urartian inscriptions. In the reign of Sarduri I, Urartian scribes used the Assyrian language and cuneiform script for their records. But subsequently, all known inscriptions were written in Urartian, with a few Urartian-Assyrian bilinguals. The contents of the inscriptions, all surviving examples of which are carved on stone, include details of military enterprises, building programmes and religious activities. However, most of what we know about Urartu's history

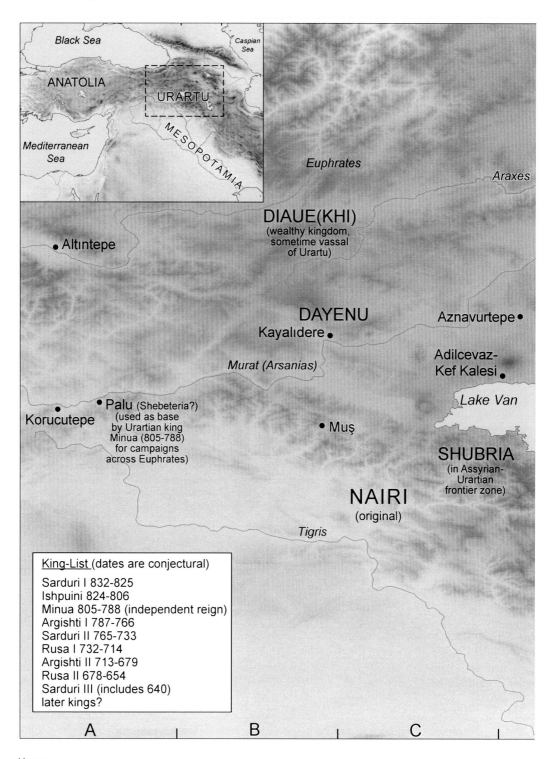

Black Sea

Caspian
Sea

ANATOLIA

URARTU

MESOPOTAMIA

Mediterranean
Sea

Euphrates

Araxes

DIAUE(KHI)
(wealthy kingdom,
sometime vassal
of Urartu)

• Altıntepe

DAYENU
Kayalıdere •

Aznavurtepe •

Adilcevaz-
Kef Kalesi •

Murat (Arsanias)

Lake Van

• Palu (Shebeteria?)
(used as base
by Urartian king
Minua (805-788)
for campaigns
across Euphrates)

Korucutepe •

• Muş

SHUBRIA
(in Assyrian-
Urartian
frontier zone)

NAIRI
(original)

Tigris

King-List (dates are conjectural)

Sarduri I 832-825
Ishpuini 824-806
Minua 805-788 (independent reign)
Argishti I 787-766
Sarduri II 765-733
Rusa I 732-714
Argishti II 713-679
Rusa II 678-654
Sarduri III (includes 640)
later kings?

A   B   C

Urartu

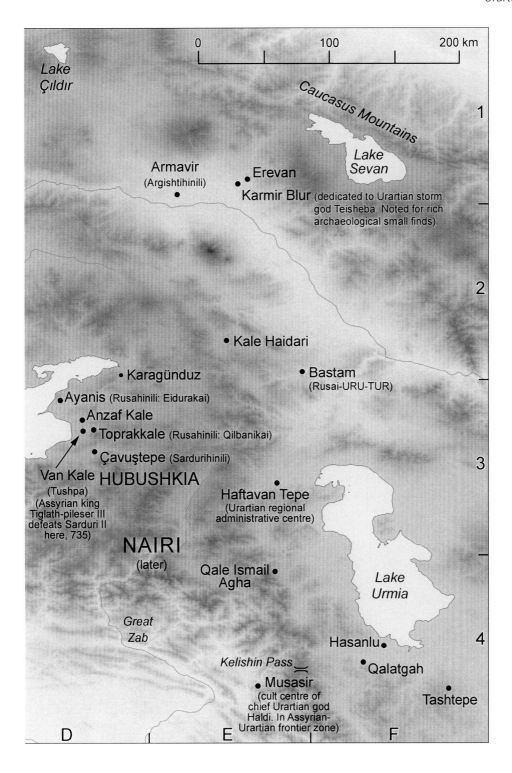

0   100   200 km

Lake
Çıldır

Caucasus Mountains

Lake
Sevan

Armavir
(Argishtihinili)

• Erevan

Karmir Blur (dedicated to Urartian storm
god Teisheba. Noted for rich
archaeological small finds)

1

2

• Kale Haidari

• Karagünduz

• Bastam
(Rusai-URU-TUR)

•Ayanis (Rusahinili: Eidurakai)

•Anzaf Kale

•Toprakkale (Rusahinili: Qilbanikai)

• Çavuştepe (Sardurihinili)

Van Kale HUBUSHKIA
(Tushpa)
(Assyrian king
Tiglath-pileser III
defeats Sarduri II
here, 735)

Haftavan Tepe
(Urartian regional
administrative centre)

3

NAIRI
(later)

Qale Ismail •
Agha

Lake
Urmia

Great
Zab

Hasanlu•

4

Kelishin Pass

• Qalatgah

• Musasir
(cult centre of
chief Urartian god
Haldi. In Assyrian-
Urartian frontier zone)

Tashtepe

D   E   F

Figure 48.1 Van Citadel, Urartu, with fortress city Toprakkale in background © Dennis Cox/Alamy.

comes from external sources, notably the Annals of the Assyrian kings, which provide valuable – if biased – information about the contacts and conflicts between Assyria and Urartu. After the reign of Rusa II, we have little written information of any kind about Urartu. The kingdom had but a few decades to run. Archaeological evidence indicates that by the end of C7 at the latest it had ended violently, with the destruction of almost all its cities by fire. We do not know precisely when this happened, or who the destroyers were.

Zimansky (*CANE* 2: 1135–46, 1998, *OHAA*: 548–59); Radner (*OHAA*: 734–51); Ayvazian (*AANE*: 877–95).

49

The Cimmerians

The Cimmerians were a nomadic people, perhaps of Indo-Iranian stock, who originally dwelt in southern Russia. But they were driven from their homeland by Scythian hordes, according to Herodotus (1.15), and thereupon, from late C8 to late C7 or early C6, they swept through and plundered many parts of the Near Eastern world. Assyrian sources report their attacks on Assyrian and Urartian subject territories, from the reign of the Assyrian king Sargon II (721–705) onwards. Several Assyrian letters from Sargon's reign record their destruction of an army from the kingdom of Urartu, then ruled by Rusa I, and the slaughter of a number of Urartu's provincial governors. But the Cimmerians were rather less successful in their confrontations with the

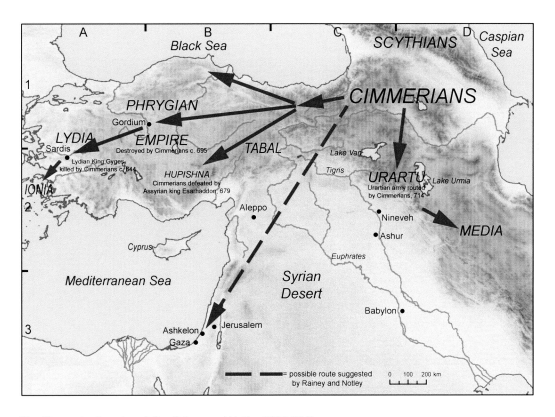

The Cimmerian invasions (after Rainey and Notley 2006: 254)

Assyrians. In 679, the Assyrian king Esarhaddon defeated their leader Teushpa in a battle in the land of Hupishna (Hubushna), an Assyrian subject territory in south-eastern Anatolia, and in 652, the Cimmerian leader Lygdamis (Assyrian Tugdammu) was defeated by Esarhaddon's successor Ashurbanipal, and later killed in Cilicia.

Westwards, the Cimmerians fought against the Phrygians and eventually destroyed their empire, c. 695. Subsequently, they were locked in a prolonged struggle with the Lydians. One of the victims of this struggle was the Lydian king Gyges, killed in a Cimmerian attack upon his kingdom c. 644. He had previously secured assistance against the invaders from Ashurbanipal, but had forfeited this when he supported Egypt's rebellion against Assyria. The Cimmerians then launched attacks upon the Greek cities along the Aegean coast. They were finally driven out of western Anatolia, in late C7 or early C6, by the Lydian king Alyattes.

SB (254–5).

50

Egypt in the Third Intermediate and Saite periods (1069–525 BC)

In the Third Intermediate Period of Egyptian history (1069–664), which followed the Ramesside era, Egypt's influence and involvement in international affairs were much reduced. There was, however, a resurgence of Egyptian claims upon the kingdom's former Palestinian territories by a ruler of Libyan origin called Sheshonq I (biblical Shishak; 945–924), founder of the 22nd Dynasty. Sheshonq restored some measure of Egyptian authority over Palestine by conquering Israel and Judah. According to his inscription on the Bubastite Gate of the temple of Karnak in Thebes, he conquered well over one hundred cities of Israel, Judah and southern Palestine. But Assyria was the great power of the age, and until its fall at the end of C7, the dominant overlord of Syria and Palestine. In 671, Egypt fell victim to it when the Assyrian king Esarhaddon, provoked by Egyptian support for Assyria's rebel vassals in the Levant, invaded and conquered the kingdom, and installed Assyrian governors there. His conquests were followed up by his successor Ashurbanipal in 664/3. But shortly afterwards, Egypt regained its independence under a new dynasty, the 26th, often referred to as the Saite dynasty (664–525). This line of rulers ushered in what scholars call the 'Late Period' in Egyptian history, which lasted until Alexander's conquests in 332.

But to back-track to the end of the Assyrian empire. In 610, the newly enthroned third ruler of the Saite dynasty, Necho II (Nekau; 610–595), set Egyptian sights afresh on the lands of Syria and Palestine – allegedly to support Assyria against the Babylonian king Nabopolassar. But collaboration with Assyria was largely a pretext. Necho's ulterior motive was to rebuild Egypt's empire and reclaim its former Syrian and Palestinian subjects. He began by launching a major land and sea campaign against the territories of northern Syria. The enterprise failed to save the Assyrians, but on his way back to Egypt Necho secured a hold over the states and cities of southern Syria and Palestine. Four years later, he returned to consolidate and extend his sovereignty there, at Babylon's expense. But a military showdown with the Babylonian crown prince Nebuchadnezzar near Carchemish on the Euphrates ended in a massive defeat of the Egyptian army and Necho's retreat home. The pharaoh was nonetheless intent on maintaining his claim over his territories in Syria and Palestine – a claim which Nebuchadnezzar, now King Nebuchadnezzar II, vigorously opposed. The matter was resolved in 601, when the Babylonian led an army south into Egypt and fought Necho's army at Pelusium in the north-east of the Delta. Both sides suffered heavy casualties, but the battle effectively ended Necho's aspirations to control any part of Syria and Palestine. Egypt was subsequently absorbed into the Persian empire, when Cambyses conducted a campaign there in 525, and defeated the pharaoh Psammetichus III in a battle outside Memphis.

Lloyd (2000: 369–83); Taylor (2000).

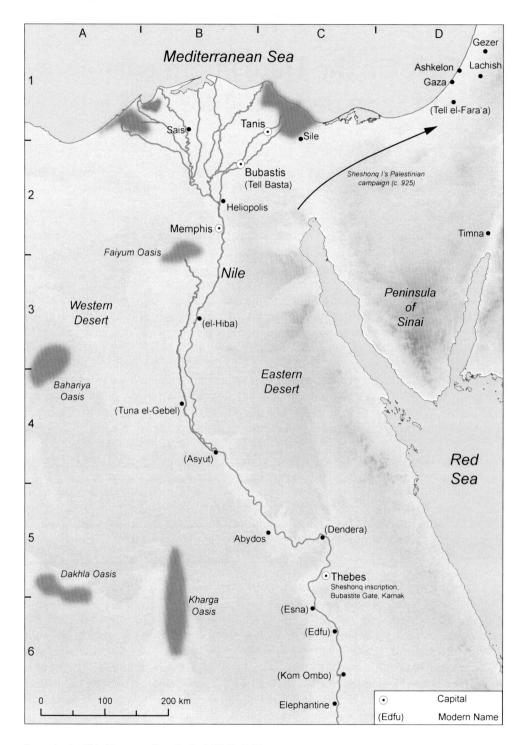

Egypt in the Third Intermediate Period (1069–747)

Part VII

The Greeks in the East

51

Aeolians, Ionians, Dorians

Note: The map of Greek eastward migrations after the Bronze Age is based primarily on Classical Greek literary sources and linguistic data. There is ongoing debate about the nature, chronology and extent of these migrations. Most scholars now regard Greek settlement in Asia Minor and the Aegean islands, after the Bronze Age as well as during it, as an incremental process involving a number of population movements over many years, indeed centuries. For a concise summary of scholarly discussions relating to the Greek migrations, see Greaves (OHAA: 508–9).

Aeolis is the Classical designation for the Aegean coastal region of north-western Asia Minor, extending from the Hellespont to the south of the Hermus river. The name was derived from a Greek population called the Aeolians, who supposedly in the last two centuries of M2 migrated eastwards from their homelands which lay in the regions later called Boeotia and Thessaly on the Greek mainland; they settled first on the island of Lesbos before occupying the coastal part of the Troad and the region to its south. Strictly, 'Aeolis' and 'Aeolian' are purely ethno-linguistic terms. They reflect neither a political nor a clearly definable geographical entity. However, the southern Aeolian settlements may have formed a league which had a religious centre in the temple of Apollo at Grynium. Cyme was the most important city in the southern Aeolian region, and perhaps the chief city of the league. (For both cities, see the map on p. 202.)

Ionia is the Classical name for the central Aegean coastal region of Anatolia extending between the bays of Izmir (Smyrna) and Bargylia (see map on p. 202) and including the offshore islands Chios and Samos. It too was allegedly settled in late M2 by refugee colonists, called Ionians, from the Greek mainland following the collapse of the major centres of Late Bronze Age civilization. The region contained twelve major cities, which had begun to develop by early M1 and probably by C9 established among themselves a league called the Panionium, reflecting the emergence of a unified cultural Ionian identity in the region. The league met at the foot of Mount Mycale, in the territory of Priene.

Dorians Classical tradition has created a view of the Dorians as latecomers to the Greek world, entering it shortly before the end of the Late Bronze Age (eighty years after the fall of Troy according to Thucydides), and occupying primarily the Peloponnese. They are regarded (by some) as one of the immediate causes of the destruction of the Mycenaean palace civilization. Henceforth they spread to other parts of the Greek-speaking world. They were allegedly the most aggressive and warlike of all Greek groups. The Homeric scholar Margalit Finkelberg comments that the tradition of the late emergence of the Dorians in southern Greece is strongly supported by the dialect map of this region. However, she notes that the widespread term 'Dorian invasion' relates to miscellaneous population movements from the periphery to the centre of the Mycenaean world at the end of the Bronze Age. The archaeological record has so far provided no evidence that the so-called Dorians were a distinctive group of late-comers to Bronze Age Greece or the possessors of a distinctive culture within the Greek world, beyond the existence of 'Doric' as one of the main dialects of the Greek-speaking peoples.

SB (104–5); Greaves and Harl (*OHAA*: 500–14, 752–74), relevant articles in *HE* by Rutherford (Aeolians and Ionians, I: 9 and II: 415–16, respectively) and Finkelberg (Dorians, I: 217–18).

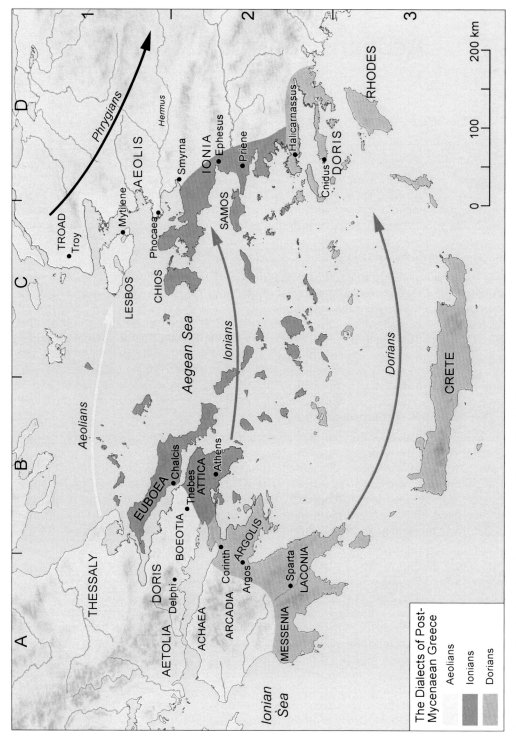

Post Bronze Age Greek migrations (after Rainey and Notley 2006: 105)

52

Two major Bronze Age–Classical sites of western Anatolia

Miletus

Once a four-harboured city on the Aegean coast, Miletus now lies in a plain 3 km inland, in the region called Milesia in Classical times. Its history of occupation extends from the Late Chalcolithic period (M4) through the Bronze Ages and the Classical Greek, Hellenistic, Roman and Byzantine periods. Called Milawata/Millawanda in Hittite texts, Miletus was for a time a vassal of the Hittite empire.

Figure 52.1 Theatre of Miletus. Photo by Trevor Bryce.

Archaeological investigations have also revealed evidence of Minoan and Mycenaean settlement there, the latter dated to late C14 and C13 when the city was subject to a Mycenaean ('Ahhiyawan') king. In later Greek tradition, Miletus figures prominently in accounts of the Ionian migrations. It was the southernmost and most important of the major Ionian settlements, and subsequently flourished as a centre of trade, commerce, culture and learning, until it initiated and played a leading role in the Ionian rebellion which broke out against Persian rule in 499. When the rebellion was crushed in 494, the Persians sacked the city, massacring or enslaving its inhabitants. In later years, Miletus became a member of the Athenian Confederacy. But it subsequently reverted to Persian sovereignty until 334, when Alexander the Great campaigned in the region, and took the city by siege. In 129 BC, it became

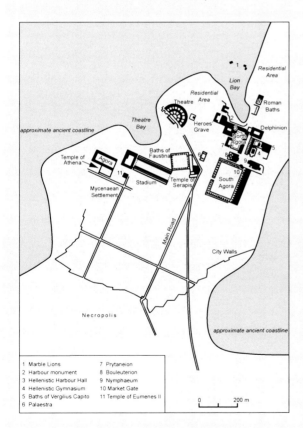

1 Marble Lions	7 Prytaneion
2 Harbour monument	8 Bouleuterion
3 Hellenistic Harbour Hall	9 Nymphaeum
4 Hellenistic Gymnasium	10 Market Gate
5 Baths of Vergilius Capito	11 Temple of Eumenes II
6 Palaestra	

0   200 m

Miletus

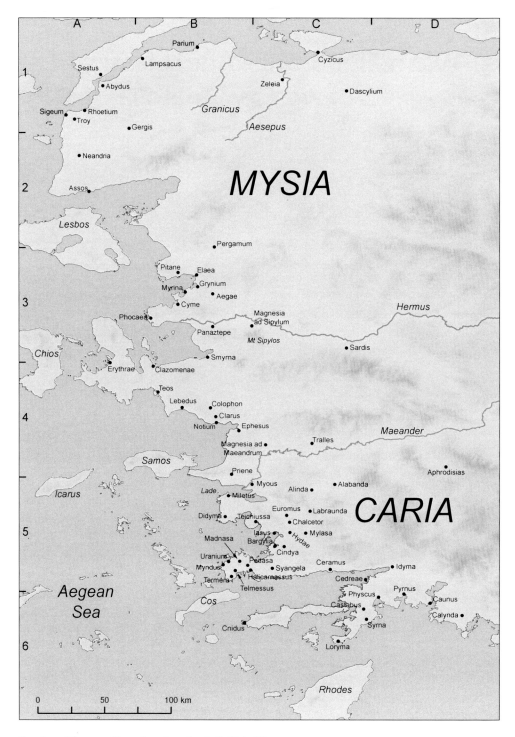

Greek and Roman cities of western Anatolia/Asia Minor

part of the Roman province of Asia. Under Roman rule, the city's former grid layout was preserved, and its C4 BC Greek theatre substantially reconstructed and considerably enlarged. Other features of Miletus' (late) Hellenistic and Roman periods include three agoras (marketplaces), the so-called Lion Harbour once flanked by two lions (now reburied for preservation), a gymnasium and stadium complex, and the relatively well preserved bath-complex dedicated to Faustina, wife of the emperor Marcus Aurelius.

Greaves (2002); *PPAWA* (472–6); Wilson (2010: 265–73).

Figure 52.2 Ephesus, reconstructed library of Celsus, 2nd cent. AD. Photo by Trevor Bryce.

Ephesus

Ephesus is first attested in Late Bronze Age Hittite texts as Apasa, capital of one of the western Anatolian Arzawa kingdoms. Recent excavations have identified what is almost certainly its remains on a hill now called Ayasuluk close to Classical Ephesus. An Ionian foundation according to Greek tradition, the city was incorporated into the Lydian empire in C7, and in C6, along with the other Ionian cities, became subject to Persia. In C5, it was for a time a member of the Athenian Confederacy, but like Miletus reverted in 386 to Persian sovereignty until 'liberated' by Alexander the Great in 334.

Ephesus is best known today for its Hellenistic and especially its Roman remains. These reflect the foundation of a new city, laid out on a rectangular grid plan by Alexander's general Lysimachus. But the famous temple of Artemis (Artemisium), built on a plain outside the Roman city and traditionally included among the seven wonders of the ancient world, had its origins many centuries earlier, probably in C8. Other notable remains of the Roman period include the theatre with a 25,000-seat capacity, the library of Celsus, built in AD 110, and the recently reconstructed Roman villas, richly decorated with paintings and mosaics. The villas were destroyed in AD 262 when Ephesus was devastated by a massive earthquake, and remained buried in a steep hillside until their excavation by Austrian archaeologists between 1960 and 1986.

Mitsopoulou-Leon (*PECS*: 306–10); Wilson (2010: 199–229).

53

The countries of southern Asia Minor in the Graeco-Roman period

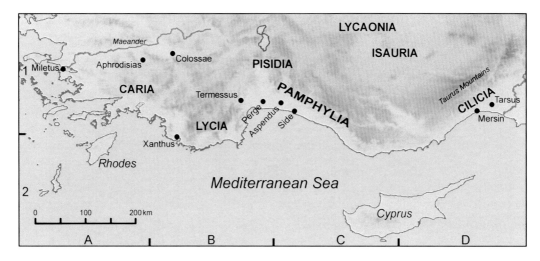

Southern Asia Minor in the Graeco-Roman period

Caria Its name perhaps derived from Late Bronze Age Anatolian Karkisa (though Herodotus claims the Carians were Aegean immigrants), Caria became subject to the Lydian empire in C6 and subsequently to Persia. Urbanization of the country progressed rapidly in C4, under the Persian-backed Hecatomnid dynasty, most notably during the rule of Mausolus (377–353) who played an important role in the spread of Greek influence through Caria, but was also concerned to preserve elements of the indigenous culture. The Carian language has survived in a number of alphabetic inscriptions, in Caria itself but mainly in Egypt, where Carian mercenaries had settled.

Graeco-Roman ***Cilicia*** consisted primarily of two distinct parts, known by the terms Cilicia Tracheia (Latin Aspera) 'Rough Cilicia', and Cilicia Pedias (Latin Campestris) 'Cilicia of the Plain'. Cilicia Tracheia was the rugged mountainous western part of the region, Cilicia Pedias the 'smoother', fertile eastern part. These regions roughly corresponded to the countries respectively called Hilakku and Que in Assyrian texts. During the first period of Persian sovereignty, from c. 542 to 401, the Cilicians appear to have enjoyed a relatively high degree of autonomy under a line of local kings called by the title Syennesis. The dynasty's seat of power may have been located at Tarsus. In the following period, from 401 to the conquests of Alexander the Great, Cilicia was directly governed by a Persian satrap.

Isauria is the Classical name for the Taurus mountain region in central-southern Anatolia, bordered by Pisidia, Lycaonia, Pamphylia and Cilicia. In the Late Bronze Age, the region lay adjacent to the kingdom of Tarhuntassa to its south. From Classical sources, we learn that its mountain peoples were noted for their banditry and their fierce resistance to outside aggressors.

Lycaonia is the Classical name of the region in south-central Anatolia located south of the Salt Lake. Its western end was probably part of the Late Bronze Age Lukka Lands. As in the Bronze Age, Lycaonia occupied strategically important territory in M1, for through it passed a major route linking western Anatolia with south-eastern Cilicia and Syria. No doubt primarily for this reason, control of the region was hotly contested by a succession of M1 powers, including Persia and the Seleucid and Attalid kingdoms.

Pamphylia is a Greek name meaning 'place of all tribes'. In Greek legendary tradition, it was settled by Greeks of mixed origin some time after the Trojan War. The Pamphylians spoke a distinctive dialect of Greek, which was related to Cypriot and Arcadian and also contained an infusion of Anatolian linguistic elements. Pamphylia no doubt became subject to Persian sovereignty c. 540 during the Persian commander Harpagus' campaigns along the southern Anatolian coast. But some time after the Athenian victory c. 466 over the Persian fleet at the Eurymedon river, whose mouth is at Aspendus in Pamphylia, a number of its cities became members of the Athenian Confederacy. From textual evidence, we know that in the Late Bronze Age the region formed the western coastal part of the kingdom of Tarhuntassa, and probably had a predominantly Luwian population.

Pisidia is the Classical name for the country occupying the mountainous region of south-western Anatolia inland from Lycia and Pamphylia. The rugged nature of the land, the strong defences of its cities, and the fierce character of its population presented a formidable obstacle to foreign aggressors. Pisidia remained independent of the Persian empire, and was never fully subjugated by the Persians' Hellenistic successors. But it eventually came under Roman control when it was incorporated into the Roman province of Galatia, created by Augustus in 25 BC. From C4 BC onwards, Pisidia's cities had become increasingly influenced by Greek civilization. But even under Roman domination, a number of elements of the indigenous Pisidian culture persisted. This applied particularly to the country's language and religious cults which continued to flourish in its rural areas.

See relevant entries in *PPAWA*.

54
Lycia

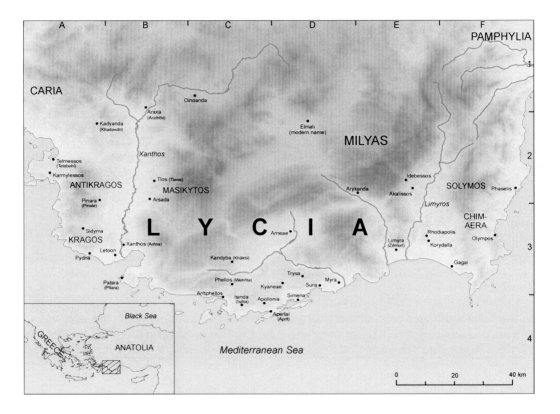

Lycia

The country called Lycia in Classical sources occupied part of the region called Lukka in Late Bronze Age Hittite texts. In their own language, the Lycians called themselves *Trm̃mili* and their land *Trm̃misa*. Their population was probably a mixture of Aegean immigrants and indigenous stock. About 540 BC, Lycia was conquered by the Persians and thereafter was part of the Persian empire (except for several decades in mid C5 when it was part of the Athenian Confederacy). A local dynasty established in the country's chief city Xanthus exercised immediate authority over much of Lycia until early C4 BC. Along with the rulers of other Lycian cities, the Xanthian dynasts issued coins which often bore their own and their cities' names as well as portrait-heads of themselves wearing Persian-type tiaras. In the 360s, Lycia participated in the abortive satrap revolt. When the uprising was crushed, Persian overlordship was resumed until Alexander the Great invaded and 'liberated' the country in 334/3. After his death in 323, Lycia came first under the control of Antigonus of Macedon, and subsequently under Ptolemaic and Seleucid rule. However, with the defeat of the Seleucid king Antiochus III by the Romans at Magnesia-ad-Sipylum in 190, Lycia came within the Roman orbit. In C2 BC, it formed a League amongst its cities which continued until C4 AD. The league discussed and decided upon matters of war, conclusions of alliances and diplomatic missions to foreign states. In AD 43, the emperor Claudius formed a Roman province from Lycia and its neighbour Pamphylia.

A native Lycian language has survived, preserved in approximately 180 inscriptions, appearing mainly on rock-cut house-like and pillar

Figure 54.1 House-shaped tombs for multiple burials, Myra in Lycia. Photo by Trevor Bryce.

tombs. Many of the tombs were used for multiple burials. Lycian inscriptions appear occasionally on steles (stone columns), more commonly on coin-legends, and, very rarely, as graffiti on metal- and ceramic-ware. The earliest inscriptions date to early C5, the latest to late C4. Lycian belongs to the Indo-European language group, and is closely related to Bronze Age Luwian. Written in a modified form of the Greek alphabet, it is still largely undecipherable. Greek inscriptions begin to appear at various Lycian sites in C5 BC, and then from C4 onwards in increasing numbers. Over 1,200 Greek inscriptions have been recorded, primarily from the Roman imperial period, along with a small number of Latin inscriptions. The most prominent native Lycian deities were a mother-goddess, called *ēni mahanahi* ('mother of the gods'), and the storm god Trqqas (a descendant of the Luwian god Tarhundas), both of Bronze Age Anatolian origin. Greek deities also appear in inscriptions and on coins from C5 onwards. Subsequently, the Letoids (Leto, Apollo and Artemis) achieved the status of the country's most important gods as the Lycian civilization became increasingly Greek in character.

Bryce (1986, *CANE* 2: 1161–72); Keen (1998); Roosevelt (*AANE*: 907–13).

55

The ten kingdoms of 1st millennium BC Cyprus

(The Esarhaddon prism referred to below is an inscription of the Assyrian king Esarhaddon, dated to 673/2 BC and providing a list of the ten known M1 kingdoms of Cyprus.)

Amathus The first substantial evidence for settlement here dates to late C10 BC. By C8, a significant Phoenician presence is reflected in strong Phoenician influence on the city's material culture and religion. Along with the rest of Cyprus, Amathus was subject to Persia for much of C5 and C4. In 498, it refused the request of Onesilus, king of Salamis, to join the other Cypriot cities in the anti-Persian Ionian revolt. The last of the kings of Amathus, Androcles, fought on the side of Alexander the Great in his siege of Tyre in 332. The city continued to prosper through the Hellenistic, Roman and Byzantine periods until its abandonment in C7 AD at the time of the first Arab invasions.

Evidence provided by tombs indicates that settlement on the site of ***Chytroi*** (Kythrea) extends back at least to the last century of M2. But it is first attested in written records on the Esarhaddon prism (there called Kitrusi), and is later mentioned by a number of Classical writers, from C4 century BC onwards. The city apparently flourished during the Hellenistic, Roman and Byzantine periods, becoming a bishopric in the last of these. It was abandoned when sacked by the Arabs in AD 912.

In early M1 BC, Phoenicians from Tyre had arrived on the site of ***Citium***, with merchants and traders paving the way for permanent settlers to establish a colony there. But despite a significant Phoenician presence in the city, Citium's population was predominantly Greek, the city's culture reflecting a blend of both Phoenician and Greek elements. Up until the Ionian revolt, Citium may have been ruled by Greek kings, probably under the last of whom Citium participated in the revolt. But following Persia's crushing victory, Phoenicians gained dominance in Citium, with Persian support. In C5 and C4, the city and kingdom were ruled by a line of Phoenician kings. Their powerful navy enabled them to play a significant role in the contests between Greeks and Persians in the eastern Mediterranean as well as providing a major source of the city's wealth. In 312 BC, the Phoenician dynasty abruptly ended when Citium fell to Ptolemy I Soter. In AD 50, Citium became part of the Roman provincial system.

Curium's history of occupation extends from the Late Bronze Age through the Byzantine period, though it is not clearly attested in written records until mid M1 BC. When Onesilus, king of Salamis, stirred other Cypriot principalities to enter the Ionian revolt against Persia in 499, Curium's king Stasanor first joined the rebels, but subsequently defected to Persia and contributed significantly to the Persians' victory. The kingdom's last known ruler Pasicrates joined Alexander the Great against the Persians in Alexander's siege of Tyre (332). During the Hellenistic and Roman periods, Curium seems to have prospered, until an earthquake destroyed much of it in AD 365.

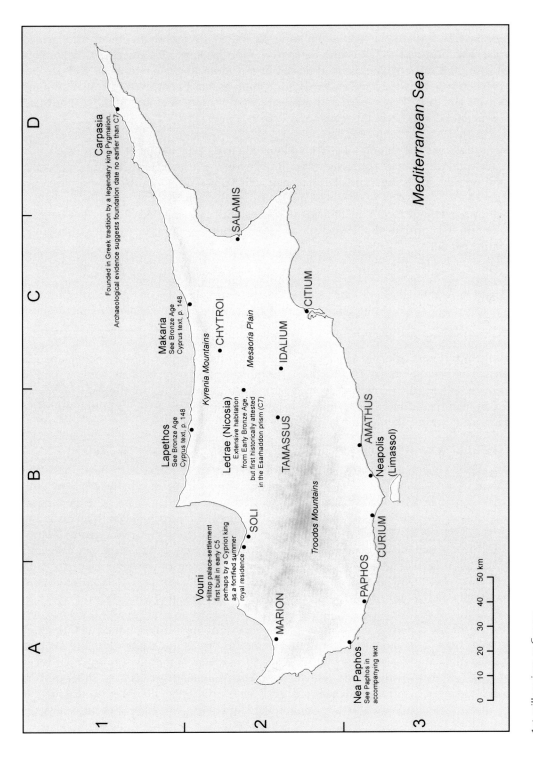

Carpasia
Founded in Greek tradition by a legendary king Pygmalion.
Archaeological evidence suggests foundation date no earlier than C7

Makaria
See Bronze Age
Cyprus text, p. 148

Lapethos
See Bronze Age
Cyprus text, p. 148

Kyrenia Mountains

CHYTROI

SALAMIS

CITIUM

IDALIUM

Mesaoria Plain

Ledrae (Nicosia)
Extensive habitation
from Early Bronze Age,
but first historically attested
in the Esarhaddon prism (C7)

TAMASSUS

AMATHUS

**Neapolis
(Limassol)**

Troodos Mountains

SOLI

Vouni
Hilltop palace-settlement
first built in early C5
perhaps by a Cypriot king
as a fortified summer
royal residence

MARION

PAPHOS

CURIUM

Nea Paphos
See Paphos in
accompanying text

Mediterranean Sea

| 0 | 10 | 20 | 30 | 40 | 50 km |

1st millennium BC Cyprus

The history of **Idalium**, first attested in written records on the Esarhaddon prism, extends from the end of the Late Bronze Age (c. 1200) to the early Roman period (C1 AD). Authority in the city appears to have been shared between a line of kings and a citizen-body (a unique arrangement on Cyprus). The former issued their own coins from shortly before 500. About 470, Idalium was captured by a joint force of Persians and troops from Citium, the latter ruled by a Phoenician dynasty. Henceforth, Idalium came under Citium's control, but it continued to flourish through the Hellenistic and early Roman periods. It was particularly noted for its cult of the Magna Mater goddess, syncretized with Greek Aphrodite and Roman Venus.

Marion, a prosperous and important city-kingdom, due to its exploitation of local copper mines and its trade with Athens, is first clearly attested in 449 when the Athenian general Cimon liberated it from the Persians, replacing its pro-Persian ruler with a pro-Greek one. The city was destroyed by Ptolemy I Soter in 312 BC, and its inhabitants transported to Paphos, on Cyprus' south-western coast. But it was refounded c. 270 by Ptolemy II Philadelphus and renamed after his wife (and sister) Arsinoe. The city prospered in Hellenistic and Roman times, and was the seat of a bishopric in the Byzantine period.

Paphos at its peak was one of the largest and wealthiest of the Cypriot city-kingdoms. Its intermixture of Cypriot, Aegean and Levantine cultural elements produced thriving craft industries with the manufacture of a range of fine ceramic ware, ivories and jewellery. Originally known simply as Paphos, it was renamed Palaipaphos ('Old Paphos') from late C4 BC onwards, to distinguish it from the harbour town Nea Paphos ('New Paphos'), founded c. 320 by Paphos' last king Nicocles, 16 km to the north-west. The 'old city' went into decline when a large part of its population was transferred to the new city, and it lost its status as the capital of the kingdom of Paphos in 294, when the Ptolemies conquered Cyprus and abolished its local monarchies. Nevertheless, Old Paphos remained an important centre of the worship of Aphrodite. In Greek mythology, Aphrodite first stepped ashore at Paphos after her birth from the sea-foam.

During the first half of M1, **Salamis** became the most important city and kingdom on Cyprus. Indeed, its C6 king Euelthon claimed to exercise sway over the entire island. In the first years of C5, his grandson Onesilus united all the cities and kingdoms under his leadership (except Amathus) against the Persians, an enterprise which ended with his defeat and death in a battle with the Persians outside Salamis in 498. The best known of all the city's kings was the pro-Greek Evagoras I, who became ruler of the city in 411, and used his links with Athens to promote Greek culture throughout Cyprus. He also maintained good relations with Persia for a time, but subsequently came into conflict with the Persian king Artaxerxes II until forced to make peace with him. Henceforth, he ruled as Persia's subject until his assassination in 374/3. In the Hellenistic period, Salamis remained a prosperous city, and in the early Byzantine period, it became the seat of a bishopric.

Settlement on the site of **Soli** probably began in the Late Bronze Age and continued until the Arab conquests in C7 AD. Throughout its history, much of the city's wealth was derived from the copper mines located in the mountains to its south. According to Plutarch, the city was originally called Aipeia, until C6 when the Athenian statesman Solon visited it and urged its king Philocyprus to shift it closer to the sea. Solon allegedly took charge of the re-establishment of the city, making it so attractive that new settlers flocked to it; out of gratitude for Solon's services, Philocyprus renamed the city after him. In historical records, the city is first significantly attested at the beginning of C5

BC, when its king Aristocyprus joined other local rulers under the hegemony of Onesilus, king of Salamis, in the abortive rebellion against Persia. Both Onesilus and Aristocyprus were killed in the conflict. Soli itself fell to the Persians after a five-month siege.

Tamassus is first attested in the Esarhaddon inscription, though settlement on the site dates back at least to the Middle Bronze Age. Our Greek sources inform us that in C4 BC it was sold for fifty talents by its ruler Pasicyprus to Pumiathon, king of Citium, but later taken from Pumiathon by Alexander the Great and handed over to Salamis' king Pnytagoras. The city appears to have prospered through the various phases of its existence, its wealth probably due largely to its exploitation of the nearby copper mines. Prior to the Byzantine era, when it became a bishopric, Tamassus was an important centre for the worship of Apollo and the Mother of the Gods. Among the very few excavated remains of the city are a temple dedicated to Aphrodite, part of the city's fortifications, installations for the production of copper, and two well-preserved 'royal built tombs' dating to the Archaic period.

For the individual kingdoms, see relevant entries in *PECS*, *OEANE* and *PPAWA*.

Part VIII

Other Near Eastern peoples and kingdoms of the 1st millennium BC

56

The Medes

The Medes were an Indo-European-speaking people whose homeland lay in western Iran. Our written information about this people, who have left us no texts of their own, comes from foreign sources, primarily the records of Assyrian and Babylonian kings and the *Histories* of the Greek historian Herodotus. Assyrian records, the earliest of the sources, report on military campaigns conducted into Media between C9 and C7 by Shalmaneser III, Tiglath-pileser III, Sargon II and Esarhaddon. However, most of what we know, or supposedly know, about the Medes comes from Herodotus' account of them, in a section of his *Histories* commonly referred to as the *Medikos Logos* (*Histories* 1.95–106). According to Herodotus, the Medes were originally independent tribal groups, who were united into a single kingdom (apparently in C7) by a certain Deioces. But Deioces' grandson Cyaxares is generally regarded as the true founder of the Median empire. Coming to the throne c. 625, Cyaxares paved the way for this empire by forming an alliance with the Babylonian king Nabopolassar, with the object of destroying the Assyrian empire. The mission was successfully accomplished in the last years of C7.

Cyaxares subsequently expanded his territories westwards across northern Mesopotamia, through the former Assyrian heartland, into north-central Anatolia. This brought him into conflict with the Lydian king Alyattes, who held sway over much of western Anatolia. An inconclusive battle fought between the two kings near the Halys river – the so-called 'battle of the eclipse' – resulted in their concluding a peace agreement, to the effect that the Halys would henceforth define the border between their kingdoms. Cyaxares was succeeded by his son Astyages, who subjected his kingdom to thirty-five years of despotic rule before he was overthrown by his 'grandson' Cyrus II (there are doubts about the alleged family link). Cyrus went on to found the Persian empire. Medes came to play an important role in the cultural and administrative activities of this empire, and in the defence of the realm.

This commonly accepted reconstruction of Median history, much of which comes from Herodotus, has recently been questioned by a number of Near Eastern scholars, who doubt or dismiss the historical validity of a 'Median empire'. They emphasize the lack of any archaeological evidence for Herodotus' account, and a perceived lack of consistency between it and contemporary treatments of the Medes in Assyrian and Neo-Babylonian sources. It has recently been suggested that after plundering and destroying the Assyrian cities, the Medians returned home, leaving to their Babylonian partners the role of reconstruction and political continuity.

Lanfranchi *et al.* (2003); *PPAWA* (461–4).

Media Atropatene

This was the name of a region located in the rugged mountainous zone south-west of the Caspian Sea. It was so called after Atropates, who governed the region between 328 and 323 BC, in the period immediately following the destruction of the Achaemenid empire by Alexander the Great. During the Seleucid empire, the country remained independent of Seleucid rule under a line of local kings.

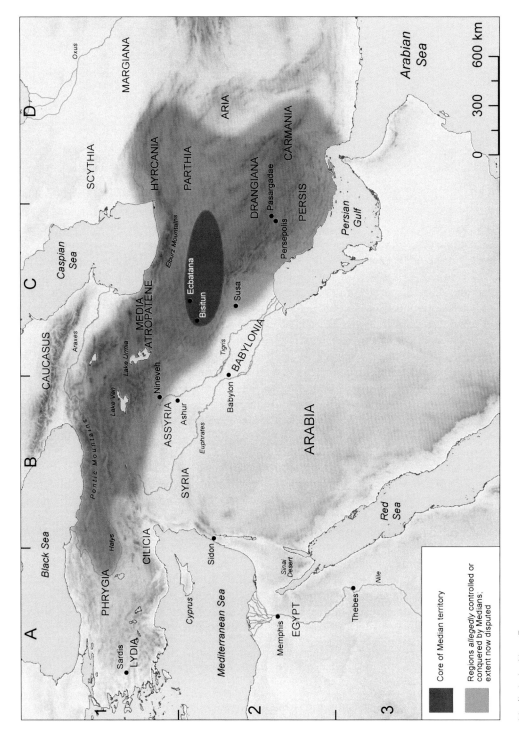

Media in its Near Eastern context

57

The Neo-Babylonian empire

In the year 626, a man called Nabopolassar seized the throne of Babylon, and became the founder of a new royal dynasty. He made an alliance with the Median king Cyaxares for the purpose of destroying the Assyrian empire. This objective was finally achieved; in 612, the Assyrian empire was effectively terminated when Babylonian and Median forces demolished its capital Nineveh (though it was to be another two years before the enemy captured and sacked Harran, the final refuge of Assyria's last king, Ashur-uballit II). The Neo-Babylonian empire, which had its genesis in Nabopolassar's reign, reached its height in the reign of his son and successor Nebuchadnezzar II, who extended Babylonian power westwards across the Euphrates to the lands in the Syrian and Palestinian regions formerly subject to Assyria and Egypt. Jerusalem was captured in 597 and after an uprising there totally destroyed in 586. The deportation of its population to Babylonia marked the beginning of the Jewish exile. Sidon and Tyre on the Levantine coast were among other cities that fell to Nebuchadnezzar. The Babylonians also extended their military operations to south-eastern Anatolia, where Nebuchadnezzar and his second successor Neriglissar campaigned in the countries called Pirindu (formerly Hilakku) and Hume (formerly Adanawa/Hiyawa/Que); but there is no clear evidence that Babylon ever established lasting control over these regions.

According to biblical sources, Nebu-chadnezzar also campaigned in Egypt. After Nebuchadnezzar's death, the empire remained relatively stable for some years, despite a series of power struggles for the royal succession. But in 539, when its throne was occupied by Nabonidus (who had extended his kingdom's frontiers into northern Arabia and resided there for ten years, in the oasis-city Tayma (Taima)), it fell to the Persian king Cyrus II. It remained under Persian sovereignty until Alexander's conquest of the Persian empire and his triumphal entry into Babylon in 331.

Leick (2003: 61–9); Arnold (2004: 87–105); Baker (*AANE*: 914–30); Van De Mieroop (*GEAW*: 70–97, 2016: 294–307)

Figure 57.1 Reconstruction of the Ishtar Gate, Babylon, built by King Nebuchadnezzar c. 575 BC. Photo courtesy of bpk/Vorderasiatisches Museum, SMB/Olaf M.Teßmer.

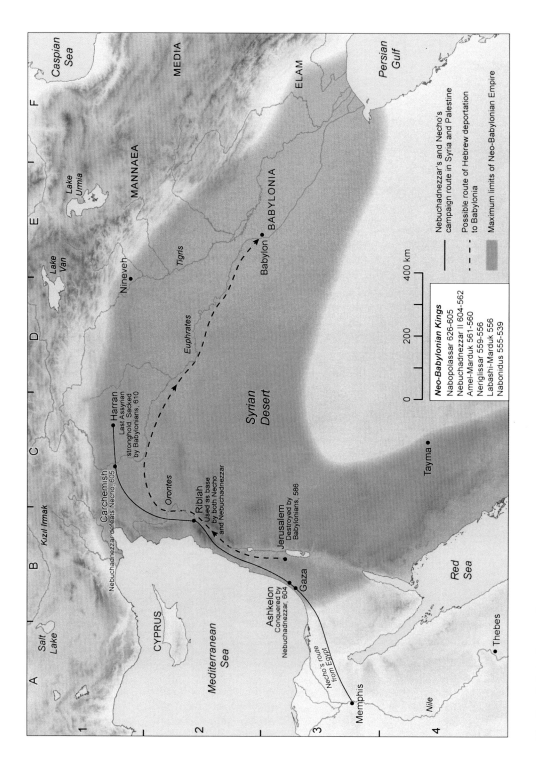

The Neo-Babylonian empire

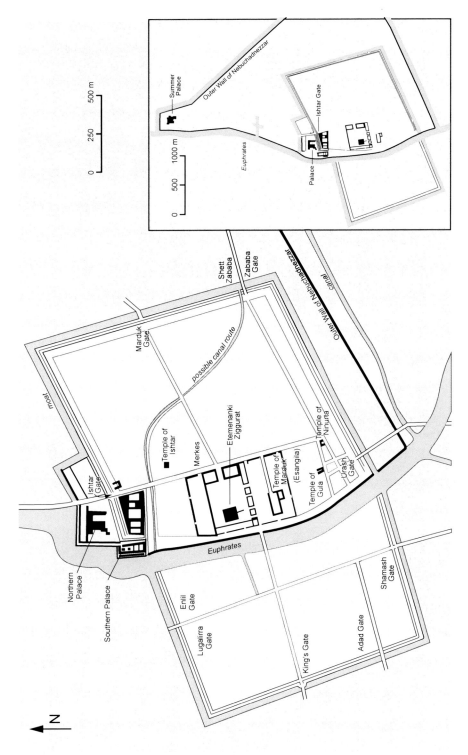

Babylon in the age of Nebuchadnezzar (after Finkel and Seymour 2008: 40)

58

The Arabs

The name *Arabia*, first attested in Herodotus, applies to a large, arid and semi-arid region extending southwards from the Syrian Desert into the Arabian peninsula. High mountains on the peninsula's western and southern sides fringe an interior plateau – mainly desert but once well watered, as indicated by its numerous ancient wadi systems. The southern part of the region was called Arabia Felix in Roman times. Further north lay the much larger Arabia Deserta. A third component of Arabia, as defined in Classical sources, was Arabia Petraea, which extended north-westwards from the peninsula of Sinai to what is now Jordan, and included the Nabataean kingdom of which Petra was the original capital. Politically and culturally, Arabia was a diverse region. But the inhabitants of many parts of it engaged in the pursuit of widespread and highly profitable international trading enterprises. Egypt, Mesopotamia, Iran, and the Indus valley were among the lands of the Near Eastern world and its neighbours with which Arabian merchants traded, by both land and sea. The land enterprises were conducted by caravaneers, using important centres like Dedan and Tayma in north-western Arabia as staging posts along their routes. Incense and spices accounted for much of the wealth they derived from their trading activities.

The name 'Arab' first appears in the annals of the Neo-Assyrian king Shalmaneser III, who reports that Gindibu the Arab joined the coalition of anti-Assyrian states that confronted him at Qarqar on the Orontes in 853. Gindibu contributed a thousand camels to the alliance. In the following two centuries, Assyrian kings had contacts and were involved in conflicts with a number of peoples called Arabs during their western campaigns. Around 740, Tiglath-pileser III included a woman called Zabibe, 'Queen of the Arabs', among his tributaries west of the Euphrates. Attempts to tap into the wealth generated by the Arabs' profitable incense trade may well have been a prime motive behind Assyrian interest in these peoples. Arab groups were almost certainly participants in the massive deportation and resettlement programmes carried out by Tiglath-pileser's successor-but-one, Sargon II, shortly after his accession. It is most likely that Arabs were part of the resettlement programmes throughout the Assyrian empire, as Assyrian kings sought to integrate them within the social and administrative structure of the empire. In the following century, the Assyrian king Esarhaddon's conquest of Egypt was facilitated by the provision of camels to him by Arabs in the Sinai region.

Until the early centuries of M1 AD, 'Arab' appears not to have had any specific ethnic significance. It simply designated groups of pastoralists and itinerant merchants, located in various regions in the Syrian desert, in the Sinai, in Jordan, in Arabia and along the banks of the Euphrates, who belonged to tribes and had a nomadic or oasis-settlement lifestyle. We know the names of some of their tribal groups at this time primarily from biblical and Assyrian sources. Though relationships between the Assyrians and these groups were sometimes hostile, when they joined enemy-alliances or rebellions, or plundered cultivated lands under Assyrian authority, they were at other times peaceful and cooperative, as illustrated by the Sinai Arabs' support of Esarhaddon's Egyptian campaign. Undoubtedly

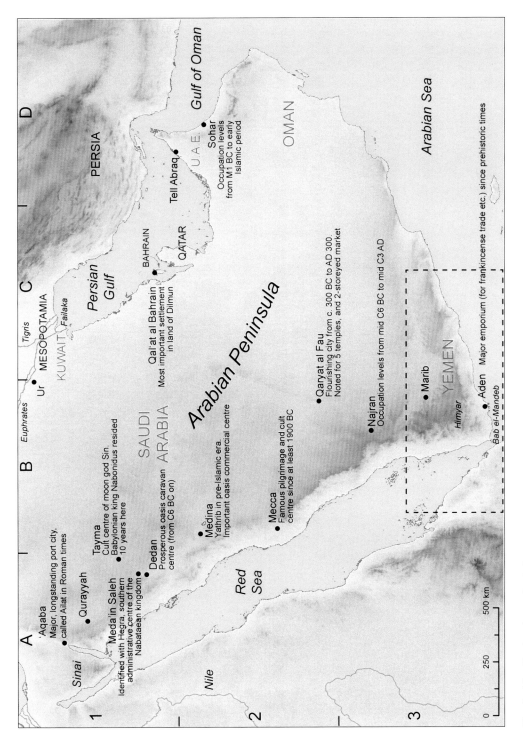

The Arabian Peninsula: ancient sites

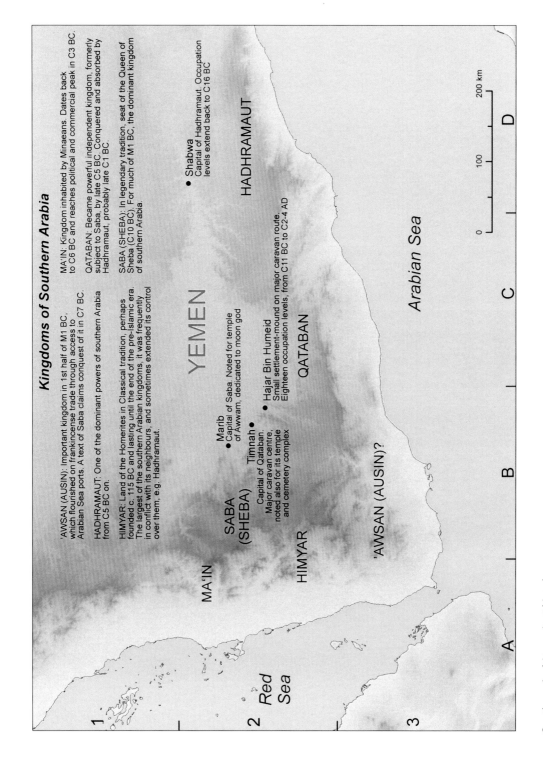

Kingdoms of Southern Arabia

'AWSAN (AUSIN): important kingdom in 1st half of M1 BC, which flourished on frankincense trade through access to Arabian Sea ports. A text of Saba claims conquest of it in C7 BC.

HADHRAMAUT: One of the dominant powers of southern Arabia from C5 BC on.

HIMYAR: Land of the Homerites in Classical tradition, perhaps founded c. 115 BC and lasting until the end of the pre-Islamic era. The largest of the southern Arabian kingdoms, it was frequently in conflict with its neighbours, and sometimes extended its control over them, e.g. Hadhramaut.

MA'IN: Kingdom inhabited by Minaeans. Dates back to C6 BC and reaches political and commercial peak in C3 BC.

QATABAN: Became powerful independent kingdom, formerly subject to Saba, by late C5 BC. Conquered and absorbed by Hadhramaut, probably late C1 BC.

SABA (SHEBA): In legendary tradition, seat of the Queen of Sheba (C10 BC). For much of M1 BC, the dominant kingdom of southern Arabia.

Southern Arabia: ancient kingdoms

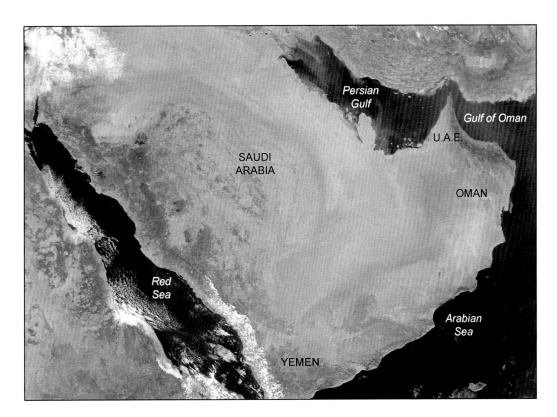

The Arabian Peninsula today (NASA satellite image)

there was a strong commercial dimension in the dealings between Assyrian kings and Arab groups; the latter must have been promised a significant degree of Assyrian protection in their commercial enterprises, in exchange for a substantial share of the profits with their overlord.

In Arabia, the term 'Arab' is first attested in C2 BC inscriptions discovered in Yemen, but was apparently not used as an ethic self-designation until C4 AD. The emergence of a specific Arab identity was associated with the use of a specific Semitic language, 'Arabic', which developed in Arabia and spread from there into various parts of western Asia and north Africa. A unifying culture developed along with the language, and from that 'Arab' came to be used as an ethno-cultural term. A high degree of literacy was characteristic of the societies of western Arabia, as attested by the tens of thousands of inscriptions and graffiti, dating from mid M1 BC onwards, that have turned up in the region. The language of the inscriptions, which is written in an alphabetic script, belongs to a north-west Semitic language group.

During M1 BC, six kingdoms emerged in south-western Arabia, in the region of modern Yemen. The earliest and most notable was Saba, better known by the name Sheba, frequently attested in biblical sources and famous in tradition for its legendary ruler, the Queen of Sheba. Saba was long dominant in southern Arabia, until its decline in C4 BC when it was eclipsed by the kingdoms of Qataban, Hadhramaut, and Ma'in. It regained its dominance with the rise of Himyar in late C2 BC, and subsequently formed with Himyar the kingdom of Saba and Dhu-Raydan. 'Awsan, which flourished in the first half of M1 BC, was another important kingdom of the region.

Relevant articles in *CANE* (2: 1335–69); *OEANE* (1: 159–69).

59
Armenia

The mountainous region called Armenia extended over a large part of eastern Anatolia. In the west, it bordered upon Cappadocia, and from there stretched eastwards, passing north of Syria and Mesopotamia, to the the lands around Lake Van, and thenceforth to the Araxes river valley where it bordered upon Media Atropatene (which included the territory of modern Azerbaijan). A number of kingdoms emerged in the region, or imposed their authority upon it, during the historical period. The earliest significant one was the Iron Age kingdom of Urartu, whose core territories radiated out from Lake Van. Armenia was subsequently incorporated into the Persian empire and became a client state of Alexander the Great. After Alexander's death, it later fell within the administrative orbit of the Seleucid dynasty.

As the Seleucid empire declined in C2 BC, Armenia came under the influence of the emerging Parthian empire. Though Parthia's rulers lacked the resources to impose direct control over it, many of them exercised an interventionist role there by propping up or disposing of local rulers. Yet sometimes Armenia's rulers strongly asserted their independence. The most notable was Tigranes II, who came to power with the support of Parthia c. 100 BC, and then in alliance with his father-in-law Mithridates VI, king of Pontus, embarked on a programme of military expansion which resulted in his occupation of Cappadocia, the north-western end of Mesopotamia, Syria and eastern Cilicia. His Syrian enterprise helped finish off the Seleucid dynasty, and inadvertently pave the way for Pompey the Great's creation of the Roman province of Syria in 64 BC. From this time on, Rome sought to extend its influence into and over Armenia, inevitably generating disputes and conflicts with Parthia for control of the region. The local rulers, or royal pretenders, often skilfully exploited the contest for their own advantage. Armenia's sympathies and affinities probably lay more with Parthia than with Rome, but its rulers were flexible in their loyalties, depending on where they felt their best interests lay. Not that they always had a say in this. Military intervention was sometimes used by one or other of the great powers to place a king of their liking upon Armenia's throne, by deposing the appointee or protégé of the other.

During the Roman period, a distinction was drawn between a Greater and Lesser Armenia. The former included all Armenian territories east of the upper Euphrates, the latter the Armenian territories north of the river, in the region inland from the south-eastern shores of the Black Sea. The issue of control over Greater Armenia was resolved, temporarily, by the Roman emperor Trajan, who annexed the region in AD 114. But in the following centuries, the Armenian question resurfaced on a number of occasions, particularly during the period of the Sasanian empire, which emerged after the overthrow of the last Parthian king in AD 224. Lesser Armenia had, from

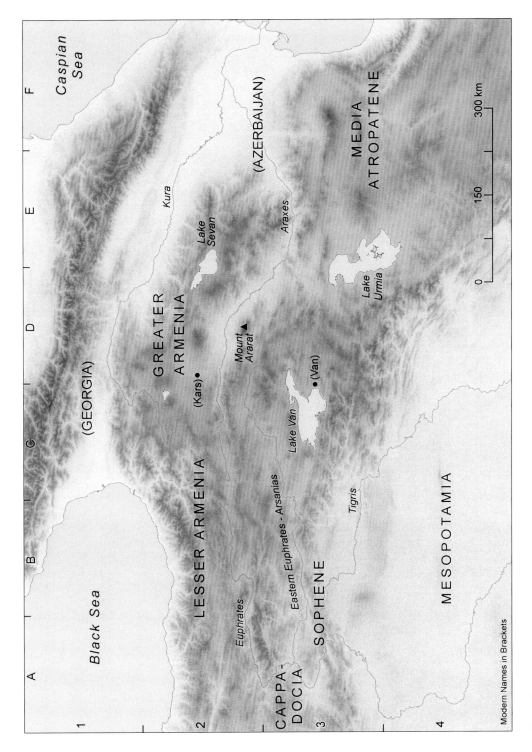

Armenia

Pompey's time, a large number of short-lived rulers – some of local origin, others the rulers of nearby states who were granted sovereignty over it by Rome – until the emperor Vespasian (AD 69–79) incorporated the region into the province of Cappadocia.

Drower *et al.* (*OCD*: 170–1); Garsoïn (*OEANE* 1: 202–7).

60

The Persian (Achaemenid) empire

In mid C6 BC a new power arose in south-western Iran, in the region of Parsa (modern Fars). Here, a man called Cyrus (II), later known as Cyrus the Great, founded an empire which lasted until 330 BC. At its peak, this first Persian empire extended from the western frontiers of India through Afghanistan, Iran, across Mesopotamia and Syria to Egypt, and westwards to Anatolia's Aegean coast. It is commonly called the Achaemenid empire, after Achaemenes, an alleged ancestor of the royal line. Cyrus took the first steps towards its creation when he united the separate Persian tribes and overthrew the Persians' despotic overlord Astyages, king of Media. Strabo claims that he established his new capital Pasargadae on the site of his victory over Astyages. Media was now incorporated into the fledgling Persian empire. Henceforth the Medes were to play an important role within it, and were acknowledged as its second most important ethnic group.

The conquest of Media paved the way for Cyrus' conquests in the regions which lay north, including perhaps the last vestiges of the former kingdom of Urartu. Subsequently, Cyrus marched westwards, into Anatolia, where he defeated the Lydian king Croesus and incorporated the territories where he held sway, including the Ionian Greek cities along the Aegean coast, into his empire. Croesus' capital Sardis became the western headquarters of the Persian administration. Then Cyrus turned his attention upon the Neo-Babylonian kingdom, now weak and divided under its current ruler Nabonidus. Babylon itself fell without a battle (539). In the following year, according to biblical sources, Cyrus issued a decree permitting the Jews to return to their homeland from their captivity in Babylonia.

The empire's subject territories east of Iran were acquired probably during a campaign which Cyrus conducted in these regions after his conquest of Babylonia. He was subsequently killed while fighting rebel forces on the eastern frontiers. But his programme of territorial expansion continued under his son and successor Cambyses (II) (530–522), who conquered Cyprus, invaded Egypt, defeated the pharaoh Psammetichus III in a battle outside Memphis, and incorporated the whole of his kingdom into the Persian empire. After a three-year stay in Egypt, Cambyses was recalled by news of a rebellion in his homeland. He died in Syria under suspicious circumstances during his homeward journey. From the resulting squabbles that arose over the royal succession, a man called Darius, formerly a commander in Cambyses' army, emerged triumphant, occupying the throne as Darius I. The first year of his reign was marked by a number of uprisings, which he ruthlessly put down, as recorded in his famous Bisitun inscription. Then he set his sights on expanding further his empire. Indeed, the Persian realm reached its greatest extent during his reign, with new campaigns in the east, the conquest of parts of northern India, and the acquisition of the region Hindush or Sind along the banks of the Indus. He now prepared to extend his empire westwards into Europe. But while he managed to establish a Persian presence

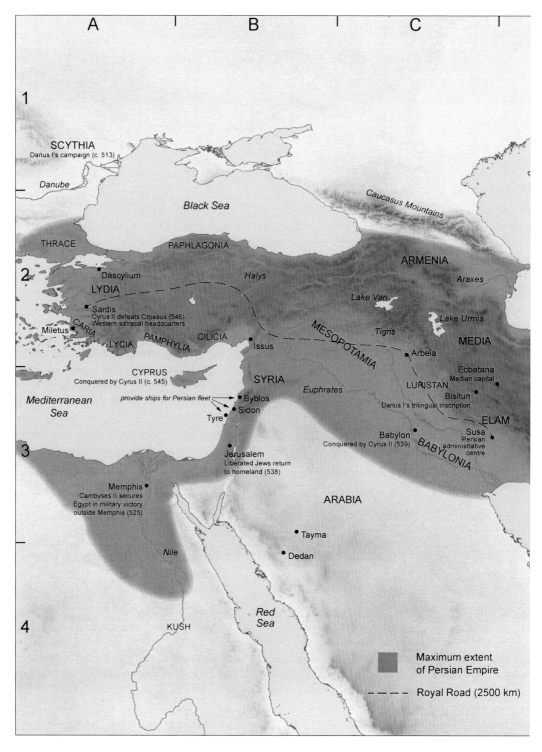

The Achaemenid empire at the end of the 6th cent. BC

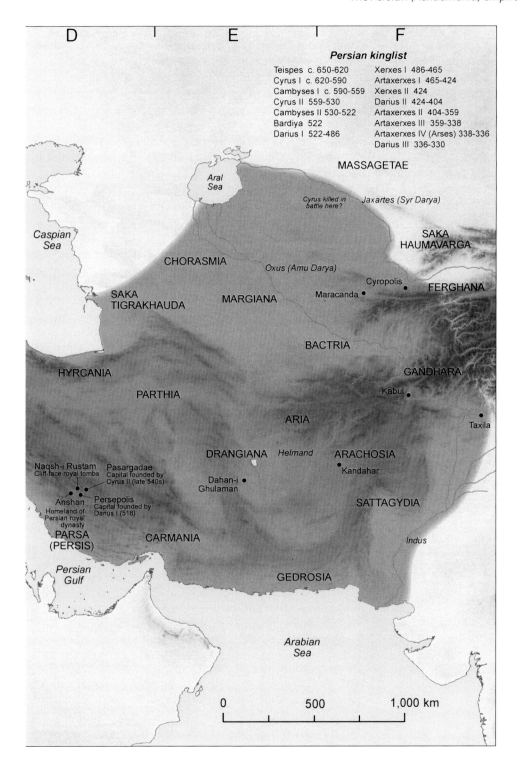

D   I   E   I   F

Persian kinglist

Teispes c. 650-620	Xerxes I 486-465
Cyrus I c. 620-590	Artaxerxes I 465-424
Cambyses I c. 590-559	Xerxes II 424
Cyrus II 559-530	Darius II 424-404
Cambyses II 530-522	Artaxerxes II 404-359
Bardiya 522	Artaxerxes III 359-338
Darius I 522-486	Artaxerxes IV (Arses) 338-336
	Darius III 336-330

MASSAGETAE

Aral Sea

Cyrus killed in battle here?   *Jaxartes (Syr Darya)*

Caspian Sea

SAKA HAUMAVARGA

CHORASMIA   *Oxus (Amu Darya)*

Cyropolis •

SAKA TIGRAKHAUDA   MARGIANA   Maracanda •   FERGHANA

BACTRIA

HYRCANIA   GANDHARA

PARTHIA   Kabul •

ARIA   Taxila •

DRANGIANA   *Helmand*   ARACHOSIA

Naqsh-i Rustam
Cliff-face royal tombs   Pasargadae
Capital founded by
Cyrus II (late 540s)   Kandahar •

Dahan-i •
Ghulaman

Anshan   Persepolis
Homeland of   Capital founded by
Persian royal   Darius I (518)
dynasty   SATTAGYDIA

PARSA
(PERSIS)   CARMANIA   *Indus*

Persian Gulf

GEDROSIA

Arabian Sea

0   500   1,000 km

in Thrace and Macedonia and the northern Aegean, his attempts, and those of his son and successor Xerxes, to impose Persian sovereignty over the Greek mainland states (between 490 and 480) ended in failure. After his withdrawal from the Greek mainland, Xerxes reigned another fifteen years, before being assassinated in a palace conspiracy in 465. In the subsequent squabbles over the royal succession, his son Artaxerxes I emerged the winner. When Artaxerxes died after a forty-year reign, the contests for the throne broke out afresh. They were in fact to be a feature of every succession until the empire's fall.

Despite royal coups and palace conspiracies, the Achaemenid empire remained a relatively stable and efficient organization until Alexander the Great ended it in 330 after defeating its last king Darius III. One of its most distinctive features was its division, by Darius I, into twenty provinces, called satrapies, governed by satraps who were often rulers of local origin. Communications between various parts of the empire were facilitated by the development of a network of major roads, the most famous of which was the 'Royal Road' linking Susa with Sardis. To help ensure the empire's stability, Darius I created a powerful standing army of professional soldiers. Its backbone was an elite force of Persians and Medes known as the Ten Thousand Immortals. For their operations by sea, the Persians had at their disposal a large navy consisting initially of ships provided by Phoenician cities along the Syro-Palestinian seaboard. The policy of Darius and his successors of employing craftsmen and artists from every part of the empire for their public works gave a rich, eclectic, cosmopolitan character to Persian material culture, to an extent unparalleled in any earlier or contemporary civilization.

Brosius (2006); Kuhrt (2007); Shahbazi (*OHIH*: 120–41); Henkelman and Khatchadourian (*AANE*: 931–83).

Persepolis

Figure 60.1 'Gate of All Nations', Persepolis. Photo by Trevor Bryce.

Persepolis was founded by Darius I to replace Pasargadae as the Persian royal capital. It became the new administrative centre of the empire, and the place where coronations, royal burials and other major ceremonies and festivals were held. The city's most distinctive feature is its great stone terrace known as the Takht (= 'throne' in Persian). On it were a number of monumental buildings, constructed by Darius and his successors. Entry was via the so-called All Nations Gate, built by Darius' son and successor Xerxes and guarded by two pairs of colossal stone bulls, one pair with wings and human heads. Columned halls and porticoes were prominent architectural features of the complex. Its most notable buildings include the so-called Hall of 100 Columns (the throne-room?), the palaces of Darius and Xerxes, the so-called harem of Xerxes, and the Apadana, a great square Audience Hall.

Persepolis was looted and destroyed by Alexander in 330. He reportedly carried off 120,000 talents of gold and silver from its treasury.

Stronach and Codella (*OEANE* 4: 273–7); *PPAWA* (538–43).

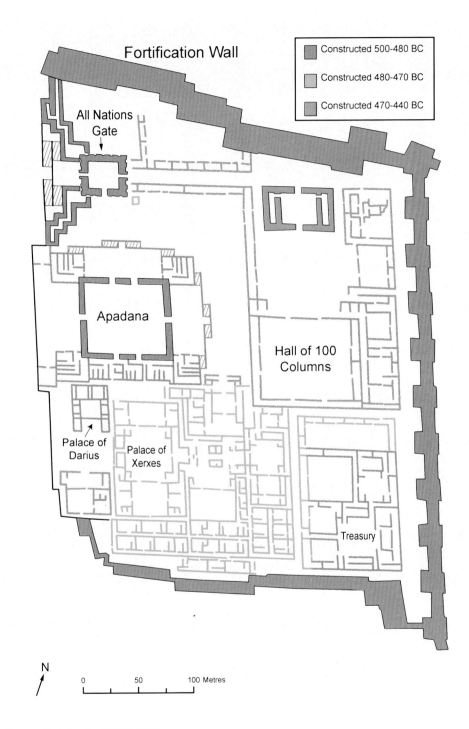

Persepolis (after Roaf 1996: 218)

61

The Persian invasions of the western Greek world

In 499 BC, a number of the Ionian Greek states in Asia Minor rebelled against Persian rule, with the support of Athens and the small state of Eretria on the island of Euboea. The rebellion was crushed by Darius I in 494, but it allegedly provided one of the prompts for Darius' naval invasion in 490 of the western Greek world, including the islands of the Cyclades and the Greek mainland. (This followed a Persian land and sea campaign to the west in 492, which resulted in the conquest of Thrace and Macedonia but was ended prematurely because of several major setbacks, including the destruction of a large part of Persia's fleet in a storm off Cape Athos.) The Persian navy gained control of a number of Cycladic islands en route, captured Eretria through an act of treachery, and anchored in the bay of Marathon in preparation for an assault upon Athens, 35 km away. Here on the Marathon plain, the Persians were resoundingly defeated by forces from Athens and Plataea (the latter lay in Boeotia in central Greece), and forced to abandon their Greek campaign. But Darius' successor Xerxes (486–465) made plans for a fresh assault upon mainland Greece, preparing a massive force for a coordinated invasion by land and sea, under his personal command, via the coast of Thrace and Macedonia. The Persians advanced with little resistance through the Greek mainland until they reached Athens, which they captured and destroyed. But they were forced to abort their invasion when they suffered major defeats by the allied Greek forces in a sea battle in the strait of Salamis just off the coast of Attica (480) and a land battle the following year at Plataea.

Miles (2010: 119–22).

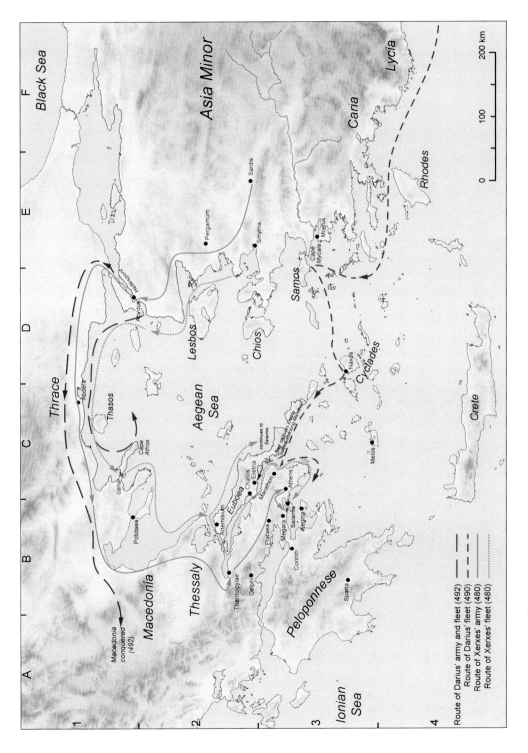

The Persian invasions of Greece under Darius I and Xerxes I (492–480)

62

Alexander the Great

In 334 BC, the young Macedonian king Alexander the Great landed his army on the north-west coast of Anatolia, the first step in his campaign to destroy the Persian empire. After paying homage at Troy to the heroes of the Trojan War, he marched 70 kms eastwards to the Granicus river where he engaged the forces of the Persian king Darius III. His decisive victory paved the way for his subsequent progress, with little resistance, along the western and south-western coast of Anatolia through Lycia, Pisidia and part of Pamphylia. From there he marched north to Gordium in Phrygia, and thence from Ancyra south-eastwards to the plains of eastern Cilicia through a pass in the Taurus mts. In Cilicia, he saved the city of Tarsus from destruction by the local Persian satrap before his next confrontation with Darius' forces, in November 333, near the town of Issus, just west of the Amanus range. Victorious once again, he marched along the Syrian coast, where he seized from Persian control the coastal Phoenician cities which provided the bulk of the Persian navy. Only the city of Tyre offered serious resistance, falling after a seven-month siege. Alexander then set his sights on the conquest of Egypt, entering it in November 332, and thereupon imposing his sovereignty upon it. Before leaving Egypt, he made a pilgrimage to an oasis in the Libyan desert called Siwah, where a famous sanctuary of the god Ammon, identified with Greek Zeus, was

Figure 62.1 The battle of Issus mosaic, Naples Museum. Photo courtesy of akg-images.

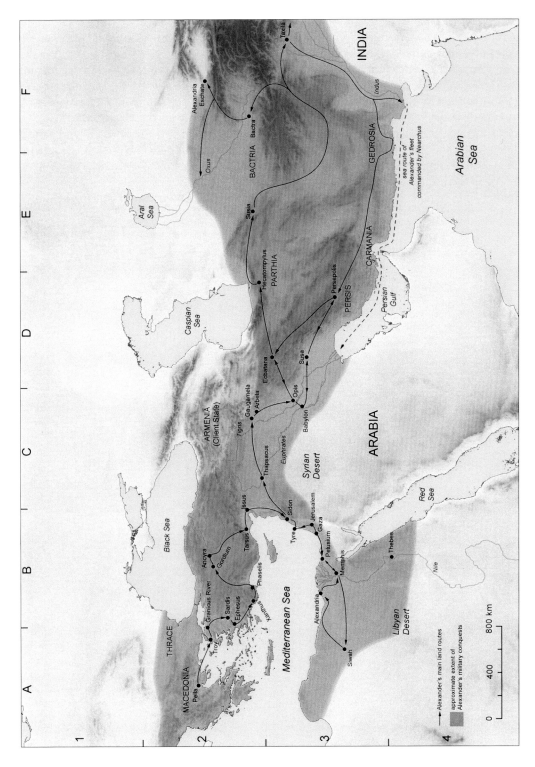

Alexander's 'empire'

located. Here he was hailed by the priests as the son of Zeus-Ammon. In the Delta he founded the city of Alexandria, the most important of a number of cities of this name established by him or in the wake of his conquests.

In the spring of 331, Alexander returned to Tyre. He paused there for a time before leading his forces to the Euphrates in preparation for his final showdown with Darius, near a village called Gaugamela, located in northern Mesopotamia just east of the Tigris (summer, 331). His decisive victory ended Darius' reign, and with it the Persian empire. Thereupon, the Macedonian marched eastwards through Iran, where he visited Susa and looted and burned the Persian royal capital Persepolis (330), and then through Afghanistan into north-western India (327) before the restiveness of his troops compelled him to turn back. He arrived in Babylon in 323, where he succumbed to a fever and died, at the age of thirty-two.

Sommer and Harrison (*GEAW*: 148–63); Miles (2010: 147–58); Venetis (*OHIH*: 142–52).

Part IX

The Hellenistic world

63

The Hellenistic age

'Hellenistic' is a term devised by a C19 scholar (J.G. Droysen) to refer to the post-Classical period of Greek civilization. This is generally identified as the period between Alexander's death in 323 and the defeat in 31 BC of the last Ptolemaic ruler, Cleopatra VII (along with her paramour and comrade-in-arms Mark Antony) by the Roman commander Octavian in the battle of Actium. The period is notable particularly for the rise of the great empires established by two of Alexander's Macedonian heirs, the Seleucid empire founded by Seleucus I and the Ptolemaic empire by Ptolemy I.

Hellenistic civilization is characterized by the spread of Greek culture through many parts of the eastern world, but also by a blend of Greek and non-Greek elements within it, as reflected in the art and architecture of many of the newly-built or rebuilt cities located across its rapidly expanding international trading network. Commerce and industry flourished. Scientific expeditions were despatched to all parts of the known world, and scientific institutions were set up in a number of cities, leading to significant advances in many fields of knowledge, from medicine to mathematics to astronomy. All this despite the fact that the Hellenistic world was frequently plunged into warfare between the competing Hellenistic states, notably the Seleucid and Ptolemaic empires, and sometimes by rival factions within them.

Ma (2013).

Alexander's heirs

Shortly after Alexander's death, a meeting was held in Babylon by most of Alexander's leading military commanders to determine how his empire would henceforth be ruled. Antipater, Alexander's chief representative in Europe, and Craterus, his highest-ranking military officer, were given joint command of Macedonia and the rest of mainland Greece. Perdiccas, another of Alexander's high-ranking officers, was appointed Chiliarch; this title literally meant 'Commander of a Thousand', but in effect it made its holder the regent of the whole empire. Other generals of the dead king were allocated rule over the regions organized as satrapies under the previous Persian administration: thus in the western half of Alexander's domains, Egypt went to Ptolemy, Antigonus got Greater Phrygia (along with Lycia and Pamphylia), Leonnatus was awarded Hellespontine Phrygia, Cappadocia and Paphlagonia were assigned to Eumenes, Lydia to Menander, Caria to Asander, Thrace to Lysimachus, and Syria to Laomedon. To begin with, these new arrangements appeared to have ensured a smooth transition of power. But before long, hostilities erupted between Perdiccas, who feared for the security of his position and sought to reinforce it with plots and intrigues, and his fellow-heirs Antipater, Craterus and Antigonus. Ptolemy was brought into the conflict when Perdiccas invaded Egypt. Here, the whole episode ended abruptly when Perdiccas' troops mutinied and assassinated him (321).

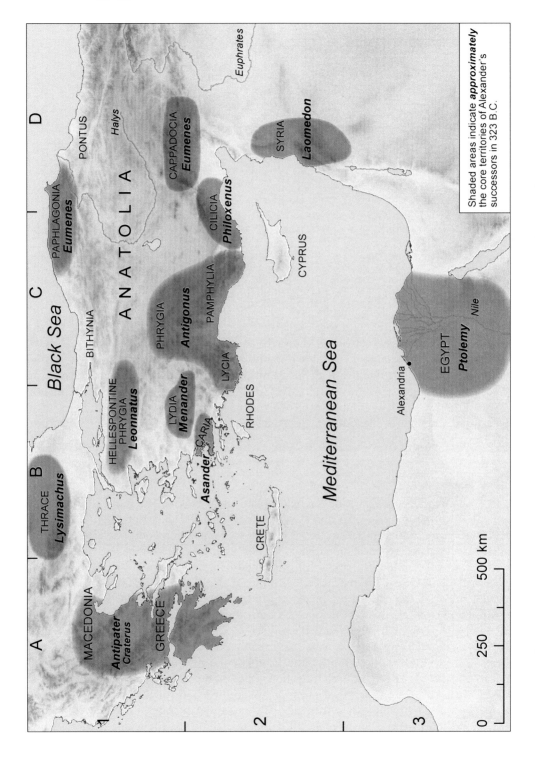

The evolution of the Hellenistic kingdoms, map 1: initial western allocations to Alexander's heirs (Babylon conference, 323)

Shaded areas indicate *approximately* the core territories of Alexander's successors in 323 B.C.

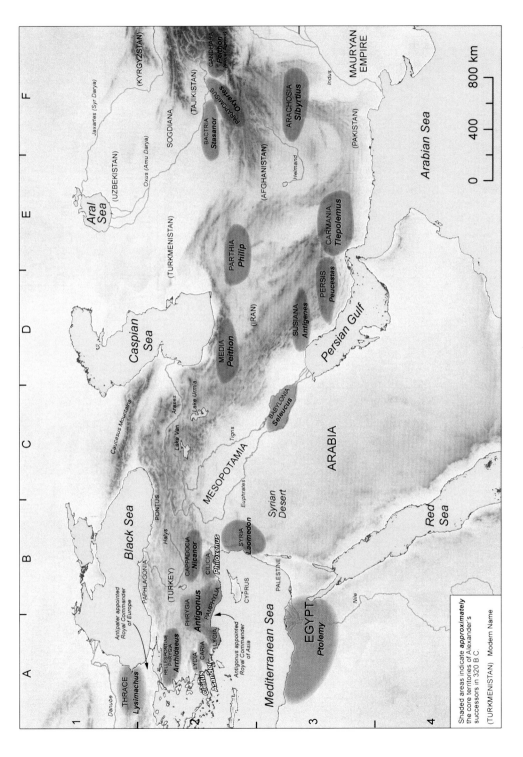

The evolution of the Hellenistic kingdoms, map 2: reallocations of Alexander's Near Eastern conquests (Triparadisus conference, 320)

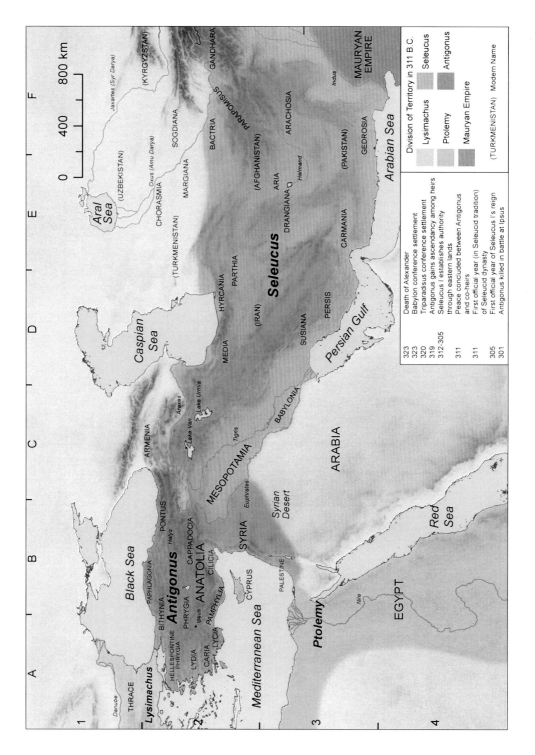

The evolution of the Hellenistic kingdoms, map 3: the main divisions of power in the Near East after the peace accord of 311

The following year, a second top-level meeting was held at a town called Triparadisus (probably located on the Orontes r.) in northern Syria. It resulted in a new agreement. Antipater became regent of the empire and confirmed as ruler of Macedonia (Craterus had been killed the previous year), Ptolemy was confirmed as ruler of Egypt, and Antigonus of Phrygia. A further outcome of the meeting was that Seleucus, one of Alexander's most steadfast comrades-in-arms, became governor of Babylonia. But after Antipater's death in 319, Antigonus provoked fresh tensions when he sought to establish his supremacy over all Alexander's conquered lands from Media in Iran through Mesopotamia to the western coast of Asia Minor. An anti-Antigonus alliance was formed, led by Cassander of Macedon, Lysimachus of Thrace and Ptolemy of Egypt, the last supported by Seleucus. In the conflicts that followed, Antigonus invaded Thrace, and sent his son Demetrius to Syria and Palestine to open up a second front. But the Antigonid cause received a major setback when Demetrius' forces were soundly defeated. Seleucus had made a substantial contribution to the victory, and was rewarded by Ptolemy with 1,000 troops with which he set out to win back control of Babylonia, seized by Antigonus, and beyond it the Iranian lands of Media and Susiana, then in the hands of rulers loyal to Antigonus.

This set the scene for further conflict with Antigonus. Seleucus could not call upon Ptolemy's support in these contests, for Ptolemy and his allies Lysimachus and Cassander had concluded a peace with Antigonus in 311, which acknowledged the latter as supreme ruler in Asia. That left Seleucus on his own to contest with Antigonus sovereignty over the lands east of the Euphrates. Several years of warfare followed, from which Seleucus finally emerged victorious, in 308. Antigonus returned to the west, where he still wielded enormous power and influence. The final reckoning was yet to come. This happened in 301, when the peace which Antigonus had made with his fellow-heirs in 311 ended abruptly, and Seleucus joined forces with Lysimachus, Cassander and Ptolemy for a final showdown with Antigonus near the small town of Ipsus in Phrygia. Antigonus was defeated and killed in the conflict.

In the wake of their victory, the allied leaders divided among themselves the territorial spoils of conquest. Lysimachus was granted a large chunk of Asia Minor, in addition to his Thracian domain, and Ptolemy was confirmed as ruler of Egypt. Seleucus was awarded Coele Syria and Phoenicia, in addition to Babylonia and the lands to the east in Iran and central Asia. Though he subsequently ceded Coele Syria and Phoenicia to Ptolemy (who was already occupying them, as he had on earlier occasions), he gained northern Syria for himself and was later to win possession of large areas of eastern and central Anatolia.

Shipley (2000); Austin (2006); Sommer and Harrison (*GEAW*: 164–73); Miles (2010: 158–79); Waterfield (2011).

Figure 63.1 Seleucus I 'the Conqueror'. Photo courtesy of akg-images/Andrea Baguzzi.

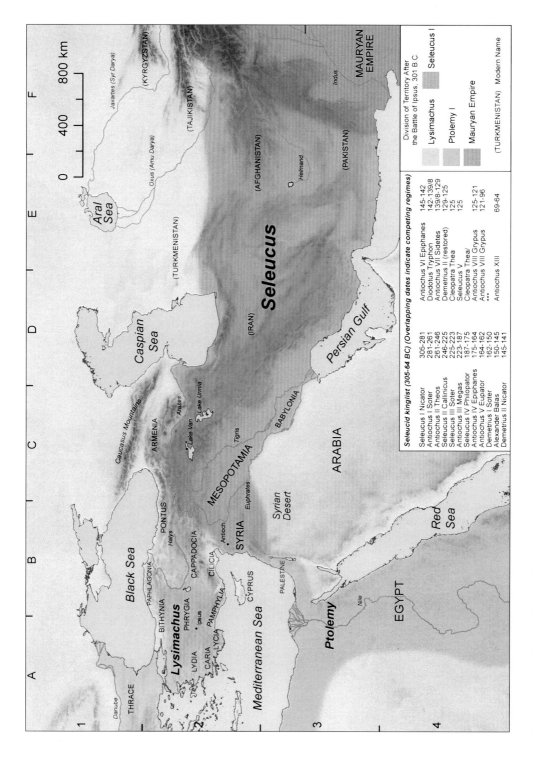

The evolution of the Hellenistic kingdoms, map 4: the territories of the three major rulers in the Near East after the battle of Ipsus, 301

64

The Seleucid empire

In 305, Seleucus laid the foundations of the Seleucid empire, following military campaigns which took his forces deep into central Asia. He was accorded the title *Nicator*, 'Conqueror', in recognition of his exploits. After declaring himself ruler of his newly created empire, he established a royal capital Seleuceia, on the banks of the Tigris. Initially, his empire extended eastwards from the Euphrates across Mesopotamia to the lands of Iran and central Asia. Subsequently, he won control also of large areas of eastern and central Anatolia, including southern Cappadocia and Commagene, and most importantly large parts of Syria. In Syria, he built a second Seleuceia – Seleuceia in Pieria – at the mouth of the Orontes. It was to serve as Syria's major port. Shortly after, 30 kms from the river's mouth, he built a city called Antioch, later to become one of the greatest metropolises of the ancient world. Seleuceia in Pieria and Antioch were but two of the many settlements Seleucus and his successors founded or refounded throughout their realm. Their new cities they populated with large numbers of Greek settlers, in line with their policy of spreading Greek culture and civilization throughout the lands subject to them. But Seleucid policy was also an inclusive one, which preserved and respected the customs and traditions of the local peoples, who were granted citizenship alongside Greeks in both the new and the old foundations. Non-Greek communities were to be recipients of benefactions and patronage from their Seleucid rulers, their religious rites, beliefs and sanctuaries protected and honoured.

Seleucus' claims of sovereignty over large tracts of the Near Eastern world did not go unchallenged. His control over Syria in particular was bitterly contested by his former mentor Ptolemy, founder of a line of rulers based in Egypt. The Ptolemies and the Seleucids frequently went to war over the territories that lay between them, notably in a series of six so-called Syrian Wars. Each side had its share of victories and defeats. On a number of occasions, Ptolemaic sovereignty extended to parts of Syria and Palestine, and sometimes as well to other parts of the eastern Mediterranean world, including Lycia and Caria on the Anatolian coast and the island of Cyprus.

Seleucid power reached its pinnacle in the reign of the sixth Seleucid king Antiochus III (223–187), known as 'the Great'. In a series of resoundingly successful military campaigns, Antiochus firmly reasserted Seleucid sovereignty over the lands of eastern Anatolia and central Asia, and established Seleucid rule over the whole of Syria by driving the Ptolemaic forces out of it in the so-called Fifth Syrian War (after suffering an earlier reverse at their hands at the battle of Raphia in southern Palestine in 217), and then evicted the Ptolemies from their subject lands in Asia Minor. Antiochus' western military operations ensured that many of Asia Minor's cities and kingdoms, claimed as Seleucid possessions from the time of the first Seleucus, were restored to Seleucid authority. But Antiochus overreached himself when he extended his campaigns to Thrace and mainland Greece. In so doing, he provoked the wrath of Rome. This culminated in

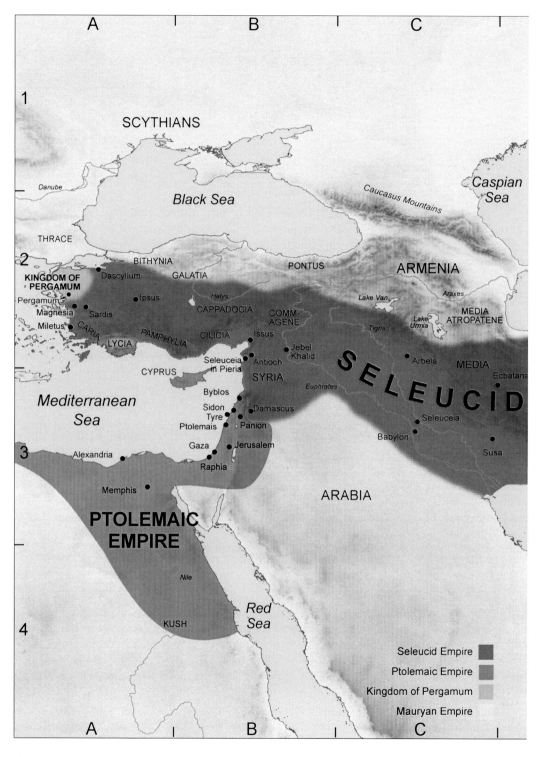

The Seleucid and Ptolemaic empires c. 260 BC

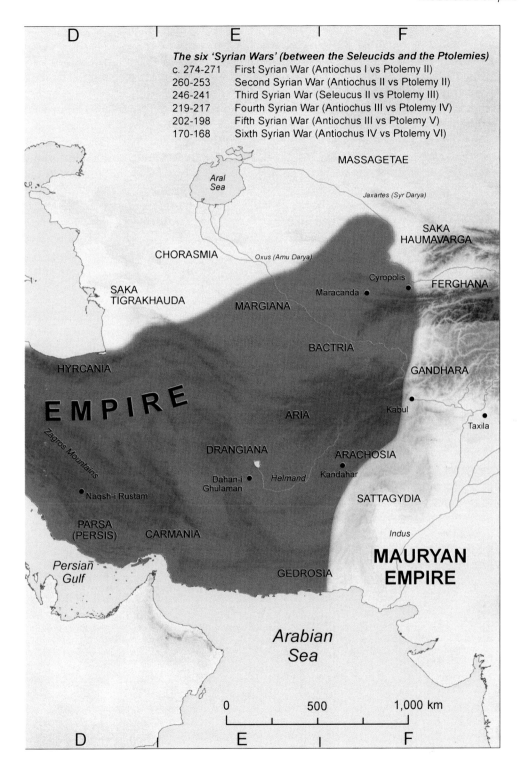

The six 'Syrian Wars' (between the Seleucids and the Ptolemies)

c. 274-271	First Syrian War (Antiochus I vs Ptolemy II)
260-253	Second Syrian War (Antiochus II vs Ptolemy II)
246-241	Third Syrian War (Seleucus II vs Ptolemy III)
219-217	Fourth Syrian War (Antiochus III vs Ptolemy IV)
202-198	Fifth Syrian War (Antiochus III vs Ptolemy V)
170-168	Sixth Syrian War (Antiochus IV vs Ptolemy VI)

MASSAGETAE

Aral Sea

Jaxartes (Syr Darya)

SAKA HAUMAVARGA

CHORASMIA

Oxus (Amu Darya)

Cyropolis

FERGHANA

SAKA TIGRAKHAUDA

Maracanda

MARGIANA

BACTRIA

GANDHARA

HYRCANIA

EMPIRE

Zagros Mountains

ARIA

Kabul

Taxila

DRANGIANA

ARACHOSIA

Dahan-i Ghulaman

Helmand

Kandahar

Naqsh-i Rustam

SATTAGYDIA

PARSA (PERSIS)

CARMANIA

Indus

MAURYAN EMPIRE

Persian Gulf

GEDROSIA

Arabian Sea

0   500   1,000 km

a final showdown between Seleucid and Roman armies at the battle of Magnesia-ad-Sipylum in western Asia Minor (late 190 or early 189). Antiochus suffered a massive defeat, and the peace accord that followed obliged him to give up a substantial part of his Asia Minor territories. But his empire remained a vast one, and his successor-but-one, Antiochus IV, came close to extending Seleucid sovereignty over Egypt as well; he had managed to occupy the northern part of it before he was intimidated into retreat by a delegation from the Roman senate demanding his immediate withdrawal from the Ptolemies' homeland.

Though his reign was not without its failures, Antiochus IV was arguably the last of the great Seleucid kings, and after his reign ended in 164, the Seleucid empire went into inexorable decline, as it became increasingly subject to external pressures, exerted primarily by the Romans in the west and the Parthians in the east, and to continuous destructive squabbles and coups within the royal dynasty's own ranks. The once vast empire dwindled though the last century of its existence, until it was confined to a small part of Syria. In 64 BC, Pompey the Great entered Antioch, unceremoniously dismissed the last Seleucid ruler Antiochus XIII, and established Syria as a Roman province.

Sherwin-White and Kuhrt (1993); Hannestad (*AANE*: 984–1000); Bryce (2014: 157–217).

Jebel Khalid

The Seleucid settlement now called Jebel Khalid (ancient name unknown) was built shortly after 300 BC by Seleucus I on an outcrop of rock, previously unoccupied, on the middle Euphrates. Its strong fortifications, which included thirty towers and bastions and a substantial gate complex, enclosed an area of 50 ha of which only 30 ha appear to have been inhabited. Other archaeological features of the site, which has been excavated since 1986 by an Australian team led by Graeme Clarke and Heather Jackson, include what is apparently a governor's palace on the acropolis, a completely excavated tenement block (insula) in the settlement's residential quarter, and a sacred area (temenos) containing a Doric temple. No inscriptions have been found, but written evidence from elsewhere suggest its ancient name may have been Amphipolis or Nicatoris. Jebel Khalid's strong fortifications and its excellent strategic location, which gave it a commanding view of the surrounding plains, suggest that the settlement was built as a garrison centre, populated with semi-retired or reserve soldiers responsible for protecting the area and closely monitoring movements within it. The site was abandoned in the second quarter of C1 BC. Since its lifespan falls entirely within the Seleucid period, it has provided us with an excellent example of a purely Hellenistic foundation.

Clarke *et al.* (2002–14); Hannestadt (*AANE*: 990–1); Wright (2011).

65

The Attalid kingdom

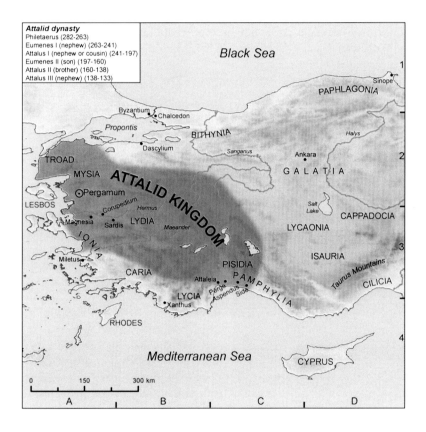

Attalid dynasty
Philetaerus (282-263)
Eumenes I (nephew) (263-241)
Attalus I (nephew or cousin) (241-197)
Eumenes II (son) (197-160)
Attalus II (brother) (160-138)
Attalus III (nephew) (138-133)

The Attalid kingdom in the mid 2nd cent. BC

In the apportionment of Alexander's empire among the Macedonian's former comrades-in-arms, Lysimachus won control of north-western Asia Minor and Thrace. He used the small city of Pergamum near the Aegean coast as a storehouse for 9,000 of the 25,000 talents taken by Alexander as plunder from his Persian conquests, and assigned the loot to the care of an officer called Philetaerus, son of Attalus. But when Seleucus (I) extended his sway from Syria into Asia Minor, Philetaerus switched his allegiance to him. And after Lysimachus was defeated and killed by Seleucus in the battle of Corupedium in Lydia (281), Philetaerus became ruler of Pergamum under Seleucus' overlordship, and founder of what became known as the Attalid dynasty. During his reign, he repulsed attacks on his city by Galatian invaders, and began expanding his city-kingdom through the neighbouring territories. He was succeeded by his nephew Eumenes I (263–241). Eumenes is generally considered the first true king of Pergamum, for he established his new kingdom's independence with a military victory over Seleucus' successor Antiochus I near Sardis in 262. His nephew (or cousin) and successor Attalus I (241–197) followed up his victories by driving the Galatians and the Seleucid forces out of western Asia Minor, and extended his own territories through much of the north-western sector of the region. The kingdom's territories were further extended in the reign of Attalus' successor Eumenes II (197–160), who bolstered his power by judicious alliances with neighbouring Greek cities and by joining forces with Rome at the battle of Magnesia, which ended in the decisive defeat of the Seleucid king Antiochus III. In gratitude for Attalid assistance, Rome handed over to Eumenes a large portion of the territory in Asia Minor won from Antiochus. At its height, the Attalid kingdom stretched to Pamphylia on the eastern Mediterranean coast, where Eumenes' successor Attalus II (160–138) founded the city Attaleia (modern Antalya). His successor Attalus III (138–133) was the last of the Attalid rulers. He bequeathed his kingdom to Rome on his death in 133.

Shipley (2000: 312–19).

Pergamum

Figure 65.1 Theatre of Pergamum. Photo by Trevor Bryce.

Built on steeply-rising natural fortifications in a valuable strategic location, and coming into high prominence during the Attalid regime, Pergamum has left a number of material remains of its Hellenistic and Roman periods. Notable among these is the Great Altar dedicated to Zeus and Athene, built to commemorate Attalus I's victory over the Galatians. The reliefs from the altar depicting the battle between giants and gods are now on display in the Staatliche Museum in Berlin. On the summit of the acropolis, next to the C4 BC temple of Athene, are the remains of the library built by Eumenes II, with housing for 17,000 parchment scrolls. There are remnants of the palaces of the Attalid kings on the acropolis' eastern edge, but the most impressive remains of the Attalid period are those of a well-preserved theatre, the steepest ancient structure of its kind in the world, with seating for 10,000 spectators. A temple of the Roman emperor Trajan provides a signal example of the Roman period of Pergamum's history. Also primarily of Roman date, in the area located in the lower part of the site, is the religious sanctuary called the Asclepieum, a famous medical centre dedicated to Asclepius, god of healing. Pergamum was the birthplace of the renowned physician Galen (c. AD 129–199).

Wilson (2010: 279–93).

66

Bactria

The country of Bactria was located between the region through which the Oxus (Amu Darya) river flowed and the Hindu Kush, in what is now north-eastern Afghanistan. Probably during the early centuries of M1 BC, Bactria developed into a wealthy and populous kingdom, perhaps the most powerful in central Asia. Its wealth was derived partly from its mineral resources, particularly silver and gold, and partly from its thriving agricultural activities. The latter were supported by large irrigation networks for which the country was noted. After *perhaps* suffering invasion and conquest by one or more Neo-Assyrian kings in C9–8 BC (we have only dubious Classical sources for this), Bactria became, in C6, one of the easternmost territories of the Persian Achaemenid empire – as attested in the inscriptions of Darius I, and by the Greek historian Herodotus (3.92). Bactria was subsequently conquered by Alexander the Great, and later came under the sway of the early Seleucid emperors, beginning with the empire's founder Seleucus I in late C4. Under Seleucid rule, the region was extensively colonized with Greek settlers. The city Bactra became its administrative capital.

The spread of Seleucid rule through Bactria, and its pervasive cultural impact upon the country, are clearly demonstrated by recent excavations of the site now called Aï Khanoum near Bactria's eastern periphery. The gymnasium, theatre, Greek temples and elite private residences of the city, founded by Seleucus c. 300, are reflective of substantial Seleucid-inspired Greek influence on Bactrian civilization. But Mesopotamian, Persian and local Bactrian elements were

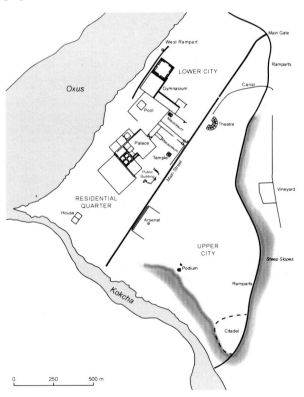

Aï Khanoum (after Bernard 2011: 82)

251

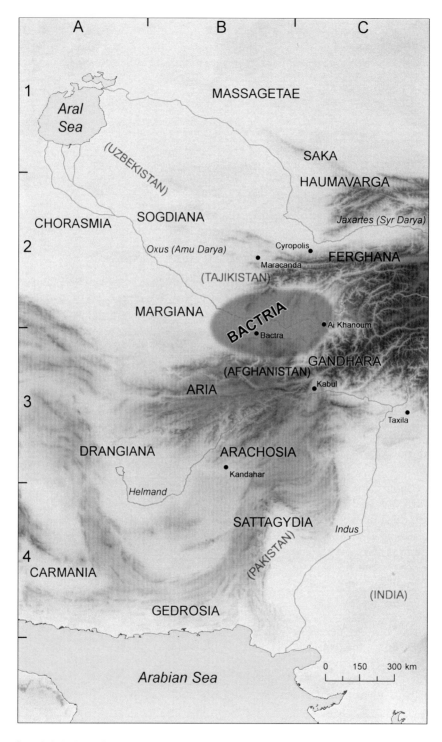

Bactria in its Near Eastern context

intermixed with the Greek, and all of them combined to produce a distinctive Graeco-Bactrian culture. This is reflected in a number of Aï Khanoum's buildings, including the large palace with porticoed courtyard which dominated the site. Huge, mud-brick fortifications and a garrisoned citadel provided Ai Khanoum with its defences.

By the early 230s, rebel satraps had broken from Seleucid control and established an independent Graeco-Bactrian kingdom. Seleucid sovereignty was reimposed over the region by Antiochus III in 206 BC. Around 145, nomadic invaders from beyond the Oxus river destroyed Aï Khanoum, and further invasions of Bactria c. 130 erased almost all traces of Greek civilization in the region.

PPAWA (109–10); Treidler and Brentjes (*BNP* 2: 455–7); Bernard (2011).

67

The Maccabean rebellion

In 167 BC, the Seleucid emperor Antiochus IV issued a proclamation to Jerusalem and other cities of Judah banning traditional Jewish religious and social customs and beliefs, and imposing Greek customs and traditions in their place. In accordance with this policy, Antiochus commanded that sacrifice be made to the Greek gods in all Judaean cities and villages, and appointed inspectors to ensure compliance. Some of these arrived in the village of Modein to carry out the order, but one of them was killed by a man called Mattathias, the village's leading resident, when he tried to enforce it. Mattathias had earlier fled to Modein from Jerusalem, with his five sons and a small group of supporters, when Antiochus' troops began massacring the city's population. Now once more he was forced to flee, this time to the hills, where he and his sons and followers prepared for a guerrilla war against Antiochus' forces. Thus began the Maccabean rebellion. It was so called after Mattathias' third son Judas Maccabaeus (the epithet probably means 'hammer') who assumed leadership of the rebels after his father's death, within a year of leaving Modein. The rebel ranks were swelled as news of the Maccabeans' defiance of Seleucid authority spread, and Judas led his troops to a number of victories over Antiochus' forces. These culminated in his reoccupation of Jerusalem in 164, and his rededication of the temple there on the 25th day of Kislev (November–December). Antiochus died the same year, and his son and successor Antiochus V issued another proclamation rescinding his father's ban on Jewish practices. Nonetheless, Judas continued hostilities with the Seleucid forces, for his ultimate aim was to establish the Jewish state's independence of Seleucid rule. But he was finally defeated and killed by a Seleucid army in the autumn of 161. For a time, the Jewish resistance continued under his youngest brother Jonathan. But relations with the Seleucid monarchy now shifted from the military to the diplomatic arena. This did not work in Jonathan's favour, for he was murdered after becoming caught up in the struggles between rival factions for the Seleucid throne. In 129 BC, the Jewish state eventually gained its independence. It is from this year until 63 BC, when Judaea was absorbed into the Roman provincial administration, that the Jewish state is said to have been ruled by the Hasmonean dynasty – so called, according to the Jewish historian Josephus, after a man called Hashmon, the great-grandfather of Judas Maccabaeus' father Mattathias.

SB (308–24); Bryce (2014: 199–206).

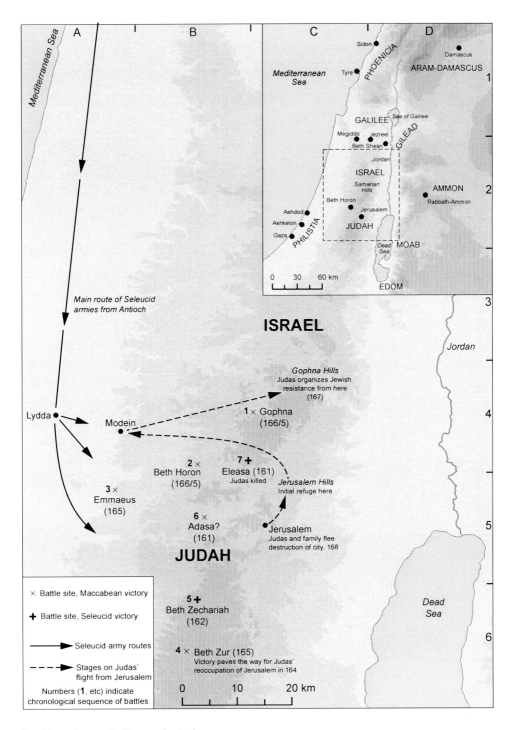

The Maccabean rebellion under Judas

Part X

The Near East in the Roman period

The following is a small sample of reference works on Rome's involvement in the Near Eastern world (full details of them are provided in the Bibliography or the List of Abbreviations): Jones (1983); Gruen (1984); Dodgeon and Lieu (1991); Millar (1993); Ball (2000); Fischer-Genz (AANE: 1021–40); Bryce (2014: 221–323). These items are not separately appended to the entries below on Roman rule in the Near East.

68

Roman rule in the Near East I

From the battle of Magnesia to the settlements of Pompey

In 192, Rome became embroiled in conflicts with the Seleucid emperor Antiochus III, culminating in the battle of Magnesia-ad-Sipylum (190/189). Antiochus' forces were routed by the Roman commander Lucius Cornelius Scipio, supported by his ally Eumenes II of Pergamum. By the terms of a treaty drawn up the following year, at Apamea in Phrygia, Antiochus forfeited most of his possessions in Asia Minor, which were apportioned by Rome between Eumenes' kingdom and the island of Rhodes. In 133 the last of the Pergamene kings, Attalus III, died, bequeathing his kingdom to the Romans. So began Roman rule in the Near East, for in the same year the Roman province Asia was established. It covered much of the western half of the Anatolian peninsula where Pergamum had held sway, from Mysia and the Troad in the north-west, southwards through Lydia to Caria, and included the Ionian city-states and offshore islands along the Aegean coast.

In the south-east of the peninsula, Cilicia became a second Roman province in Asia Minor c. 80 BC. Here, the Roman commander Pompey was wintering with his troops in 67–66 BC, after his success in eliminating piracy from the Mediterranean and Black Seas, when Rome assigned him a more wide-ranging task – that of settling the political and military affairs of the eastern lands. In response, Pompey embarked on a series of campaigns which took him through much of the Near Eastern world as the Romans knew it. In northern and eastern Anatolia, a combination of force and diplomacy were used to bring to heel the troublesome kingdoms of Pontus and Armenia. Then Pompey set his sights upon Syria. Brushing aside the last feeble Seleucid emperor, he established, in 64, the Roman province of Syria. Antioch on the Orontes was its administrative centre. The following year, Pompey expanded the province's boundaries by incorporating within them a large part of the former kingdom of Judaea. Syria's territory now extended from the southern border of the kingdom of Commagene in the north southwards through Judaea. In this same year, Bithynia and Pontus in Asia Minor were combined into a Roman province. But under Roman patronage and protection, a number of lands in the region, like Commagene, retained their own rulers and a fairly high degree of autonomy – for the time being.

Figure 68.1 Pompey the Great. Courtesy of the Ny Carlsberg Glyptotek.

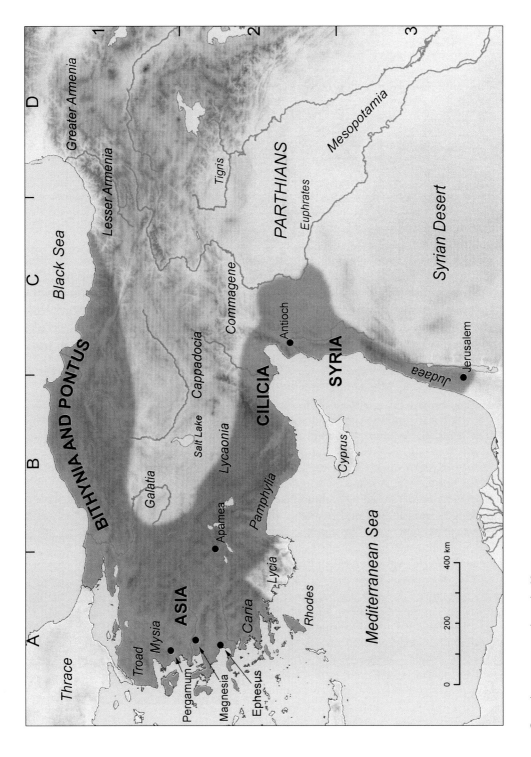

Rome's eastern provinces in 60 BC

69

Roman rule in the Near East II

From Pompey to Augustus

Roman civilization spread rapidly through many of Rome's eastern territories, and with Romanization came all the major amenities and diversions of Roman life, including baths, theatres and stadiums. Under Roman rule, hundreds of towns and cities were built from scratch, or refounded on the sites of earlier settlements, especially in Asia Minor, Syria and northern Mesopotamia. Roman military veterans as well as local peoples provided populations for these rapidly developing urban centres and village communities, in accordance with a Romanization programme particularly associated with Julius Caesar, and subsequently with his nephew, the emperor Augustus. The cities and smaller settlements, both old and new, were connected by a much upgraded road network. Major features of this were the north–south Via Maris ('The Way of the Sea') which linked Egypt with Palestine and coastal Syria, the Via Nova Traiana, the former King's Highway which linked the Gulf of 'Aqaba to Damascus, and a west–east route that connected Damascus with the Euphrates via Palmyra.

But inevitably, Rome was drawn further eastwards as it sought to establish effective defence zones against enemies and potential enemies who threatened its frontiers – particularly the Parthians. The first major test of strength between Roman and Parthian forces was won by the latter when they routed Crassus' army at Carrhae in 53 BC. Subsequently, the Parthian king Orodes launched invasions into Roman territory on two occasions – the first into Syria in 51, the second into Syria, Palestine and Asia Minor in 40. The invaders were defeated and driven out by the Romans on both occasions. But a subsequent attempt by Mark Antony to take the war deep into Parthian territory, in 36, failed disastrously. Terms of peace between Rome and Parthia were finally agreed in 20 BC, through negotiations conducted on the Roman side by Tiberius, stepson and representative of Rome's first emperor Augustus, and the Parthian king Phraates IV. The peace accord was formalized in a ceremony on an island in the Euphrates in AD 1. The river now became the official boundary between the two empires.

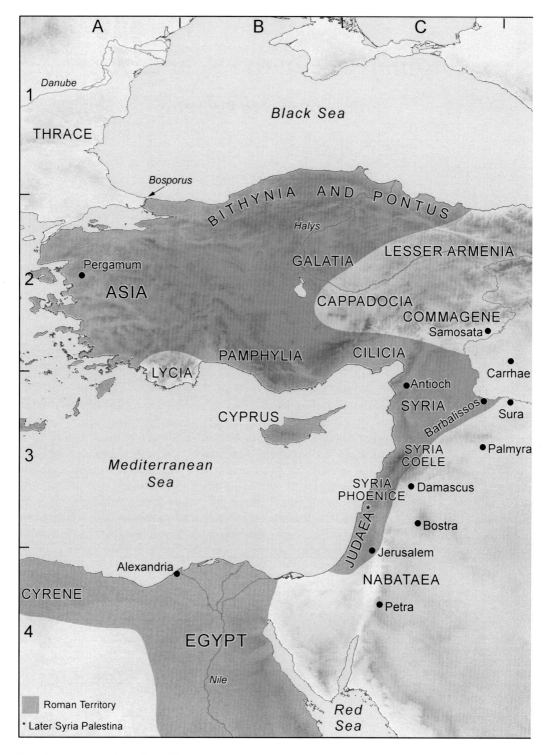

Rome's eastern provinces in AD 14

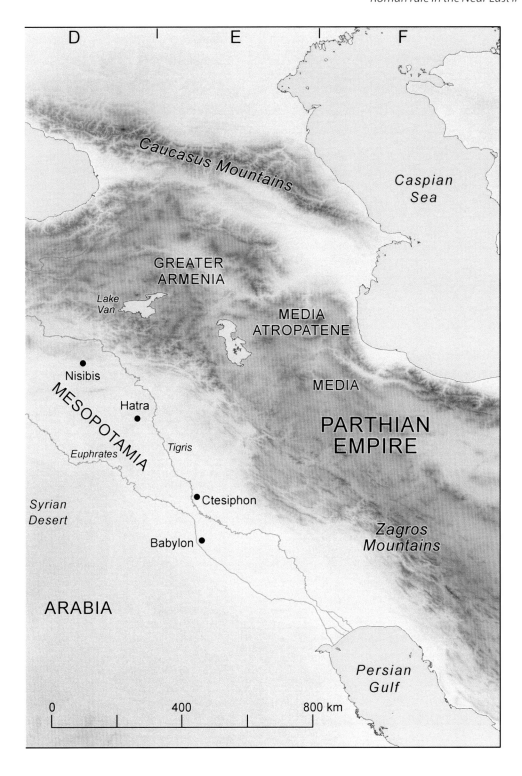

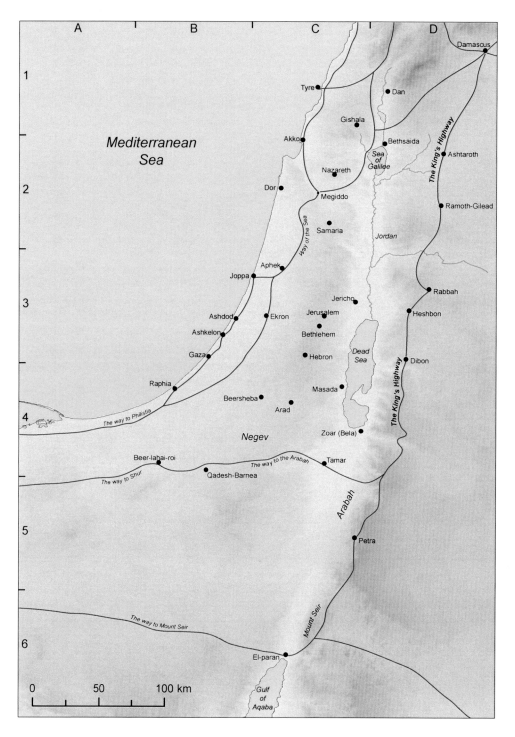

Highways predating Roman rule (after Barnes 2010: 47)

Baalbek

The city of Baalbek, so named after the Semitic god Baal, lay in the Biqa' Valley of what is now Lebanon. It was renamed Heliopolis, 'City of the Sun', after Alexander the Great's conquest of the region in 334. Becoming an important pilgrimage site, the city was made a Roman colony in 31 BC, by Octavian (the later Augustus), who used it as a place to settle some of his military veterans. Shortly after, work on the temple of Jupiter began. Today, the site is particularly noteworthy for its monumental temple ruins; indeed it became one of the largest religious sanctuaries of the Roman empire. The gods worshipped there, the triad of Jupiter,

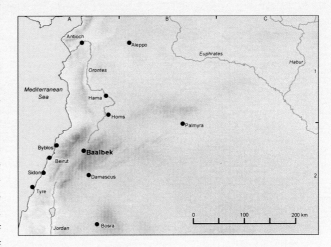

Baalbek in its broader context

Venus and Bacchus, were equated with the local deities Hadad, Ashtarte and a young male god of fertility. Reflecting this syncretism, the temples' architectural and sculptural features display a mixture of Roman and Oriental elements. The temple of Jupiter was built during the Augustan era, the temple attributed to Bacchus (there is no clear evidence for this attribution) dates to the reign of Antoninus Pius in C2 AD, and the temple of Venus, with its unique circular design, was built in C3 AD. Remains of a fourth temple, dedicated to Mercury, are located on a nearby hill.

Rey-Coquais (*PECS*: 380–2).

Figure 69.1 Temple of Jupiter, Baalbek. Photo by Trevor Bryce.

70

Herod the Great

In 40 BC, Rome appointed a 25-year-old youth called Herod as ruler of the kingdom of Judaea. This was after its forces had restored Roman control over Syria and Judaea following a period of Parthian occupation of these lands. Herod had hitherto been a minister of Antigonus, a member of the Hasmonean dynasty and the Parthian-appointed ruler of Judaea. He had now to justify his title as King of the Jews by seizing his throne from Antigonus – who was executed by the Romans at his successor's request. Nonetheless, Herod maintained his connections with the Hasmonean family by marrying Mariamne, granddaughter of Antigonus' uncle and predecessor John Hyrcanus II (she was but one of Herod's ten wives). From 37 until his death in 4 BC, Herod remained King of the Jews, and throughout that period a loyal ally of Rome. He proved an effective administrator and managed his kingdom's finances well, partly through imposing a heavy tax burden on his subjects, which provided a major source of revenue for his grandiose building projects, including the rebuilding of the Temple of Jerusalem. His ten wives produced a large family who engaged in many intrafamilial disputes, some of which led Herod to take brutal action against those members who fell out of favour with him, or were accused of plotting against him. Thus he executed Mariamne and her two sons. Continuing instability within his family after his death caused the Romans to intervene and divide his kingdom among his surviving children.

Ball (2000: 47–56); *SB* (334–48).

Jerusalem

Jerusalem's history began with a Chalcolithic settlement on the Ophel Ridge (located to the south of the 'Old City's' eastern side). But it was not until the Middle Bronze II period (C18–17) that the site assumed the character of a city, which appears to have flourished during the Late Bronze Age, when it is attested in a number of letters in the C14 Amarna archive. At this time, it was the seat of a local king, appointed by the pharaoh. In biblical tradition, the city first came into high prominence when King David established it as his royal capital. David's son Solomon continued his father's building programme in the city, and it was in his reign that Jerusalem's First Temple was constructed. But by the end of the reign, Solomon's kingdom was falling apart. The partitioning of it on his death saw a substantial reduction in the status of Jerusalem, which now became merely the capital of the tribal lands of Judah and Benjamin. (We have no independent evidence to corroborate the biblical narrative which covers the above events.)

An assault upon the city in 701 by the Assyrian king Sennacherib was apparently repulsed, at least according to the biblical account of it in 2 Kings 18–19 (though Assyrian records claimed success for

(continued)

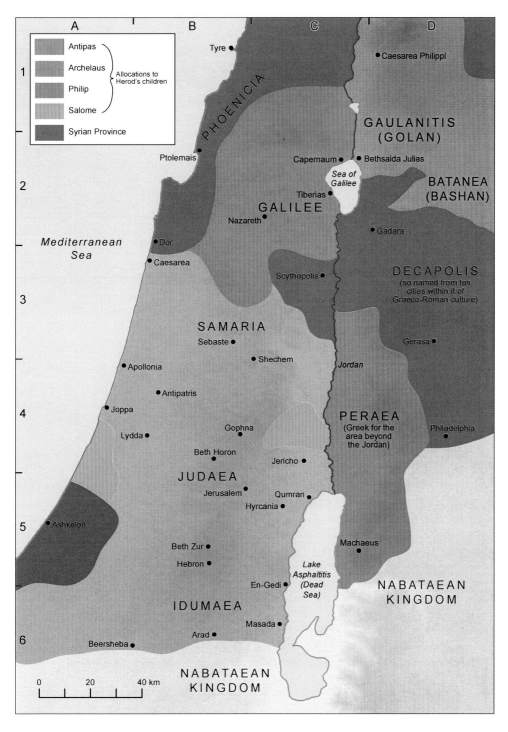

Herod the Great's kingdom and the apportionment of it to his heirs (after Bang and Scheidel 2013: 182)

(continued)

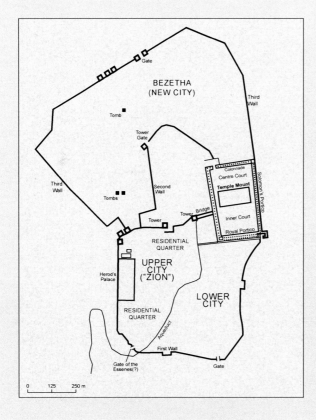

Herodian Jerusalem (4 BC–AD 70) (after Cline 2004: 103)

Sennacherib). But it fell to the Babylonian king Nebuchadnezzar II in 597, who deported to Babylonia (according to the biblical account) 10,000 of its inhabitants, along with its king Jehoiachin, leaving a puppet ruler Zedekiah in his place (2 Kings 24:14–17). Zedekiah eventually rebelled. Jerusalem was again attacked, and this time destroyed by Nebuchadnezzar's forces (586). Thus ended the First Temple period, with further mass deportations of the Jewish population to Babylonia. When the Persian Cyrus II conquered the Babylonian empire in 539, he allowed the Jews to return to their homeland, where they began the task of rebuilding Jerusalem. But Jerusalem's history remained a chequered one. The city was again destroyed in 167 by the Seleucid king Antiochus IV in the wake of factional uprisings in the city. It rose to new heights the following century when Herod was appointed by the Romans as king of the Jews (40 BC). Herod's substantial rebuilding programme in his kingdom included the construction of a new Temple of Jerusalem (begun in 20 BC but not completed until AD 62). This Second Temple period in Jerusalem's history was a shortlived one, for in response to repeated Jewish uprisings against Roman authority, the city, along with its temple, was again destroyed, in AD 70, by Titus, on the orders of his father, the emperor Vespasian.

In 131, the emperor Hadrian provoked a further rebellion among the Jews when he established on Jerusalem's site a new Roman colony called Aelia Capitolina. Within it, he ordered the construction of a temple to Jupiter Capitolinus – in the place where the revered Second Temple of Jerusalem had stood. Under the leadership of a messiah-like figure called Bar Kochba, 'Son of the Star', the Palestinian Jews rose up against their rulers and for a few brief years an independent Jewish state was established. But the uprising was finally crushed by Rome's superior forces, who systematically destroyed the rebels' towns and villages, and massacred or enslaved their inhabitants. The land once called Judaea was given a new name: Syria Palestina. The remnants of the Jewish people who survived the Roman onslaughts were henceforth forbidden to set foot in Jerusalem. Effectively stripped of their identity and forbidden to practise their ancestral customs, the Jews faced the prospect of further decline and indeed extinction. But their fortunes improved when Hadrian's successor Antoninus Pius became emperor. Antoninus allowed the Jews to revive and maintain their religious beliefs and customs and to practise their traditional forms of worship.

Bahar (*OEANE* 3: 224–38); Geva (2000); Cline (2004).

71

Parthia

The country called Parthia in Classical texts (Parthava in Persian texts) lay in north-eastern Iran, to the south-east of the Caspian Sea. It became subject to the Persian Achaemenid empire shortly after the empire's foundation by Cyrus II in mid C6. Though it participated in the widespread and ultimately abortive uprisings against Cyrus' third successor Darius I on his accession in 522, Parthia generally remained submissive to Persian rule throughout the Achaemenid period, which ended in 330 BC.

In the Hellenistic period, Parthia became a province of the Seleucid empire. But a new era in its history began when it came under the control of a band of nomadic invaders called the Parni, from the grasslands of central Asia. The newcomers were not mere plunderers and adventurers, but rapidly integrated with the country's existing inhabitants, adopting their name and culture and language. Shortly after their arrival, one of their leaders Arsaces founded in 247 BC a royal dynasty, called the Arsacid dynasty, which marked the beginning of the Parthian empire. The empire lasted until AD 224, thus spanning much of the Seleucid and the Roman imperial periods. At its peak, it held sway over a broad expanse of territories extending eastwards from the Euphrates to the frontiers of modern Afghanistan, and southwards from the Caspian to the Arabian Sea. Its trade and diplomatic links reached as far east as China. And its links with the western world were reflected in the policies of a number of its early rulers who showed themselves highly receptive to Greek cultural influences, using Greek inscriptions on their coins and explicitly identifying themselves as philhellenes ('lovers of Greek culture'). Many Greek settlers were readily accepted into Parthian society, often forming communities of their own within the kingdom.

Pompey the Great's establishment of Syria as a Roman province in 64 BC led inevitably to tensions and conflicts with Parthia. Disputes over the boundaries between Roman and Parthian territory were a central issue. An early test of the matter came in 53 BC, at Carrhae in north-western Mesopotamia, when a contingent of

Figure 71.1 Coin of Parthian king Artabanus II (AD 10–38). From the collection of Trevor Bryce.

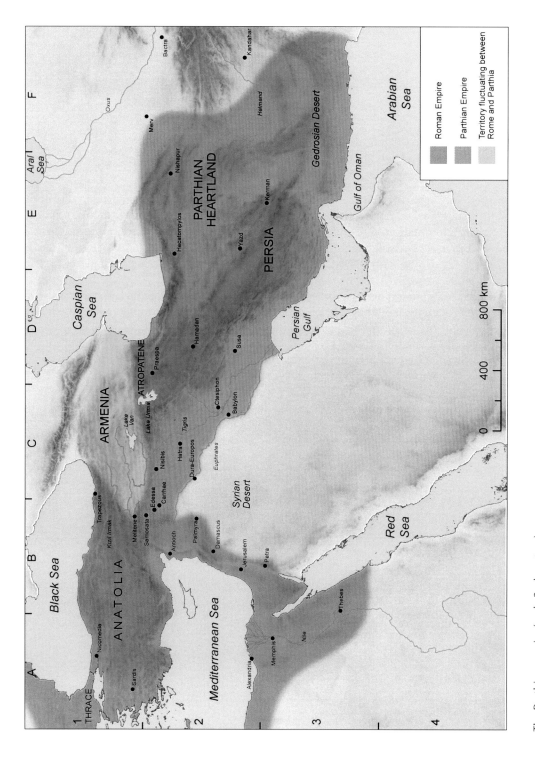

The Parthian empire (early 2nd cent. AD)

Parthian archers annihilated the forces of the Roman commander Crassus. This episode in particular consolidated Parthia's hold on all its territories up to the Euphrates, and established a clear division between Roman and Parthian territory along the river, subsequently confirmed in a peace agreement between Rome and Parthia in the reign of Augustus. But C2 and early C3 Roman emperors, notably Trajan (98–117), Septimius Severus (193–211) and his son Caracalla (211–217), resumed campaigns across the river, intent on expanding their territories through Babylonia to the Tigris and beyond, and once again provoked a series of conflicts with Parthia. The expansionist wars of Severus and Caracalla in particular contributed significantly to the crippling of the Parthian regime, and as a consequence the serious undermining of the regime's control over its regional governors. In AD 224, the last Parthian king Artabanus IV was overthrown by one of these governors, Ardashir, satrap of Persis, who became the founder of the Sasanian empire.

Kaizer (*GEAW*: 174–86); Hauser (*AANE*: 1001–20); Dabrowa (*OHIH*: 164–86).

72

The Nabataeans

When Persia's Achaemenid kings ruled the Near East, large groups of nomadic Arab herdsmen and merchants, called Nabataeans, left their desert homelands in north-eastern Arabia and settled, peacefully and gradually, in the southern regions of Transjordan. During the Hellenistic and Roman periods, the Nabataeans developed a powerful and prosperous kingdom which at its peak controlled an extensive span of territories, stretching between southern Syria and Transjordan in the north and the peninsula of Sinai in the south. The famous rose-red city Petra was the capital of this kingdom.

Figure 72.1 The Khazneh (commonly known as 'The Treasury'), Petra. X via Wikimedia.

Beginning with a highly profitable trade in frankincense and myrrh, which they acquired from their original homelands, the Nabataeans rapidly expanded their repertoire of merchandise to include a wide range of exotic and luxury products, including spices and incenses of many kinds, ivory, sugar, precious and semi-precious stones. There was an insatiable demand for these products, especially among wealthy clientele, in the western as well as the Near Eastern worlds. The Nabataeans obtained them through the trading links they established with countries as far afield as Han Dynasty China, by means of caravan routes which passed through Arabia to the Persian Gulf and thence to the lands of the east. Petra served as a reprocessing centre for many of the raw products acquired in these trading enterprises, converting oils and balms and incenses into medicinal and cosmetic products, which were then sold on to the Nabataeans' international customers.

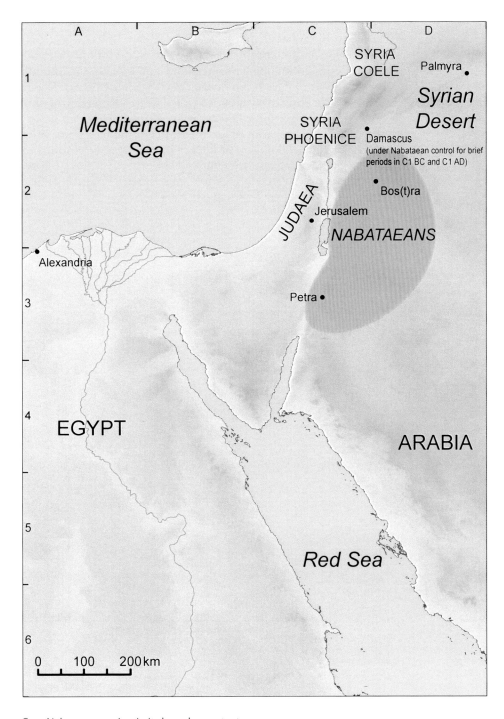

Core Nabataean region in its broader context

Some 4,000 Nabataean inscriptions have been found, widely distributed throughout the Mediterranean and Near Eastern worlds. Though the Nabataeans were an Arabic people, the language of these inscriptions is Aramaic. Understandably so, since Aramaic was the most widely used international language of the day. Along with literary sources and coin legends, the inscriptions inform us that the Nabataeans for most of their history were ruled by a line of kings. Beginning c. 170 BC with a ruler called Aretas I, the royal dynasty ended with the reign of Rabbel II (70–106), on whose death the Roman emperor Trajan absorbed the Nabataean kingdom into his newly created province Arabia (Petraea). Bosra, a Nabataean city located 140 km south of Damascus, was the capital of his new province. Already in the reign of Rabbel II, if not earlier, Bosra (Roman Bostra) had become the chief city of the Nabataean kingdom.

Markoe (2003); McKenzie (2005); Taylor (2012).

73

Roman rule in the Near East III
From Augustus to Trajan

Overall, the Augustan era was one of peace, stability and consolidation. Augustus wanted no further territorial expansion – and indeed none of any significance occurred until the reign of Trajan, early in C2. Before then, Rome generally remained on peaceful terms with its eastern neighbours, though Armenia remained problematic, and the accord with Parthia intermittent. The Euphrates provided Rome with no practicable line of defence against its eastern enemies, for it was easily fordable and would have required massive military resources to defend it with a string of effective military garrisons. Instead, the Romans relied on a series of buffer states to help secure its eastern frontiers, and during C1 AD, a number of the client kingdoms and semi-autonomous states in the regions between Roman and Parthian spheres of control were converted or absorbed into Roman provinces.

Thus in AD 72, the emperor Vespasian deprived Commagene of its client status and incorporated it into the province of Syria. Further to the north, he placed the client kingdom Lesser Armenia and with it Cappadocia under the authority of the governor of Galatia. The result of these extensions was that direct Roman authority now reached the northernmost limits of the Upper Euphrates, and beyond that the south-eastern shores of the Black Sea. Subsequently, Trajan annexed the Nabataean kingdom and created in its place the *Provincia Arabia (Petraea)*, with Bosra (Trajana Bostra Metropolis) as its capital (106). Shortly after, some time between 107 and 113, he established the new province of Cappadocia with Pontus, a union which lasted until the reign of Diocletian at the end of C3. He then became the first emperor to confront the problem of the porous Euphrates frontier by conducting military operations across the river in 115 and 116, marching through northern Mesopotamia, now also declared a Roman province, and further afield into western Iran. His campaign culminated in the capture of Parthia's winter capital Ctesiphon on the Tigris. But uprisings among the recently captured territories and a major rebellion in Judaea forced him to abandon his eastern enterprises and return home. His successor Hadrian (117–138) relinquished all the trans-Euphrates territories over which he had claimed control, and brought the Roman frontier back to the river. Nonetheless, Trajan had shown that the Euphrates need no longer be considered the ultimate territorial limit of Rome's power. Later emperors would be inspired by his example and campaign afresh in the lands east of the Euphrates.

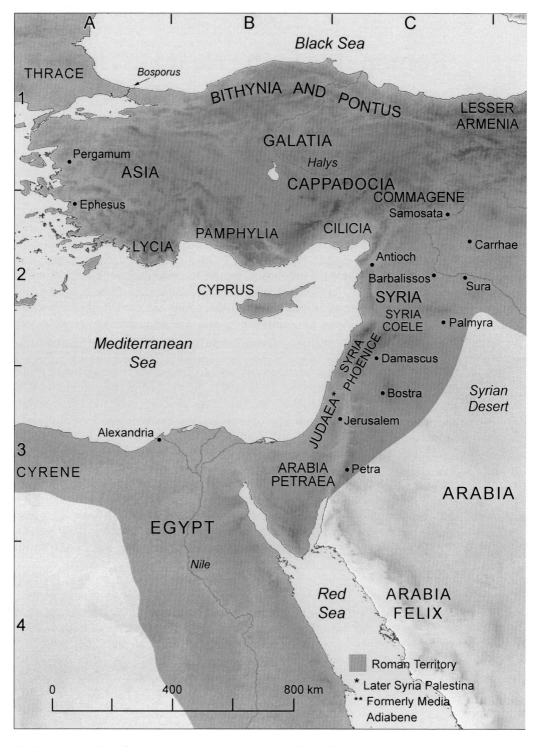

The Roman Near East after Trajan's eastern campaigns (AD 115–116)

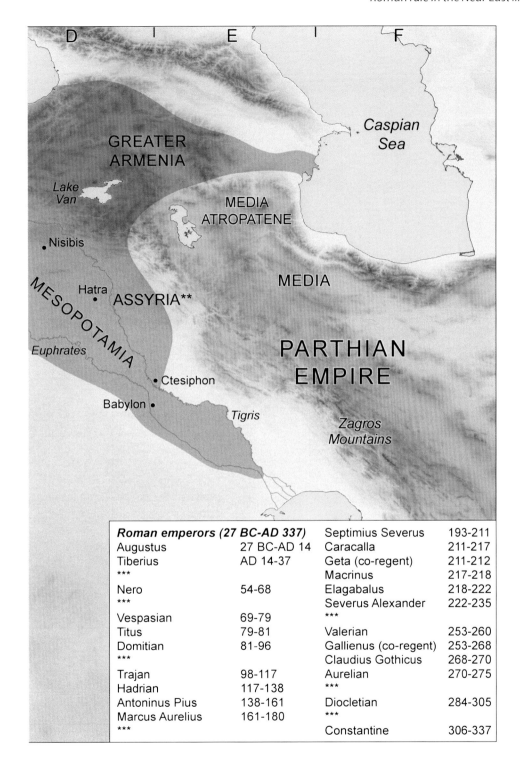

Roman emperors (27 BC-AD 337)		Septimius Severus	193-211
Augustus	27 BC-AD 14	Caracalla	211-217
Tiberius	AD 14-37	Geta (co-regent)	211-212
***		Macrinus	217-218
Nero	54-68	Elagabalus	218-222
***		Severus Alexander	222-235
Vespasian	69-79	***	
Titus	79-81	Valerian	253-260
Domitian	81-96	Gallienus (co-regent)	253-268
***		Claudius Gothicus	268-270
Trajan	98-117	Aurelian	270-275
Hadrian	117-138	***	
Antoninus Pius	138-161	Diocletian	284-305
Marcus Aurelius	161-180	***	
***		Constantine	306-337

Jerash

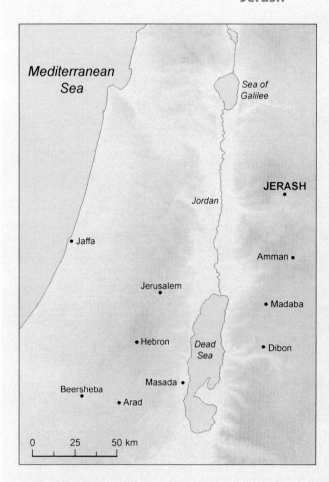

Jerash in its broader context

Located in the Gilead region of Transjordan, the city of Jerash first came into prominence in the Hellenistic period, under its Greek name Gerasa. In 64 BC, the city and its peripheral territories were annexed to the Roman province of Syria, newly established by Pompey. 170 years later, it became part of a new Roman province, Arabia (Petraea), created by Trajan in 106. Jerash played a significant role in this province, and flourished for the next century as a major commercial and trade centre, close by the great international trade-route, the Via Nova Traiana (formerly the King's Highway). The peace, security, and wealth that came with Romanization stimulated intense building activity in Jerash throughout C2. A hallmark structure of this era was the great triumphal arch which celebrated the emperor Hadrian's visit there in 129–130. Twenty years later, work began on a massive sanctuary dedicated to the goddess Artemis. Taking thirty years to build, the temple-complex became renowned as one of the most spectacular religious sanctuaries of the Near Eastern world. Other monumental structures built in C2, and still for the most part well preserved, include two theatres, two sets of baths, a temple of Zeus, a number of smaller temples, and a distinctive circular colonnaded forum, which is connected to the city's north gate by its main thoroughfare, the colonnaded *cardo maximus*. At its maximum extent, Jerash covered 800,000m², enclosed within a set of walls which incorporated 101 towers built at regular intervals along it. A large hippodrome lay outside the walls. C2 marked the peak period in Jerash's existence. Decline set in early the following century, but the city experienced a brief revival under the emperor Justinian (527–565).

MacDonald (*PECS*: 348–9); Aubin (*OEANE* 3: 215–19).

74

The Sasanians

The Sasanian empire was the third of the great Iran-based powers of the ancient world. It began in AD 224 when the last Parthian ruler, Artabanus IV, was overthrown by one of his governors, Ardashir, satrap of Persis. Under Ardashir's leadership, the Sasanian empire was founded, so called after Sasan, a legendary ancestor of Ardashir's royal line. It lasted until the Islamic conquest of Mesopotamia and Iran in AD 651. The Sasanian kings claimed descent from the rulers of the Achaemenid empire, founded by Cyrus the Great,

Figure 74.1 Shapur I monument, Naqsh-i-Rustam. X via Wikimedia.

and they sought to re-establish their authority over the lands (or a substantial portion of them) which had been subject to Cyrus and his successors. In pursuit of this ambition, they made serious inroads into Rome's eastern territories. At its height, their empire extended from the Indus river through large parts of central Asia, to Mesopotamia and the Persian Gulf. On occasions they occupied parts of Syria and Asia Minor as well, as illustrated by the western campaigns of Ardashir's son and successor Shapur I; these culminated in Shapur's capture of Rome's Syrian headquarters at Antioch. In a trilingual inscription carved in three versions (Parthian, Middle Persian, and Greek) on a cliff-face at Naqsh-i-Rustam, Shapur records victories over three Roman armies, led successively by the emperors Gordian III, Philip the Arab and Valerian.

Conflicts between the Romans and the Sasanians continued intermittently over the following centuries, with Sasanian power reaching further peaks in the reigns of Shapur II in C4 and Chosroes II (whose conquests extended to Palestine and Egypt) in late C6 and early C7. But by the end of Chosroes' reign in 628, the empire was entering its final decades. Twenty-three years after his death, it fell to the Arabs.

Kaizer (*GEAW*: 186–95); Mousavi and Daryaee (*AANE*: 1076–94); Daryaee (*OHIH*: 187–207).

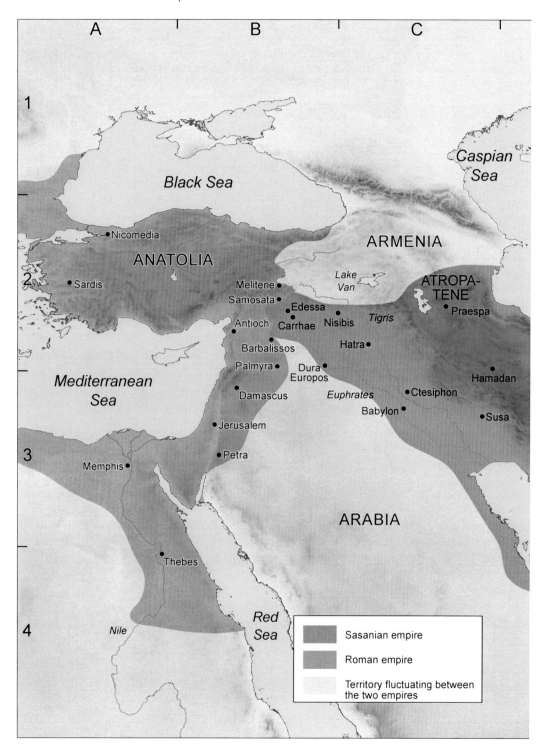

The Sasanian empire (mid 3rd cent. AD)

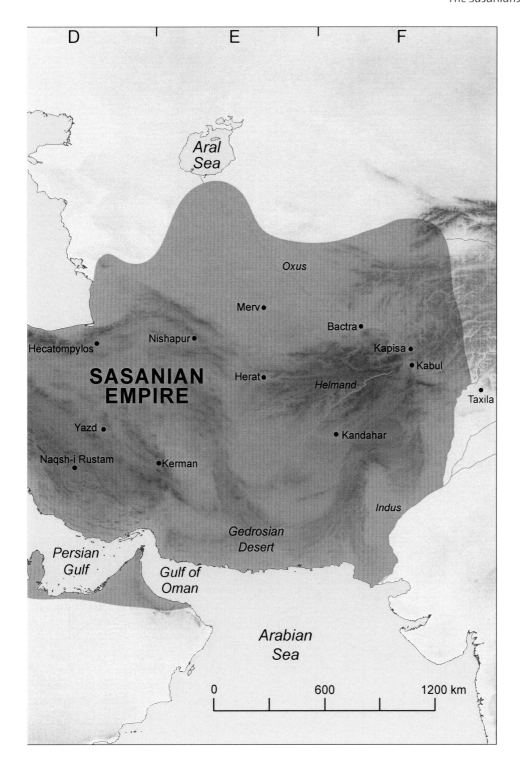

75

Zenobia

Zenobia (al-Zabba' in Arabic) was the second wife of Odenathus, ruler of Palmyra. His death in 267/268 paved the way for her accession as Palmyra's next ruler. But initially, Zenobia occupied the Palmyrene throne merely as regent for her and Odenathus' son Vaballathus (Arabic Wahballath) who was still a minor. Whether or not she ever planned to hand over her powers to Vaballathus remains unknown because of the brevity of her reign. The first two to three years of this reign she devoted to peaceful enterprises, above all to boosting Palmyra's image as a cultural centre. Then probably in the spring of 270, she embarked upon a pro-gramme of westward military expansion which took her armies into the Roman province of Arabia, and beyond it into the broader region the Romans called Arabia Felix. Up to this point, Zenobia could claim to be acting as Rome's representative in the east, by securing its territories in the Syrian-Arabian region while the emperor was preoccupied with problems in the west. But most importantly, Zenobia was seeking to establish control over the region which gave her forces access to the Red Sea and the Nile Delta. With that accomplished, her next objective lay immediately ahead – the conquest of Egypt. After two unsuccessful attacks upon the Egyptian forces, Zenobia's general Zabdas finally conquered the land, enabling Zenobia herself to enter it in triumph.

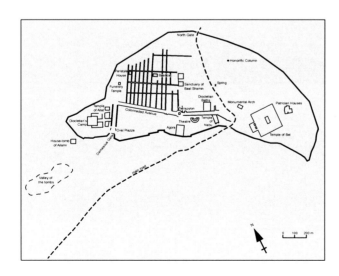

Palmyra (after Stoneman 1992: 55)

This set the stage for conflict with Rome, for Egypt was Roman subject territory. Zenobia claimed, theo-retically on her son's behalf, that she sought no more than partner-ship with the Roman emperor (now Aurelian), as protector of the east-ern half of the empire. Her military successes in both Arabia and Egypt demonstrated the credibility of her claim. But Aurelian had no inter-est in accepting either Zenobia or her son as his co-regent, and in late 271 he set out for the east to reassert Roman authority over Egypt and other territories won by Zenobia. By this time the Palmyrene queen had returned to Syria, where she made preparations for the invasion

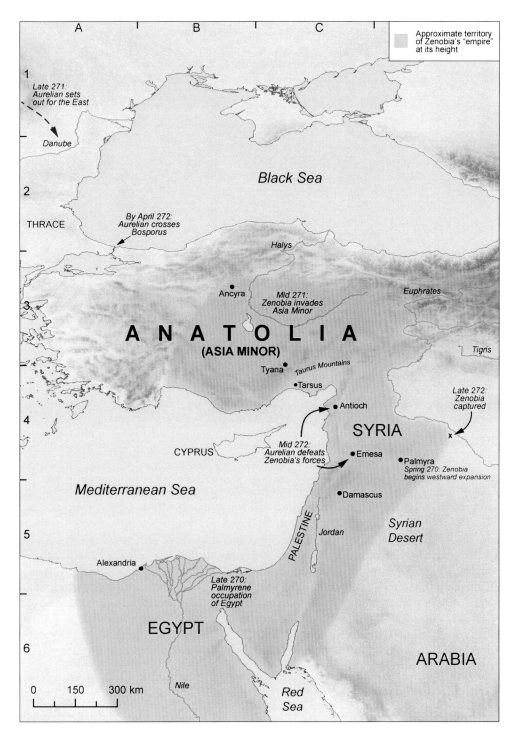

Approximate territory
of Zenobia's "empire"
at its height

Late 271:
Aurelian sets
out for the East

Danube

Black Sea

THRACE

By April 272:
Aurelian crosses
Bosporus

Halys

Euphrates

•Ancyra

Mid 271:
Zenobia invades
Asia Minor

A N A T O L I A
(ASIA MINOR)

Tigris

Tyana• *Taurus Mountains*

•Tarsus

Late 272:
Zenobia
captured

•Antioch

SYRIA

x

Mid 272:
Aurelian defeats
Zenobia's forces

CYPRUS

•Emesa

•Palmyra
Spring 270: Zenobia
begins westward expansion

Mediterranean Sea

•Damascus

PALESTINE

*Syrian
Desert*

Jordan

Alexandria•

Late 270:
Palmyrene
occupation
of Egypt

EGYPT

ARABIA

0   150   300 km   *Nile*   *Red
Sea*

Zenobia's 'empire'

Figure 75.1 Palmyra, Grand Colonnade. Photo by Trevor Bryce.

and occupation of Asia Minor. But she probably got no further than Ancyra before being forced to retreat to Syria, very likely on receiving news that Aurelian's army was rapidly approaching. By April, 272, the emperor had crossed the Bosporus into Asia Minor, and then proceeded through the Anatolian plateau and along the south-eastern coast into Syria. Two military confrontations between Aurelian's and Zenobia's armies near Antioch and Emesa resulted in decisive victories for Aurelian, who then pursued the queen back to Palmyra. The city was placed under siege, but held out until Zenobia was captured by a Roman cavalry detachment while trying to escape across the Euphrates into Sasanian territory. She was taken back to Rome where she provided a star attraction (along with the captured Gallic chieftain Tetricus) in Aurelian's triumph (274) to celebrate his victories over both the Palmyrene and the rebel Gallic empires. Our sources provide different accounts of Zenobia's ultimate fate, ranging from her execution after the triumph to a comfortable retirement in Rome or nearby Tivoli.

Stoneman (1992); Southern (2008); Bryce (2014: 275–317).

76

Roman rule in the Near East IV

From Diocletian to the Islamic invasions

Fresh stability for the Roman empire came with the accession of Diocletian, a battle-hardened warrior from the imperial bodyguard, in 284. One of the great accomplishments of his reign, which he shared with three other rulers (Maximian, Galerius and Constantius, forming a so-called tetrarchy) was the peace he secured in 297 with the Sasanian king Narseh (Narses) in the so-called treaty of Nisibis. In accordance with this peace, Rome's eastern frontier was shifted east of the Euphrates, to the Habur river. In Syria, Diocletian strengthened the frontier areas with a series of fortifications, and rebuilt a number of Syria's strategically important roads, thus greatly facilitating communication-links and rapid movement of troops in the empire's eastern regions. This contributed much to Syria's sense of stability and well-being during Diocletian's reign, greatly enhancing, through the peaceful conditions thus created, the region's overall prosperity.

During C4 and early C5, there were further wars between the Roman/Byzantine and Sasanian empires, seriously draining the resources of both sides. They ended when the emperor Theodosius II (408–450) agreed upon a 'hundred-year peace' with his Sasanian adversary. But warfare erupted again in the reign of Justinian (527–565), once more exacting a heavy toll on its protagonists. Ultimately, both were weakened beyond recovery. And that paved the way for a new intruder upon the scene. After the death of Muhammad on 8 June 632, the prophet's political and administrative successor Abu Bakr determined an aggressive new course for the armies gathered beneath the banner of the new religion Islam. He set his sights first of all on the conquest of the lands to the north of Arabia, and in 634, Muslim forces invaded Syria, and briefly occupied

Figure 76.1 The tetrarchy of Diocletian and his co-emperors. Photo by Trevor Bryce.

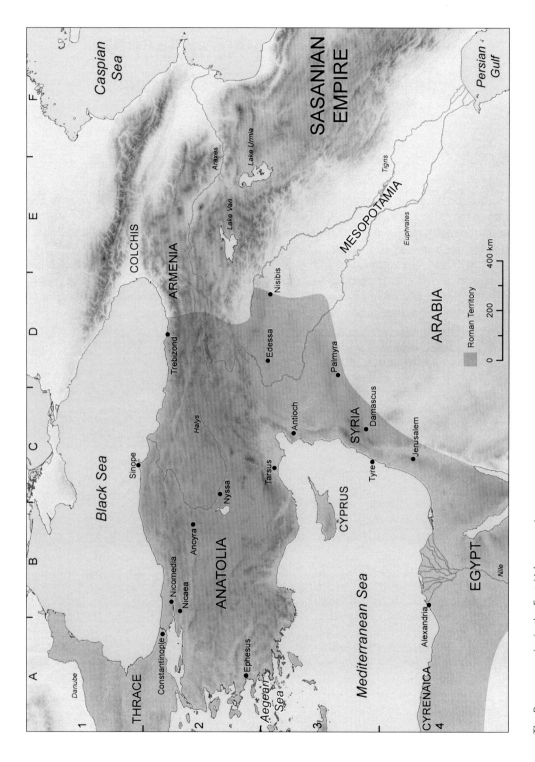

The Roman empire in the East (4th cent. AD)

Damascus. Two years later, a showdown took place at Yarmuk, near the present border between Jordan and Syria, between an Islamic army, and an army despatched by the Roman emperor Heraclius. The engagement lasted six days, but in the end Heraclius' forces were routed. Yarmuk proved a major turning point in world history. The Islamic peoples were here to stay. In 661, Damascus became the capital of the first Muslim empire. Thus began the Umayyad period of Islamic history.

Timeline

Prehistoric periods

Geological terms

Pleistocene: 2.588 Ma–0.0116 Ma (2,500,000–11,600 BP)
Holocene: 9,600 BC (11,600 BP)–present

Cultural terms

Epipalaeolithic (or terminal Palaeolithic): 20,000–9600 BC
Near Eastern Neolithic period: 9600–4500 BC
Pre-Pottery Neolithic: 9600–6900 BC
Transition to Ceramic Neolithic: 6900–6000 BC
Halaf and Ubaid periods: 6500–4200 BC
Uruk period: 4200–3100

Historical periods

BC	*Early Bronze Age (c. 3100–2000 BC)*
c. 3100–2900	Jemdet Nasr period
c. 3000–2125	Early Dynastic and Old Kingdom Egypt
c. 2900–2334	Sumerian Early Dynastic period
c. 2334–2193	Akkadian kingdom
mid M3	Beginning of Old Elamite period
c. 2112–2004	Ur III kingdom
	Middle Bronze Age (c. 2000–C17/16 BC)
c. 2055–1650	Egyptian Middle kingdom
c. 2025–1763	Period spanned by Isin and Larsa kingdoms
c.2000–1763	Old Assyrian period
C20–18	Assyrian merchant colonies
c. 1880–1595	Old Babylonian kingdom
c. 1810–1762	Period spanned by Mari royal dynasties
early C17	Beginning of Hittite kingdom

Late Bronze Age (C17/16–early C12 BC)

C17–early C12	Hittite kingdom
c. 1570–1155	Kassite Babylonian kingdom
1550–1069	Egyptian New kingdom
C16–13	Mitanni/Hanigalbat kingdom
c. 1500–1100	Middle Elamite period
betw. 1184–1153	Pharaoh Ramesses III repels Sea Peoples' incursions

Iron Age (period covered here: C12–end C7 BC)

→ 1069	Egyptian New kingdom
mid C12–late C8	Neo-Hittite kingdoms
c. 1100–mid C6	Neo-Elamite period
late C11	Saul establishes united kingdom of Israel (bibl. tradition)
1069–525	Egyptian Third Intermediate and Saite periods
by end M2	Emergence of Aramaeans
C10	Reigns of David and Solomon (bibl. tradition)
934–610	Neo-Assyrian kingdom
720	End of kingdom of Israel
610	Babylonian–Median alliance ends Neo-Assyrian Empire

Neo-Babylonian and Persian Achaemenid periods (626–330 BC)

626–539	Neo-Babylonian kingdom
586	Babylonian destruction of Jerusalem
559–330	Achaemenid kingdom, founded by Cyrus II
539	Cyrus ends Neo-Babylonian kingdom
490–479	The Persian invasions of the Greek mainland
334–323	Alexander the Great's campaigns in the East
330	Fall of the Persian empire to Alexander

The Hellenistic and Parthian kingdoms (late C4–late C1 BC)

305–64	The Seleucid kingdom
305–30	The Ptolemaic kingdom
263–133	The Attalid kingdom
c. 274–168	Period spanned by the six 'Syrian Wars' (Seleucids vs Ptolemies)
c. 247 BC–AD 224	The Parthian kingdom
Dec 190 or Jan 189	Antiochus III defeated by Rome in battle of Magnesia
166–142	Maccabean rebellion

Rome's involvement in the East (from 133 BC–AD 661)

133	Attalus III bequeaths his kingdom to Rome
64 BC–AD 14	From the settlements of Pompey to the death of Augustus
37–4	Rome's appointee Herod rules Jewish state
20	Rome reaches accord with Parthia

AD

14–117	From Augustus' death to the end of Trajan's reign
70	Romans, led by Titus, destroy Jerusalem

106	Trajan annexes the Nabataean kingdom
193–235	Severan dynasty
224	Parthian dynasty ends; Sasanian empire begins (founded by Ardashir I)
224–mid C7	The Sasanian kingdom
267/68–273	Reign of Palmyrene queen Zenobia
271–273	Aurelian's campaign against and victory over Zenobia
284–661	From Diocletian to the dawn of the Islamic era
313	Christianity officially recognized by Constantine
324	Constantine refounds Byzantium as Constantinople
636	Muslim victory at Yarmuk
661	Damascus becomes capital of first Muslim empire

Bibliography

Prehistoric section

Barker, G. (2006), *The Agricultural Revolution in Prehistory*, Oxford: Oxford University Press.

Bender, B. (1978), 'Gatherer-Hunter to Farmer: A Social Perspective', *World Archaeology* 10: 204–22.

Binford, L. and Binford S. (eds) (1968), *New Perspectives in Archaeology*, New York: Academic Press.

Braidwood, R.J. and Howe, B. (1960), *Prehistoric Investigations in Iraqi Kurdistan*, Chicago: University of Chicago Press.

Childe V.G. (1928), *The Most Ancient East*, London: Kegan Paul, Trench, Trubner and Co.

Dietrich, O. and Schmidt, K. (2011), 'A Radiocarbon Date from the Wall Plaster of Enclosure D of Göbekli Tepe', *Neo-Lithics: A Newsletter of South-West Asian Lithics Research* 2(10): 82–3.

Edwards, P.C. (2007), 'A 14,000 Year-Old Hunter-Gatherer's Toolkit', *Antiquity* 81: 865–76.

Flannery, K. (1969), 'Origins and Ecological Effects of Early Domestication in Iran and the Near East', in P. Ucko and G.W. Dimbleby (eds), *The Domestication and Exploitation of Plants and Animals*, London: Duckworth, 73–100.

—— (1973), 'The Origins of Agriculture', *Annual Review of Anthropology* 2: 271–310.

Gates, C. (2011), *Ancient Cities*, Abingdon: Routledge.

Garrod, D. (1932), 'A New Mesolithic Industry: The Natufian of Palestine', *Journal of the Royal Anthropological Institute* 62: 257–70.

Hodder, I. (1982), *Symbols in Action*, Cambridge: Cambridge University Press.

—— (1990), *The Domestication of Europe*, Oxford: Basil Blackwell.

—— (2006), *The Leopard's Tale: Revealing the Mysteries of Çatalhöhük*, London: Thames & Hudson.

Kenyon, K. (1957), *Digging Up Jericho: The Results of the Jericho Excavations, 1952–1956*, New York: Praeger.

Lieberman, D.E. and Shea, J.J. (1994), 'Behavioural Differences between Archaic and Modern Humans in the Levantine Mousterian', *American Anthropologist* 96 (2): 300–32.

Liverani, M. (2014), *The Ancient Near East: History, Society and Economy*, New York and Abingdon: Routledge.

Peregrine, P.N. and Ember, M. (eds) (2002), *Encyclopedia of Prehistory*, vol. 8, New York and Boston: Kluwer Academic/Plenum.

Roaf, M. (1990), *Cultural Atlas of Mesopotamia and the Ancient Near East*, Oxford: Andromeda.

Rosenberg, M. and Erim-Özdoğan, A. (2011), 'The Neolithic in Southeastern Anatolia', *OHAA* 125–49.

Scarre, C. (ed.) (2013), *The Human Past*, London: Thames & Hudson (3rd edn).

Sherratt, A. (1981), 'Plough and Pastoralism: Aspects of the Secondary Products Revolution', in I. Hodder, G.L. Isaac and N. Hammond (eds), *Pattern in the Past: Studies in Honour of David Clarke*, Cambridge: Cambridge University Press, 261–306.

Stein, G. and Rothman, M.S. (eds) (1994), *Chiefdoms and Early States in the Near East: The Organizational Dynamics of Complexity* (No. 18), Madison: Prehistory Press.

Zohary, D. and Hopf, M. (2000), *Domestication of Plants in the Old World*, Oxford: Oxford University Press (3rd edn).

Historical section

Akkermans, P.M.M.G. and Schwartz, G.M. (2003), *The Archaeology of Syria: From Complex Hunter-Gatherers to Early Urban Societies (c. 16,000–300 BC)*, Cambridge: Cambridge University Press.

Arnold, B.T. (2004), *Who Were the Babylonians?*, Atlanta: Society of Biblical Literature.

Atici, L., Kulakoğlu, F., Barjamovic, G. and Fairbairn, A. (eds) (2014), *Current Research at Kültepe-Kanish, Journal of Cuneiform Studies Supplemental Series No. 4.*

Austin, M. (2006), *The Hellenistic World from Alexander to the Roman Conquest*, Cambridge: Cambridge University Press (2nd edn).

Ball, W. (2000), *Rome in the East: The Transformation of an Empire*, London and New York: Routledge.

Bang, P.F. and Scheidel, W. (eds) (2013), *The Oxford Handbook of the State in the Ancient Near East and Mediterranean*, Oxford and New York: Oxford University Press.

Bard, K.A. (2000), 'The Emergence of the Egyptian State (c. 2300–2686 BC)', in I. Shaw (ed.), *The Oxford History of Ancient Egypt*, Oxford: Oxford University Press, 61–88.

Barnes, I. (2010), *The Historical Atlas of the Bible*, London: Cartographica.

Beckman, G., Bryce, T.R. and Cline, E.H. (2011), *The Ahhiyawa Texts*, Atlanta: Society of Biblical Literature.

Bernard, P. (2011), 'The Greek Colony at Aï Khanum and Hellenism in Central Asia', in F. Hiebert and P. Cambon (eds), *Afghanistan, Crossroads of the Ancient World*, London: British Museum, 81–130.

Brosius, M. (2006), *The Persians*, London: Routledge.

Bryce, T.R. (1986), *The Lycians in Literary and Epigraphic Sources*, Copenhagen: Museum Tusculanum Press.

—— (2002), *Life and Society in the Hittite World*, Oxford: Oxford University Press.

—— (2005), *The Kingdom of the Hittites*, Oxford: Oxford University Press (2nd edn).

—— (2006), *The Trojans and Their Neighbours*, Abingdon: Routledge.

—— (2009/2012), *The Routledge Handbook of the Peoples and Places of Ancient Western Asia: From the Early Bronze Age to the Fall of the Persian Empire*, Abingdon and New York: Routledge, cited as *PPAWA*.

—— (2012), *The World of the Neo-Hittite Kingdoms*, Oxford: Oxford University Press.

—— (2014), *Ancient Syria: A Three Thousand Year History*, Oxford: Oxford University Press.

Burns, R. (2009), *The Monuments of Syria*, London and New York: I.B. Tauris.

Charpin, D. (2012), *Hammurabi of Babylon*, London and New York: I.B.Tauris.

Clarke, G.W., Jackson, H., Tidmarsh, J. *et al.* (2002–14), *Jebel Khalid on the Euphrates*, Sydney: Mediterranean Archaeology (4 vols).

Cline, E.H. (2004), *Jerusalem Besieged, from Ancient Canaan to Modern Israel*, Ann Arbor: University of Michigan Press.

—— (2013), *The Trojan War*, New York: Oxford University Press.

—— (2014), *1177 B.C.: The Year Civilization Collapsed*, Princeton and Oxford: Princeton University Press.

Cohen, R. and Westbrook, R. (2000), *Amarna Diplomacy: The Beginnings of International Relations*, Baltimore and London: Johns Hopkins University Press.

Collins, B.J. (2007), *The Hittites and Their World*, Atlanta: Society of Biblical Literature.

Crawford, H. (2004), *Sumer and the Sumerians*, Cambridge: Cambridge University Press (2nd edn).

Dodgeon, M.H. and Lieu, S.N.C. (1991), *The Roman Eastern Frontier and the Persian Wars AD 226–363: A Documentary History*, London and New York: Routledge.

Finkel, I.L. and Seymour, M.J. (eds) (2008), *Babylon, Myth and Reality*, London: British Museum.

Geva, H. (ed.) (2000), *Ancient Jerusalem Revealed*, Jerusalem: Israel Exploration Society (expanded edn).

Greaves, A.M. (2002), *Miletos: A History*, London and New York: Routledge.

Gruen, E.S. (1984), *The Hellenistic World and the Coming of Rome*, Berkeley, Los Angeles and London: University of California Press.

Haywood, J. (2005), *The Penguin Historical Atlas of Ancient Civilizations*, London: Penguin.

Heimpel, W. (2003), *Letters to the King of Mari*, Winona Lake: Eisenbrauns.

Jones, A.H.M. (1983), *The Cities of the Eastern Roman Provinces*, revised by M. Avi-Yonah, Amsterdam: Adolf M. Hakkert (2nd edn) (repr. of Oxford University Press publication, 1973).

Keen, A.G. (1998), *A Political History of the Lycians and their Relations with Foreign Powers, c. 545–362 B.C.*, Leiden, Boston and Cologne: Brill.

Kitchen, K. (1982), *Pharaoh Triumphant: The Life and Times of Ramesses II*, Warminster: Aris and Phillips.

Kuhrt, A. (2007), *The Persian Empire: A Corpus of Sources from the Achaemenid Period*, Abingdon: Routledge (2 vols).

Lanfranchi, G.B., Roaf, M. and Rollinger, R. (eds) (2003), *Continuity of Empire(?) Assyria, Media, Persia* (Procs. of a conference held in Padua, 26–28 April 2001), Padua (History of the Ancient Near East, Monographs V): S.a.r.g.o.n. Editrice e Libreria.

Latacz, J. (2004), *Troy and Homer*, Oxford: Oxford University Press.

Laughlin, J.C.H. (2006), *Fifty Major Cities of the Bible*, London and New York: Routledge.

Leick, G. (2003), *The Babylonians*, London and New York: Routledge.

Lipiński, E. (2000), *The Aramaeans, Their Ancient History, Culture, Religion*, Leuven, Paris and Sterling: Peeters.

Lloyd, A.B. (2000), 'The Late Period (664–332 BC)', in I. Shaw (ed.), *The Oxford History of Ancient Egypt*, Oxford: Oxford University Press, 369–94.

Ma, J. (2013), 'Hellenistic Empires', in P.F. Bang and W. Scheidel (eds), *The Oxford Handbook of the State in the Ancient Near East and Mediterranean*, Oxford and New York: Oxford University Press, 324–57.

McKenzie, J. (2005), *The Archaeology of Petra*, Oxford: Oxbow books (repr.).

Malek, J. (2000), 'The Old Kingdom (c. 2686–2125)', in I. Shaw (ed.), *The Oxford History of Ancient Egypt*, Oxford: Oxford University Press, 89–117.

Markoe, G.E. (2000), *Phoenicians*, London: British Museum Press.

Markoe, G.E. (2003), *Petra Rediscovered: Lost City of the Nabataeans*, London: Thames & Hudson.

—— (ed.) (2003), *The Luwians*, Leiden: Brill.

Mieroop, M. Van De (2005), *King Hammurabi of Babylon*, Oxford: Blackwell.

—— (2016), *A History of the Ancient Near East*, Oxford: Blackwell (3rd edn).

Miles, R. (2010), *Ancient Worlds*, London: Allen Lane.

Millar, F. (1993), *The Roman Near East 31 BC – AD 337*, Cambridge, MA and London: Harvard University Press.

Moran, W. (1992), *The Amarna Letters*, Baltimore and London: Johns Hopkins University Press.

Oren, D. (ed.) (2000), *The Sea Peoples and Their World: A Reassessment*, Philadelphia: University of Pennsylvania.

Potts, D.T. (1999), *The Archaeology of Elam*, Cambridge: Cambridge University Press.

Powell, B. (2007), *Homer*, Oxford: Blackwell (2nd edn).

Radner, K. (2015), *Ancient Assyria: A Very Short Introduction*, Oxford: Oxford University Press.

Rainey, A.F. and Notley, R.S. (2006), *The Sacred Bridge: Carta's Atlas of the Biblical World*, Jerusalem: Carta, cited as *SB*.

Roaf, M. (1996), *Cultural Atlas of Mesopotamia and the Ancient Near East*, Oxford: Andromeda.

Robinson, A. (1995), *The Story of Writing*, London: Thames & Hudson.

Roth, M.T. (ed.) (1997), *Law Collections from Mesopotamia and Asia Minor*, Atlanta: Scholars Press (2nd edn).

Rothman, M.S. (ed.) (2001), *Uruk Mesopotamia and Its Neighbours: Cross-Cultural Interactions in the Era of State Formation*, Oxford: James Currey; Santa Fe: School of American Press.

Roux, G. (1980), *Ancient Iraq*, Penguin: London (2nd edn).

Sallaberger, W. and Westenholz, A. (eds) (1999), *Akkade-Zeit und Ur III-Zeit*, Göttingen: Vandenhoeck and Ruprecht; Freiburg: Universität Freiburg.

Sandars, N.K. (1985), *The Sea Peoples*, London: Thames & Hudson (rev. edn).

Shaw, I. (ed.) (2000), *The Oxford History of Ancient Egypt*, Oxford: Oxford University Press.

Sherwin-White, S. and Kuhrt, A. (1993), *From Samarkhand to Sardis: A New Approach to the Seleucid Empire*, London: Duckworth.

Shipley, G. (2000), *The Greek World after Alexander: 323–30 BC*, London and New York: Routledge.

Southern, P. (2008), *The Empress Zenobia: Palmyra's Rebel Queen*, London and New York: Continuum.

Spalinger, A.J. (2005), *War in Ancient Egypt*, Oxford: Blackwell.

Steel, L. (2004), *Cyprus Before History: From the Earliest Settlers to the End of the Bronze Age*, London: Duckworth.

Stoneman, R. (1992), *Palmyra and Its Empire: Zenobia's Revolt against Rome*, Ann Arbor: University of Michigan Press.

Taylor, J. (2000), 'The Third Intermediate Period (1069–664 BC)', in I. Shaw (ed.), *The Oxford History of Ancient Egypt*, Oxford: Oxford University Press, 330–68.

—— (2012), *Petra and the Lost Kingdom of the Nabataeans*, Cambridge, MA: Harvard University Press.

Tubb, J. (1998), *Canaanites*, London: British Museum Press.

Veldhuis, N. (2011), 'Levels of Literacy', in K. Radner and E. Robson (eds), *The Oxford Handbook of Cuneiform Culture*, Oxford: Oxford University Press, 68–89.

Waterfield, R. (2011), *Dividing the Spoils: The War for Alexander the Great's Empire*, Oxford: Oxford University Press.

Westenholz, A. (1999), 'The Old Akkadian Period: History and Culture', in W. Sallaberger and A. Westenholz (eds), *Akkade-Zeit und Ur III-Zeit*, Göttingen: Vandenhoeck and Ruprecht; Freiburg: Universität Freiburg, 17–117.

Westenholz, J.G. (1996), *Royal Cities of the Biblical World*, Jerusalem: Bible Lands Museum.

Wilhelm, G. (1989), *The Hurrians*, Warminster: Aris and Phillips.

Wilson, M. (2010), *Biblical Turkey: A Guide to the Jewish and Christian Sites of Asia Minor*, Istanbul: Ege Yayınları.

Wright, N.L. (2011), 'The Last Days of a Seleucid City: Jebel Khalid on the Euphrates and Its Temple', in K. Ericksen and G. Ramsey (eds), *Seleucid Dissolution: The Sinking of the Anchor*, Wiesbaden: Harrassowitz, 117–32.

Yon, M. (2006), *The City of Ugarit at Tel Ras Shamra*, Winonan Lake: Eisenbrauns.

Zimansky, P.E. (1998), *Ancient Ararat: A Handbook of Urartian Studies*, Delmar and New York: Caravan Books.

A select bibliography of ancient sources in translation

From the Early Bronze Age to the Achaemenid period

Chavalas, M.W. (ed.) (2006), *The Ancient Near East: Historical Sources in Translation*, Oxford: Blackwell.

Glassner, J.-J. (2004), *Mesopotamian Chronicles*, Writings from the Ancient World Number 19, Atlanta: Society of Biblical Literature.

Grayson, A.K. (1987–96), *The Royal Inscriptions of Mesopotamia: Assyrian Periods*, Toronto, Buffalo and London: University of Toronto (3 vols).

Hallo, W.W. and Younger, K.L. (eds) (1997, 2000, 2002), *The Context of Scripture*, Leiden, New York and Cologne: Brill (3 vols), cited as *CS*.

Pritchard, J.B. (1969), *Ancient Near Eastern Texts Relating to the Old Testament*, Princeton: Princeton University Press (3rd edn).

Roth, M.T. (ed.) (1997), *Law Collections from Mesopotamia and Asia Minor*, Atlanta: Scholars Press (2nd edn).

Late Bronze Age

Beckman, G. (1999), *Hittite Diplomatic Texts*, Atlanta: Scholars Press (2nd edn).

Moran, W. (1992), *The Amarna Letters*, Baltimore and London: Johns Hopkins University Press.

Iron Age

Frame, G. (1995), *The Royal Inscriptions of Mesopotamia. Babylonian Periods, Vol. 2. Rulers of Babylonia from the Second Dynasty of Isin to the End of Assyrian Domination (1157–612)*, Toronto, Buffalo and London: University of Toronto Press.

Persian (Achaemenid) period

Brosius, M. (2000), *The Persian Empire from Cyrus II to Artaxerxes I*, London: The London Association of Classical Teachers.

Kuhrt, A. (2007), *The Persian Empire: A Corpus of Sources from the Achaemenid Period*, Abingdon: Routledge (2 vols).

Hellenistic period

Austin, M. (2006), *The Hellenistic World from Alexander to the Roman Conquest*, Cambridge: Cambridge University Press (2nd edn).

Bagnall, R.S. and Derow, P.S. (2004), *The Hellenistic Period: Historical Sources in Translation*, Oxford: Blackwell (2nd edn).

Greece and Rome in the Near East

Sherk, R.K. (1984), *Rome and the Greek East to the Death of Augustus*, Cambridge: Cambridge University Press.

Later Roman period

Dodgeon, M.H. and Lieu, S.N.C. (1991), *The Roman Eastern Frontier and the Persian Wars* AD *226–363: A Documentary History*, London and New York: Routledge.

Gazetteer

Page nos in **bold** indicate main refs.

Index

Personal names are briefly defined. Page nos in **bold** indicate main refs. m.c. = military commander; r. = ruler.